You Must Be Joking
The Game of Presidential Elections

George Kahale, III

Copyright © 1998 by George Kahale, III

All rights reserved under International and Pan American Copyright Conventions. No part of this book may be reproduced or transmitted in any form, by any means, electronic or mechanical, including photocopying, recording, or any information retrieval system, without permission in writing from the publisher. Published by Axelrod Publishing of Tampa Bay, Inc., 1304 DeSoto Avenue, Tampa, FL 33606

Book and Cover design by Drawing Board Studios
Edited by Margie Weber
Printed in the United States of America

Publishers Cataloging-in-Publication
(Prepared by Quality Books Inc.)

Kahale, George.
    You must be joking : the game of presidential elections / George Kahale.—1st ed.
    p. cm.
    ISBN : 0-936417-58-7
    LCCN : 97-074612

    1. President—Election. 2. Elections—United States. I. Title.

JF285.K34 1997   324.7
                                      QBI97-41059

To My Parents

Table of Contents

GETTING ACQUAINTED   1
THE CLINTONS   6
THE REPUBLICANS   12
TOO EARLY FOR THE REFORMERS   25
SITTING IT OUT   29
KICKOFF   37
LET THE GAMES BEGIN   42
A BREAK IN THE ACTION   62
THE REPUBLICAN DILEMMA   73
THE CUBAN MINICRISIS   78
THE REPUBLICANS BEGIN SORTING THINGS OUT   86
THE MIDDLE EAST HEATS UP   91
SUPER JUNIOR TUESDAY   96
THE MINEFIELD ABROAD   101
DOLE GOES OVER THE TOP   108
BAD NEWS FOR BOTH SIDES   112
CALIFORNIA HAS ITS DAY   121
CHARACTER   124
NOT JUST AN AMERICAN PHENOMENON   128
THE REPUBLICANS NEARLY SELF-DESTRUCT   133
THE WHITE HOUSE OR HOME   138
GUILTY   143
A TEARFUL FAREWELL   145
ANOTHER GATE   150
SEESAW   152
HE'S BACK!   158
THE BATTLE OF THE PLATFORMS   160
HELMS-BURTON COMES INTO EFFECT   166
HALFTIME   171

THE GAMBLE 176
THE CHOICE 182
THE PRELIMS 185
SAN DIEGO 189
CHICAGO 193
MAKE MY DAY 198
THE REAL CAMPAIGN 205
THINGS GET UGLY 210
THE DEBATES 214
THE HOME STRETCH 220
LESSONS 227

APPENDIX 247

Chapter 1

Getting Acquainted

Given the trend in modern political writing, I felt I owed somewhat of a disclaimer at the outset. I've never held or run for public office, cashed a government paycheck other than for National Guard duty, managed a political campaign or otherwise been actively involved in politics, and have no clue who's been smoking what in the White House, who's been sneaking in or out of it and what really happened to those missing records. In other words, I've got no dirt to tell, beans to spill or inside dope to sell and wouldn't like the idea of doing so even if I did. If that's what you're looking for, stop here and ask for a refund. Read on if you don't mind looking through the eyes of an outsider at the game of U.S. presidential elections. The convenient framework for analysis will be our most recent game experience, a spectacle that held the world's attention for an entire year and one they'll be talking about for years to come, albeit in less than flattering terms.

There's no doubt that U.S. presidential elections fascinate and captivate Americans and foreigners alike, even more than the Simpson murder trial, which had far too many lulls and far too much motion practice for the taste of its addicted viewers. Like its predecessors, Election '96 was the Super Bowl of politics, better than anything Hollywood had to offer, better than *An American President*. We saw Bill Clinton become an early favorite for

Comeback Player of the Year when he rose from the depths of political depression in 1995 to take a 20-plus point lead over Bob Dole in the first quarter of 1996. We saw Dole nearly collapse early in the primaries, only to come back strong and wrap up the Republican nomination before the end of March, and then collapse twice more before Labor Day. We saw Democrats acting like Republicans, Republicans acting like Democrats, supply-siders merging with deficit hawks, liberals turning conservative and the emergence of a powerful new definition of "extremism." Scandals, hearings and politically sensitive trials and investigations kept the action moving during the slow times, and the drama continued all the way to Election Day. Although we knew or should have known something was very wrong, we were enjoying the ride.

There's no point in denigrating the entertainment value of our politics, but there's also no denying the serious problems that seem to have worsened over time and were painfully evident during Election '96. My favorites include, inter alia, ideological stagnation; the "sportification" of politics—don't look it up; the exaltation of form over substance, an ill normally associated with my own profession; the imbalanced roles of money and the media; the inherently *undemocratic* nature of the candidate selection process; the increasing irrelevance of true presidential issues to the political debate; the ugliness and meanness surrounding the campaigns; and the overall volatility and consequent unpredictability of the system. Since these are basically the same reasons that make elections exciting and entertaining, no real corrective action is likely to be taken until we figure out exactly what we want out of our politics.

Even before these problems became magnified in the '90s, they had led many to suggest importing practices and concepts from other countries and transplanting them into our political system—the parliamentary system of government, a longer presidential term, a ban on reelection, shorter campaigns, free television. It's not at all clear that these transplants would take, at least not without unforeseen adverse side effects. In addition, in considering whether to tinker with the system we should be mindful of the fact that many of these so-called solutions have not been working very well elsewhere, and that in 1996 alone we saw at least two examples of the adoption of American political practices in important foreign elections. Nevertheless, at some point we have to ask ourselves some basic questions, such as why so attractive a job as president of the United States attracts so few attractive applicants, why do so few people choose to participate in selecting the person who will be in a position to wreak havoc at home and abroad at the drop of a hat, how many of those who do have any clue whom or what they're voting for and when do we start caring enough to reorder our priorities to place policy above entertainment.

Not being a political scientist, historian, journalist or pundit by trade, I don't purport to have the answers to these cosmic questions. I've got a job that requires hopping around this global village Pat Buchanan loves to lambast, leaving me with time to kill at 35,000 feet. So I decided to follow the action last electoral season a little more methodically than in the past and use some of that time to write it up my way. In the course of recording this minihistory, I tried to identify with greater precision what it is that bothers me about the process in the hope that there was wisdom to be gleaned from this heightened awareness. It was good fortune that Election '96 turned out to be the best possible case study for this analysis, modern history's most embarrassing display of democracy in action.

Having skipped the preliminaries, I joined the action in 1996. By then, I had already missed much of the fun: California Governor Pete Wilson's aborted campaign, which was going to sweep first the Republican Party and then the country riding the back of the affirmative action issue until it experienced a personality outage; Colin Powell's teasing book tour that ended in a "Thanks, but no thanks"; and a third-party circus conducted by Ross Perot, which saw politicians from both sides racing to Dallas in search of the Texan maverick's blessing. But the real fun was just beginning.

What was my perspective on the proceedings? That of a lawyer, a misunderstood and much-maligned breed in modern

American society. A year of O.J. didn't do much to improve that image. Fortunately, there are two sides to every story, and lawyers are no exception. While the jabs proliferate, clients continue to seek out lawyers and both Hollywood and television are now in love with the law, all of which is good news for me because I don't expect to earn a living as a writer.

I'm an international lawyer. Along with basketball and movies, that area of practice remains an American specialty in great demand abroad—which means travel, hundreds of thousands of miles, and subspecialization in airports and flight connections. Did you know you could leave the Persian Gulf in the wee hours of the morning, write a chapter or two, catch a few zzz's, have a brief meeting in Paris and walk into your New York office bright and early that same morning for a full day's work? If you like breakfast, you can have it three times before you greet the receptionist in New York. Pat Buchanan's protestations aside, there really is something to this global village concept.

That's right, I'm a New Yorker, another misunderstood and much-maligned breed. They say you can't live in New York. Of course, most people saying that haven't lived there. The defense of New York typically starts with the song—make it there and you can make it anywhere. It's a weak defense. A lot of New Yorkers make it there and are lost anywhere else. We should just acknowledge that New York is different, unique, part of the United States only in a technical sense.

A final piece of background information before beginning—I'm not a Democrat, Republican or Reformer and, while the candidates in 1996 weren't exactly holding their breaths on this one, I hadn't decided to throw my support to any of them when I started writing at the Mexico City airport early in the season. Ironically, Election '96, an election sat out by a *majority* of eligible voters, was one of the few occasions that I bothered to take time out to vote. I never spent much time analyzing why I had sat out previous elections. Maybe it had something to do with a gut feeling that participation in a sham was not really meaningful, a distortion of democracy rather than a manifestation of it. Maybe it had something to do with the shows put on by candidates and political parties in past campaigns, which left many of us feeling sick and a stunned international community staring in disbelief. And maybe it had something to do with the fact that the choices offered tended to leave voters entering the polling booth holding their noses, an expression used by one observer to describe the state of mind of Clinton supporters in 1996. Whatever the excuse in the past, I was able to press the lever this time. My bet is you won't easily be able to guess for whom.

Now it's time to review the field as it stood at the beginning of the race and get on with the action.

Chapter 2

The Clintons

To the surprise of those unfamiliar with Bill Clinton's history, the President opened the 1996 season in great shape, unchallenged in his own party and comfortably ahead of all Republican challengers. It was a remarkable story, as barely a year earlier this campaigner extraordinaire had been pronounced irrelevant to American politics. The Republicans had just regained control of the House of Representatives, something I thought I would never see in my lifetime, and the country was catching right wing fever. The President seemed to be just standing by as Newt Gingrich, the brash young leader of the Republican Revolution, was trying hard to fulfill his Contract with America. The only question was how low could Bill go?

The wonder of this bizarre process is that things change, and quickly. Observers all over the world have always had trouble with this concept because nowhere is the electoral process as volatile as it is in this country. Wherever I travel during an election year, people want to know who's winning, who's losing, who will next call the White House home. Whether in January or June, the answer always seems to involve a multiplicity of factors and events that can affect the outcome, the unpredictability of their occurrence and the speed with which they can change the fortunes of individual candidates. None of this is particularly satisfying to anxious observers in other countries, many of whom are more deeply affected by our choice for president than we are and nearly all of whom seem mystified by the process.

Remember 1991-92? George Bush was unbeatable. Not only did he have all the advantages of an incumbent, he was also basking in the glow of victory in the Gulf War. I'm sure some public official someplace was as popular as Bush going into the election season, but I can't recall one. All the leading Democrats saw it the same way and decided to stay away, waiting for 1996 rather than risk humiliation in the tradition of Walter Mondale and Michael Dukakis. I recall a cocktail party where I met one of those Democrats who had missed the boat. The tide had just begun to turn, but it was too late to jump into the race. "You really blew that one, didn't you?" lurched uncontrollably, as McLaughlin would say, into the conversation. I couldn't resist; he was someone I could have voted for.

In a few short months, Bush's poll figures plummeted. When Ross Perot threw his hat into the ring, Bush couldn't beat the Young Turk from Arkansas. At the end, I wasn't even sure he could win the D.C. Republican Club vote. The attitude of many Republicans I knew was that four years of Bill Clinton was just the right tonic to reinvigorate the Republican Party and condition the country for the next twelve years of Reaganomics. The Republican successes in the 1994 midterm elections did nothing to disprove that theory.

George Bush was involved in another amazing turnaround of recent vintage, this time as beneficiary. In 1988, this eminently qualified but uninspiring professional seemed uneasy in his bid to continue the Reagan Revolution. Reagan had stumbled badly toward the end of his second term; he seemed to run out of steam and ideas at the same time. Without a major boost from Reagan, the Bush campaign was in deep trouble. Michael Dukakis had fought his way valiantly through the Democratic primaries and, after the Democratic National Convention in midsummer, stood miles ahead of the Republican nominee to be.

What happened? Television—a few mean commercials starring a convict named Willie Horton, an ill-advised ride in a tank that made Dukakis look silly on camera, and plop. Inside three months, Dukakis had snatched defeat from the jaws of victory.

Bill Clinton set a fine example for his 1996 comeback with his own performance during the 1992 campaign for the Democratic nomination. When none of the principal Democrats dared enter the fray in 1991, he established himself as the best of the rest in a who cares contest to select the next Democrat to suffer ignominious defeat. Then came Gennifer Flowers and, suddenly, the Clintons were doing a lot of explaining on network television. In a stunning performance, husband and wife appeared together on "60 Minutes" to discuss their marriage and save the campaign.

There are some countries where a little sleeping around is both accepted and expected of presidents. I'm not sure whether it's actually a job requirement in France. In the U.S.A., however, an indiscretion or two can put a real damper on a political career. (See Gary Hart-1987.) Since Gennifer Flowers sounded like a lot more than an indiscretion or two, you could be forgiven for assuming it was all over for Bill Clinton when she went public with her story. Yet, in one of the most remarkable turnarounds in memory, he came back to win the Democratic nomination, with a lot of help from Hillary Clinton.

As the 1996 electoral season opened, Bill Clinton was on top again, having earned his position the old-fashioned way. Taking beating after beating—health care, Whitewater, the Paula Jones sexual harassment lawsuit, the midterm fiasco—he never quit. It was the Clinton way. In Arkansas, he had rebounded from electoral defeat to regain the governorship. The scandal he had overcome in Campaign '92 would have put most other politicians away for good. And now he had fought and won his unique battle with irrelevancy and appeared more than ready to take on all comers.

Impressive political strength wasn't the only clear distinction between Clinton's position in early 1996 and his standing at the same point in 1992. The impact of Hillary Rodham Clinton was another. In 1992, she stood by her husband, allowing him to win. Perhaps it was only fitting that in January 1996 she stood as potentially the biggest obstacle to his reelection. Far too much attention was focused on her activities at her former Arkansas law firm, how her long-subpoenaed billing records materialized in a White House reading room, whether she directed the firing of the

White House travel staff (aka. Travelgate—I expect the next edition of *Webster's* to add White House scandal to the definition of "gate") and a seemingly endless series of minor mishaps transformed into major problems through either mismanagement or arrogance. All this led to an unscheduled campaign stop, the grand jury, and seemed headed toward a showdown with Al D'Amato's Senate Committee on Whitewater.

The fact is people were never fully comfortable with Hillary Clinton. She is an intelligent, opinionated woman— conventional wisdom has it we're not ready for that, for women in leadership positions, for women who don't want to stay home and bake cookies. It does seem odd that in the home of the feminist movement no woman has ever made a serious bid for national office (assuming you don't count Geraldine Ferraro's 1984 vice-presidential run as a serious bid), while other countries with less-established feminist traditions have been led by women. I cannot explain why female leadership came to Argentina, Bangladesh, India, Israel, Nicaragua, Pakistan, Sri Lanka, The Philippines and Turkey before the United States, not to mention Maggie Thatcher's reign in the mother country. Something told me, however, that there was more to this than a preference for female-baked cookies. I think most of us couldn't care less whether Hillary Clinton bakes or orders take-out as long as our intelligence is not insulted, and our intelligence was insulted when we were told her difficulties were attributable to our unpreparedness to deal with opinionated women.

Of course, Hillary Clinton wasn't merely viewed as opinionated; her opinions were perceived as too liberal, out of step with the rest of the country. Being a liberal was still legal in this country, but there was a feeling that this liberal had far too much influence for the country's good, that she had been the only White House resident with the character, vision and ability to promote ideas that could not otherwise have been promoted through the electoral process. The suppressed fear was that Bill Clinton owed her too much for 1992 and was too inclined to pay his debt.

Whatever the explanation, the bottom line on Hillary Clinton is that she was once widely admired and respected, but not liked. When she was no longer as widely admired or respected, she was liked even less. So, at least as long as Al D'Amato was enjoying himself, there was little doubt we would continue to hear more about her role in Travelgate and Whitewater, about what had happened to the papers in the office of former White House Counsel Vince Foster following his suicide, and about what happened to her own papers. Did columnist William Safire step over the line when he called her a congenital liar? Yes, but I suspected the best (or the worst, depending on your point of view) was yet to come.

Hillary Clinton wasn't the President's only problem as the 1996 electoral season began. The man himself was carrying around a lot of baggage. Remember all those questions in 1992 concerning his character, his soul, his core beliefs, whether he could control his natural impulses and whether he inhaled? Everyone expected them to return with a vengeance (well, maybe not the last one). Despite the President's uncanny ability to rebound from adversity, it was not at all certain he would be able to overcome the next scandal to arise during the course of the campaign, and one had the feeling the Republicans were searching long and hard to find one.

If that weren't sufficient reason to anticipate trouble ahead, there was always the uncertainty surrounding foreign affairs. Even though that area had not been as troublesome as might have been expected for the inexperienced Arkansas governor, it remained a wild card.

For a candidate who couldn't wait to return leadership's focus home, Bill Clinton the President devoted a lot of attention to foreign affairs in his first three years in office. Ironically, while Clinton's domestic record had been less than spectacular, he had had success and made gutsy calls in foreign affairs. The showdown over Haiti ended without war, with President Aristide restored to power and without too many people questioning why the strongest nation on earth was preoccupied with General Cedras and company; the world witnessed the incredible scene of Yasir Arafat, Yitzhak Rabin and Shimon Peres shaking hands on the White House lawn; much to Pat Buchanan's chagrin, Mexican newspaper headlines read "VIVA CLINTON" following the loan package arranged by

Clinton to assist Mexico out of the economic crisis triggered by the 1994 peso devaluation; and the long-awaited decision to use air power in Bosnia changed the course of that war and led ultimately to the Dayton Accords among Bosnia, Serbia and Croatia.

The overall record was not unimpressive for a guy whose experience in international affairs, according to Pat Buchanan, consisted principally of breakfast at the International House of Pancakes. However, things have a way of getting out of control in places we don't understand, and that can put a dent in any president's reelection bid. (See Jimmy Carter and Iran.) Bosnia was one of those places. With thousands of American troops sent to Bosnia to keep the fragile peace hammered out in Dayton, danger was always lurking just around the corner on the campaign trail. And in case Bosnia for some inexplicable reason was not to become a mess, the world was full of other trouble spots, any one of which could give Bill Clinton a bumpy ride on his train to the 21st century.

In other words, things couldn't have looked worse for Clinton after the 1994 midterm elections, but they got better; they couldn't have looked better in early 1996, but there was a sense, almost an expectation, that they would get worse. Given the volatility of the process and the length of the campaign, Clinton's fortunes could and would change several times more before the election in November. As in pro basketball, the last two minutes often decide the game.

Chapter 3

The Republicans

In many respects, Bob Dole was the opposite of Bill Clinton. We knew much more about him at the outset of the 1996 campaign than we knew about Clinton in 1992. He was a bona fide war hero, savvy and experienced legislator, reasonably conservative conservative and self-deprecating humorist who could hold his own with David Letterman and Jay Leno. He also had a mean streak that frequently got him into trouble. Overall, a decent fellow with a remarkable career. The decent part, of course, was only a guess. Yet some comfort could be derived from the fact that Bob Dole had been around awhile without a major scandal to his credit.

What was wrong with Bob Dole? Well, for one, we'd seen him before in national campaigns, both as Gerald Ford's running mate in 1984 and as a Reagan and Bush rival for the Republican presidential nomination. What did anyone take away from those experiences aside from that mean streak and a nasty temper? Elizabeth Dole, owner of a distinguished career in public service and reportedly once on the list of potential Republican vice-presidential candidates (how history might have changed if George Bush had selected her over Dan Quayle), at times seemed a better bet to win a national election. In fact, many felt that if Bob Dole could only manage to survive the grueling nomination process and pull within striking distance of the President, the sharp contrast between Elizabeth Dole and Hillary Clinton might provide the uncharismatic candidate with the boost he would sorely need in the general election, a theory that acquired more subscribers after Elizabeth's riveting performance during the Republican National Convention in San Diego.

Bob Dole's critics mercilessly attacked him for an alleged lack of a vision for America. They accused him of being merely a lawmaker, a sort of legislative technocrat. You didn't have to be a big fan of Dole's to be puzzled by that criticism. True, Dole didn't come across as a visionary, but didn't history teach us to be wary of politicians with visions? Rather than worry about Dole's vision deficit, we might have found something comforting about his lack of vision, his reliance on experience and knowledge of the processes of government; it should have told us that if by chance this man wound up fulfilling his dream, there was at least some possibility of his maintaining touch with reality.

Unfortunately for Dole, his brand of knowledge and experience was hard to sell. It wasn't the vision that was missing; it was the energy, excitement and enthusiasm, indispensable ingredients of any political campaign not driven by ideology. Although his sometimes biting humor was appreciated by some audiences, he had difficulty energizing crowds in his monotone. When he wanted to stress a point, he had an annoying habit of simply stating a word or expression thrice, as in his characterization of the Democrats' tactics on the Medicare issue: "Mediscare; Mediscare; Mediscare." All it got him was some extra attention by comedians on "Saturday Night Live" and "the Tonight Show," the kind of attention that can destroy a candidate's image and devastate a political campaign.

Despite his deficiencies as a campaigner, Dole's lengthy public career and his stature as a respected Senate majority leader made him the front-runner for the Republican nomination the moment he announced he would make one last run at the White House. However, he had to overcome several obstacles (aside from the vision thing). First, as was the case with Bush, Dole wasn't fully trusted by much of the right. The right, of course, covered a lot of territory. There was the economic right, the guys who wanted to balance the budget, cut taxes and dismantle big government; the populist right, who believed in Fortress America, America First and a whole bunch of other Americas, and who didn't care for immigrants, big corporations or free trade; and the religious right, which stood against abortion, for school prayer and for something called Values. So it was anticipated that Dole would curb his instinct to compromise, trash Boutros Boutros Ghali and the United Nations and fire a few salvos on Hollywood to shore up his "right" flank.

Second, Dole was the ultimate Washington insider at a time when Washington's popularity seemed to be at an all-time low. There are few serious professions where experience is considered a handicap. Fresh faces are always important, but in most jobs you'd better learn quickly how it's been done before lest you find out the hard way. Even if you are very creative, you shouldn't have to apply that creativity to constantly reinventing the wheel. In any event, while Dole would be able to modify his positions on issues to suit the voters, he couldn't run away from his experience. So why not use it? As one Iowa voter asked, if you wouldn't hire a politician to run General Motors, why would you hire a businessman (*e.g.*, Steve Forbes) to run the government? Dole tried to pick up on the theme, asking whom would you call to fix your leaky faucet. Maybe it was for the best that he couldn't drive home the message; in the fall, only one candidate would be able to claim almost four years of experience in the White House, and it wouldn't be Bob Dole.

Last, though by no means least, Dole suffered from the continuous predictions of his eventual downfall, either due to some mean outburst or simply the lack of a spark, a feeling that his time had come and gone. After all, only Ronald Reagan could get away with that line about not exploiting the youth of his opponent (Walter Mondale in 1984) for political purposes. In the electronic age, where perception and reality are often confused, such predictions have a nasty habit of becoming self-fulfilling prophecies.

As we entered 1996, there was a subtle change in Dole's position as front-runner. He was still leader of the Republican pack, only now the perception of him as the likely nominee was growing. With Jack Kemp, Dan Quayle, Dick Cheney and others sitting it out and the Colin Powell distraction over for the time being, Dole looked like the only serious candidate for the Republican nomination, like it or not. The main reaction elicited by the other pretenders was: who are these guys and what are they doing here?

*   *   *

Steve Forbes was one of those guys. Sitting second to Dole in January, he was a complete unknown outside the business world only a short time earlier. Never having held elective office, he had no particular political credentials. He was the opposite of Dole, the ultimate Washington outsider, and was having surprising success holding Dole's experience against him.

Forbes came to the race with strong ideas and the intelligence to present them effectively. More importantly, he brought money to the table, plenty of it. While neither the White House nor Congress has a For Sale sign hanging outside, there's no denying the central role of money in American politics. As Campaign '96 was to illustrate more vividly than any other in history, the first objective of any campaign is to attract money, not votes. The money doesn't guarantee that the votes will come later, but they certainly won't be there if the money isn't.

Raising millions at $1,000 a clip is no easy task even for the best of moochers. Yet Congress did its best to ensure that the talent, stamina and stomach for perpetual fund-raising were job requirements for all except the most financially self-sufficient political aspirants when it imposed that limit in the Federal Election Campaign Act of 1971. The job requirements are particularly burdensome for those vying for a party's nomination without access to the millions of "soft" dollars contributed to the party itself rather than to a particular candidate. Many fine would-be candidates were either unwilling or unable to fulfill those requirements in 1996 (see Jack Kemp). Lamar Alexander, one of those awaiting the fall of Dole, lamented having to spend 1995 begging for money rather than doing what he should have been doing to prepare for the job he coveted. Steve Forbes had more freedom. That's what money can do for you. While we could not (legally) provide him with more than $1,000 each to sell his ideas, he was free to provide himself with as much as he wanted. And, of course, you can't get around the restriction by slipping 10 hundred dollar bills to each of your friends in envelopes addressed to your favorite politician.

The long-standing debate over the role of money in modern American politics, a debate that has intensified in direct proportion to the increasing power of the mass media, stems from the inherent conflict between the desire to avoid any restrictions on our personal freedom and the need to maintain some degree of integrity in the political process. Part of us sees the evil money can spawn; another part just doesn't like the idea of anyone telling us how to spend it. Instinctively, we feel there must be something in the Constitution that unequivocally establishes our freedom to spend our money any way we want. Although that freedom isn't specifically listed in the Bill of Rights, the First Amendment comes close enough, at least if you're spending your *own* money on your *own* campaign. When you're spending on someone else's campaign, close may no longer be good enough. If you want to know why, check out *Buckley v. Valeo*.

In that 1976 decision, the Supreme Court upheld the constitutionality of restrictions on campaign *contributions* because, even though those restrictions impinge on our First Amendment rights, they don't *directly* limit the quantity of speech. Mindful of the abuses surfacing after the 1972 election, the Court gave precedence to the compelling governmental interest in protecting against both corruption and the appearance of corruption in the electoral process: "To the extent that large contributions are given to secure a political *quid pro quo* from current and potential office holders, the integrity of our system of representative democracy is undermined. . . . Of almost equal concern as the danger of actual *quid pro quo* arrangements is the impact of the appearance of corruption stemming from public awareness of the opportunities for abuse inherent in a regime of large individual financial contributions." In other words, since politicians can't be trusted to bite the hand that feeds them, Congress has the right to make sure they're not fed too much.

When it came to assessing the constitutionality of limitations on *expenditures*, rather than *contributions*, the Court was much less sympathetic with Congress: "A restriction on the amount of money a person or group can spend on political communication during a campaign necessarily reduces the quantity of expression by restricting the number of issues discussed, the depth of their exploration, and the size of the audience reached. This is because virtually every means of communicating ideas in today's mass society requires the expenditure of money. The distribution of the humblest handbill or leaflet entails printing, paper, and circulation costs. Speeches and rallies generally necessitate hiring a hall and publicizing the event. The electorate's increasing dependence on television, radio, and other mass media for news and information has made these expensive modes of communication indispensable instruments of effective political speech." Thus, since limiting the amount that may be spent on a campaign directly and necessarily reduces the quantity of political expression, the statutory limitations on campaign *expenditures* were held unconstitutional. So if a Steve Forbes wants to run for president, he can. If you (at least most of you) harbor any such notion, forget it. That's democracy.

But let's not blame Steve Forbes for either having money or exercising his constitutional right to spend millions of it. Last time I checked the codes, wealth hadn't yet been criminalized. Nor does it in and of itself make good ideas bad.

The idea most associated with Forbes (several others espoused a variation of it) was the flat tax, a sort of declaration of war on the Internal Revenue Code. The flat tax proceeds from two basic premises: (1) the tax code is a nightmare most of us can do without and (2) all of us are paying far too much to the feds. If you disagree with either premise, you have no use for the flat tax.

Personally, and with apologies to my tax lawyer friends, I have long found the idea attractive. My colleagues in the tax department generate millions of dollars in legal fees brilliantly guiding clients through the maze that is the Internal Revenue Code and I do not wish to sound in the least bit ungrateful. Still, I can't in good conscience object to any attempt to reform (*i.e.*, simplify) the Code. Maybe that's because I've been sentenced to read more than my share of it. Before you dismiss the flat tax as passing fancy, pick up the Code—or even better, the Regulations—and try reading any ten consecutive pages. No cheating allowed. You must read ten full pages, every sentence (there won't be many), all in one sitting. When you finish, it'll be time to ask yourself what you really think of the flat tax.

Although people frustrated by their annual battle with the tax forms began warming to the flat tax concept, there were a lot of problems with Forbes' version of it. As fellow Republican candidate Phil Gramm said, Americans would not accept a proposal that taxed income derived from hard work and exempted unearned income such as dividends on your IBM stock, even though the income generating those dividends had already been taxed once (the corporate income tax paid by IBM). It may also be that the 17 percent rate proposed by Forbes was simply too low. (Do I hear 18 percent?) Deductions for home mortgage interest, charitable contributions and other items raised serious policy issues that deserved months of expert attention, and the transition problems alone were daunting. As important as those issues were, however, they were details. The big picture remained quite clear. Any law that couldn't be read was in for a major overhaul sooner or later.

Structure was not the only issue in the tax debate led by Forbes. As Forbes recognized, the amount of taxes, flat or otherwise, was at least as painful as the headache of calculating them. On this issue the debate had taken on a new twist.

Democrats have never been comfortable talking about taxes. Taxes are, after all, unpopular. But cutting taxes puts pressure on government spending, the cornerstone of Democratic politics for more than half a century. As the popularity of government spending approached that of taxes, more Democrats seemed anxious to line up on the side of tax cuts. Unfortunately, that common ground with Republicans wasn't wide enough to build on; it merely shifted the tax debate to the uglier ground of class warfare. Suddenly, every discussion of taxes sounded like a sociology class. Taxes and tax cuts no longer meant anything unless they were linked to the wealthy, the middle class or the poor. The borders separating the classes were not always clearly defined, but one thing was certain: you didn't want to get caught taxing the poor to give to the rich. Playing Robin Hood was always sound political strategy.

Fear of the Robin Hood strategy drove a large part of the intra-Republican debate on taxes during the primaries, as Steve Forbes seemed to be the only candidate who wasn't paranoid about the public's reaction to a tax reform proposal that did not *increase* taxes on the wealthy. The silliest aspect of the debate was the attack on Forbes for failing to disclose his tax returns. For some reason, his opponents seemed to assume that personal tax savings constituted his primary motivation in pushing the flat tax. What a great idea—run for president so you can lower your own taxes. Motive having been established, there was no need to deal with the merits of the issue. You didn't have to support Steve Forbes to realize how ridiculous that argument was.

I was willing to assume that Forbes, like many others, would benefit from the flat tax. Given his rather lofty income level, I also assumed the benefit would be substantial. The logic broke down there. As Forbes pointed out with some degree of credibility, we didn't have to worry about him—he would do just fine with or without the flat tax. The material issue was the percentage of our respective incomes that should go to the government whatever may be the size of our balance sheets. If that percentage has us working from January into June just to pay taxes, we can intuitively sense it's time for a basic reassessment of tax policy.

Of course, as one of my non-tax partners pointed out to me in a discussion of the flat tax, slaving away for Uncle Sam would go down more easily if he ever said thank you and if politicians would stop making us feel bad for the percentage we keep rather than good for the percentage we pay. Not even cost-cutting conservatives would mind if the IRS instituted a new kind of mailing to address my partner's concern. No "Dear Taxpayer"; it would be a personalized note as follows: "Dear Mr./Ms._____:

Thank you for your generous contribution this year. We know you work hard for your money and, though we've never put much of it to good use, we'll do our best to do so this time. Keep up the good work." Isn't that a lot nicer than just receiving your label?

*   *   *

When he challenged George Bush in 1992, he couldn't have been serious about winning. In 1996, even though he was still widely regarded as a sideshow, people came to appreciate that Pat Buchanan was indeed very serious.

Buchanan had many impressive qualities. Like Forbes, he was articulate, intelligent and the proud owner of a clearly defined set of beliefs. Unlike Forbes, Buchanan didn't have virtually unlimited resources to spend on his campaign. He capitalized on his television experience and debating skills to get his message across—from the right, as they say on CNN's "Crossfire." Whereas Dole appeared uncomfortable and Forbes awkward on camera, Buchanan couldn't wait to get to the next interview. Every television appearance for him was a free commercial, and he made the most out of each one.

Buchanan's main problem was that he was more suited to his former role as "Crossfire" cohost and newspaper columnist than presidential candidate. Throughout his career, he had expressed strong opinions both in print and on the air, never holding back. "Crossfire" was the perfect vehicle for Buchanan, a show whose popularity and success was dependent on the ability of its highly opinionated hosts to debate controversial issues aggressively on a nightly basis. In print, he was much the same. His columns were hard-hitting though frequently unpopular. Whether or not you agreed with him, it was hard to ignore Pat Buchanan. He was going to challenge you, partly because he felt passionately about his politics and, I suspect, partly because he was a warrior who harbored a Patton-like passion for the battle itself.

That kind of warrior is appreciated in many fields of endeavor. Generally, however, U.S. presidential politics isn't one of them. Ronald Reagan aside, candidates with strong ideological positions, right or left, typically don't do well in national politics. While they make colorful, provocative TV, they tend not to attract votes in sufficiently large numbers to carry the day.

The difficulty in using ideology to motivate the American electorate is underscored by our impressive record of political apathy. Americans are famous for their low voter turnouts. One can get suspicious of 99 percent plus turnouts, but when barely a majority of eligible voters actually vote—would you believe the 55 percent turnout in 1992 was considered *good*—it's safe to say you don't have a fired up electorate.

That doesn't mean Americans don't care about politics. In spurts, we can and do get worked up over issues people around the world often find trivial, such as flag-burning and uniforms for schoolchildren. Nevertheless, the overriding fact remains that there is broad consensus in American society on first principles. We are not faced with fundamental choices among political or economic systems from election to election and, with relatively few exceptions, we are not concerned that the wrong choice would have a dramatic impact on our lives. The chances are fairly good that whoever wins, our basic freedoms will remain intact, as will the structure of our political institutions and economy.

This state of affairs places us in an often unappreciated comfort zone few other societies have experienced for any length of time. It also tends to lull us into feeling it makes no difference who wins a presidential election. In effect, the country is on automatic pilot (Peter Sellers in *Being There*). Under these circumstances, one can sympathize with politicians seeking to distinguish themselves in presidential campaigns. It's not an easy task, searching constantly for issues that might capture the public's imagination without crossing into new ideological territory, manufacturing those issues if necessary, and then exaggerating their importance to make us believe the future of the nation turns on them.

Every now and then a set of positions is linked in a train of thought sounding vaguely like a new ideology—Barry Goldwater's conservatism in 1964, George McGovern's liberalism in

1972—and is invariably rejected, primarily for that reason; it *sounds* like a new ideology. That sound, typically amplified by the proponent's opponents, is not music to the ears of an electorate uninterested in rocking the boat. In 1996, Pat Buchanan's populist conservatism sounded like a new ideology and his opponents, both Democrats and Republicans, were going to make sure everyone heard it that way. He had no chance.

*   *   *

Phil Gramm had high hopes entering 1996. Having started almost a year earlier and been successful in fund-raising, he was looking forward to a strong run for the Republican nomination based on his solidly conservative record. Unlike Buchanan, this conservative came to the party with credibility as a politician. He was a United States senator; he deserved to be taken seriously.

Gramm's candidacy underscored another truth about American politics, namely, the importance of image. No, image isn't everything, and it isn't the only thing, but it is important. If you don't look like a president, chances are you won't become one, no matter what you believe or say. Conversely, if you look like a president and can solve the money problem, you just might have a chance. What you believe or say won't be completely irrelevant, but those things can be taught, the same way Crash Davis taught the young pitcher in *Bull Durham*.

Ronald Reagan is probably the best example of this principle in operation. Reagan was conservative, in many respects simplistically so. He was therefore the exception that proves the rule about the role of ideology in American politics. Why was he able to do that and to have such a profound and lasting effect on both the domestic and international scenes? Image. He played a good president.

Remember how much difficulty Reagan seemed to have with the facts? They never got in the way of his message. Reporters seemed frustrated following him on the campaign trail, trying to pin him down on the specifics of his speeches. They were missing the point. The specifics didn't matter; nobody cared. People liked what they saw and heard, and that was enough. This sort of immunity from scrutiny stuck to the "Teflon President" throughout his presidency. Americans wanted him to succeed and weren't interested in negative comments, regardless of whether the facts pointed in another direction. Reagan took a bullet for the country, and the country was going to win one for the Gipper.

That's not to say Reagan was not substantive; he most assuredly was. The changes taking place during his presidency were material. The highest tax rate was slashed from 50 percent (can you believe it had previously been 70 percent and at one point had reached as high as 90 percent) to 28 percent. When you measure reduction in your taxes in the thousands rather than the hundreds, you have something worth arguing about. On the international level, Reagan made clear who the good and bad guys were and spent the Soviets into oblivion. The Iron Curtain may have fallen on George Bush's watch, but it was Reagan who did the damage. Try telling people living in former Soviet bloc countries that wasn't a substantive change.

Acknowledging Reagan's substantive beliefs and accomplishments doesn't mean they were responsible for either of his remarkable victories. Ronald Reagan won in 1980 mainly because he made us feel better about ourselves than Jimmy Carter did, not a difficult task after all that honest talk about the malaise in America, and he won in 1984 because we liked him better than Walter Mondale, another straight shooter who didn't mind talking about a tax *increase* in an election year.

While Phil Gramm saw himself as Reagan's successor, he didn't strike the same chord. He could have been reading the same speeches, but the effect was radically different. We were not predisposed to listen to Phil Gramm. We were not pulled to him by some natural force of attraction. So he had to win us over with ideas, and ideas, particularly those emanating from the far end (either one) of the political spectrum, just aren't enough to win over a largely apathetic electorate. Despite this handicap, Phil Gramm wouldn't give up easily; his mamma wouldn't let him and, as he said, even his wife turned him down twice before saying yes.

* * *

Lamar Alexander was the last of the serious (meaning having a chance) candidates for the Republican nomination. A Washington lawyer, former governor of Tennessee and former secretary of education, he projected himself as a Washington outsider, frequently donning red and black checkered shirts and jackets presumably in an effort to drive home the point. Why was this man literally walking across states in the middle of winter? Because he actually believed he had a chance to win. The oddity was he did, even though it looked awfully slim in January.

Many thought Alexander combined center-right support with the charismatic appeal to match the youthful campaigning talents of Bill Clinton. When Bob Dole stumbled, conventional wisdom had it, the path would be clear for a fresh face to gather momentum and capitalize on the country's overall tilt to the right. Great strategy; wrong candidate.

* * *

Believe it or not, there were four other Republican candidates as we approached the first caucuses and the New Hampshire primary: Senator Richard Lugar, a seemingly decent man who preferred calm discussion to rolling around in the mud, a disqualifying trait for the battle that lay ahead in the Republican primaries; former Ambassador Alan Keyes, whose fiery preaching about the moral crisis in America would win him some social conservative support, making his preaching more fiery and at times downright disturbing; Representative Bob Dornan ("B-1 Bob"), who had no business being there and managed eventually to lose his own seat in the House of Representatives; and businessman Morry Taylor, who never should have left his business. That wasn't counting the guys who had already dropped out—Wilson of California, whom many had mistakenly expected to do well, and Senator Arlen Specter, Anita Hill's questioner, who never had a chance. Let's just say none of these fine gentlemen would have a major impact on the race.

Chapter 4

Too Early for the Reformers

In January, no one was seeking the nomination of the newly formed Reform Party. The main question on Reform-watchers' minds was whether—or rather when—Ross Perot, the party's indomitable and wealthy founder, would announce his candidacy for a second run for the White House, this time with the backing of a formally organized political party. Former Colorado Governor Richard Lamm, who was later to seek the Reform Party nomination when he mistakenly assumed Perot was putting it up for grabs, wasn't on the scene when the 1996 season opened. When he did try to fill the illusory void on the Reform Party ticket, he found out quickly where the power in the party rested.

Ross Perot's power in national politics, which was considerable in 1992 and remained potentially significant in 1996, was a reflection of American dissatisfaction with traditional politics and political parties. Oh yes, it was also a reflection of the power of money. Perot has money, which means if he has something to say, you will hear it. (See Steve Forbes and the *Buckley* case.) And Perot always seems to have something to say.

Bill Clinton owed much to Ross Perot and his 1992 presidential campaign; it's not often you get a four-year pass to the White House with 43 percent of the popular vote (see Richard Nixon's victory over Hubert Humphrey in 1968, another year in which a third candidate, George Wallace, drew a substantial block of votes). As far as George Bush had fallen in 1992, there was no way he would have lost that election were it not for Ross Perot. How would Clinton repay Perot? Perhaps by inviting him to the party once again because, once again, his presence was expected to hurt the Republicans. With the entire liberal vote going to Clinton, his 43 percent seemed solid; the question was whether he could obtain majority support absent a third party candidate.

While there was some uncertainty as to whether there would be a Perot candidacy in 1996, most experts were confident that if there was, it wouldn't capture the impressive percentage (19 percent) of the vote it did in 1992. Perot's popularity had peaked before he temporarily withdrew from the 1992 race. Remember the shock and disappointment of his supporters when he announced his withdrawal to protect his daughter? It never quite added up in my mind, so I figured he would return. He did, of course, with all his folksy stories, but it was never quite the same. He had let his people down and the criticism began to stick. Although he was still riding high through the 1992 elections, that was more a sign of weakness on the part of the main candidates than any positive force generated by Perot.

Then came the great debate on the North American Free Trade Agreement (NAFTA), the treaty that would break down trade barriers among the United States, Canada and Mexico, thereby creating the world's largest free trade zone. I don't completely understand why Bill Clinton chose NAFTA as the vehicle for demonstrating that he does indeed have character (at least under one of the many definitions of the term that unfolded during the 1996 campaign). Many saw NAFTA as a no-win situation for him. If it passed, he wouldn't get the credit since NAFTA would always be known as George Bush's treaty. If it didn't, Clinton's support would have alienated the traditional Democratic power base for nothing. Considering all the difficulties Clinton was having getting programs through Congress in his first year in office, NAFTA was a headache he could do without. Yet for some reason, after some early wavering, he staked his leadership on the treaty's ratification. It was a gutsy call, much like his later decision to provide loan guarantees to help Mexico out of its economic crisis.

Notwithstanding Clinton's support, NAFTA encountered stiff opposition from labor and most Democratic leaders, including House Speaker Dick Gephardt and Majority Whip David Bonior. Party discipline, never strong in American politics, had vanished. In the midst of it all, the colorful Perot was having a field day asking people whether they could hear the giant sucking sound of jobs headed south of the border. Some bold move had to be made to save NAFTA and, many were saying, the entire Clinton presidency. That bold move was a NAFTA debate between Vice-President Al Gore and Perot on CNN's "Larry King Live."

The gamble paid off big time for the Administration as Gore won the debate handily. The debate yielded three direct results. First, the treaty passed, and there's little doubt the debate was the turning point in the battle. Second, by placing his Administration on the line and then avoiding defeat, Clinton appeared presidential for the first time in his presidency. Third, Ross Perot's stock plummeted after his poor performance. He didn't seem comfortable when challenged by the energetic Gore and exhibited a mean streak that made him seem less folksy, less fun, less likeable. The camera, so instrumental in Perot's rise, was no longer kind to him. The irony was that this setback occurred on the very television show that had served as the launching pad for Perot's 1992 presidential campaign.

It's hard to keep a good man down; it's even harder to keep down a man with an iron will and pockets of gold to back it up. Ross Perot hadn't invested all that time and money since 1992 just to play the role of an interested observer in 1996. He had more to say and wasn't going to let either of the main parties say it for him. The whole point of his movement purportedly was the inability of Democrats and Republicans to address the issues of the day honestly and effectively.

But January was far too soon for Perot to make his move. Unlike the established parties, the Reform Party nomination would not be won through the bizarre primary system; the nominee would be selected through a vote of party members taken over a one-week period much later in the year. Under those circumstances, jumping into the race early was both unnecessary and dangerous, as it would expose Perot to more scrutiny by the public and the media, scrutiny he had managed to avoid for much of 1992. All indications were that early scrutiny was not conducive to a successful Perot candidacy in 1996. In contrast to the Republicans, not a single one of whom could afford to wait as late as January to announce his candidacy, Perot couldn't afford to announce that soon. The field was therefore left to the main parties in January, giving them every opportunity to demonstrate on their own that there was indeed a need for a third party in American politics.

Chapter 5

Sitting It Out

Before picking up the action, several noncandidates deserve mention precisely because they were sitting it out, in some cases after publicly and agonizingly contemplating their potential candidacy. Testing the waters for a presidential run and backing off is neither unusual nor disturbing. What is disturbing is the possibility that those who might have had a realistic chance of winning a fair race backed off for reasons that reflect a serious malfunctioning of the democratic process. If it is true that many qualified individuals sat out only, or in some significant part, because of money (or the lack of it), the need to protect one's family from vicious campaign attacks, the virtual impossibility of engaging in honest debate on the campaign trail without jeopardizing one's chances of success or any of the other ills afflicting the presidential election process, then a reassessment of that process would obviously be in order. The right to vote means nothing if those ills are depriving us of candidates to vote for.

* * *

On the Democratic side, Bill Bradley, senator from New Jersey, may have been wondering whether he had made the same mistake leading Democrats made in Campaign '92, staying away because of an unbeatable incumbent. There had been noise emanating from the Bradley camp that he might mount a challenge for the Democratic nomination. Being pronounced irrelevant can do that to a president. In the end, Bradley decided against a run. Too bad.

I like Bill Bradley. He's always had a calm, clear-minded approach to his job, even when he worked in short pants. If you want proof, watch a tape of Game 5 of the 1970 NBA championship, when Willis Reed went down early and Bradley and the rest of the overmatched Knicks played David to the Lakers' Goliath. I have a clear recollection of that night in Clancy's (not many houses were wired for cable then); the whole place was vibrating with every basket as mighty Wilt Chamberlain and the rest of the powerful Laker squad crumbled. Bradley's jersey now hangs in Madison Square Garden, together with those of other key players from that championship team. Featuring teamwork rather than individual talent, the 1970 Knicks are recognized as one of the most intelligent basketball teams ever, in no small part thanks to the man they called "Dollar Bill."

Popularity of sports heroes is not unique to the United States. Europeans love their soccer stars. Tennis stars are virtually idolized. Michael Jordan has a strong following outside the United States. And Muhammad Ali once owned the world. But nobody loves sports heroes like Americans and no place is the transition from the world of sports to politics smoother than in the United States. Bill Bradley and Jack Kemp are two examples of the operation of this principle at the highest level; Ronald Reagan, who played a football hero in a Grade B tearjerker, almost counts as a third. Of course, if you have the misfortune to have a ground ball pass through your legs in the World Series, your political plans might have to be put on hold. Bill Buckner, in many respects a hero, won't be running for mayor of Boston.

Bradley hadn't even retired from professional sports when people started talking about him as a future presidential candidate. It was therefore no surprise when he ran for senator from New Jersey, and no surprise when he won. But now, instead of preparing for either reelection to the Senate or a challenge for the presidency, he was giving up his Senate seat and joining the crowded ranks of authors. Questioned on national television about the state of American politics and his temporary retirement at age 52, he referred to the importance of money in politics, the increasing meanness and negativism of campaigns, the mercenary conduct of the media and the lack of privacy. It was a powerful indictment of a political system that discourages participation, driving potential candidates away out of fear and disgust.

Yet, when asked whether he would consider a future run for president, he responded affirmatively and did not even close the door on 1996. Don't take Bradley's withdrawal from the Senate as the end of his political career. One night down the road there might be a rally in a packed Garden, with Bradley standing at center court pointing up to the banners and speaking of the need to bring teamwork to Washington. The camera and spotlight will move from jersey to jersey, settling in on No. 24, and New York will again belong to Dollar Bill.

* * *

Going back to 1992, there had been word that Senator Sam Nunn of Georgia was considering a run for the presidency. Like Bradley, Nunn was widely respected in the Democratic Party and had credibility as a potential presidential candidate. As former chairman of the Senate Armed Services Committee, he actually had experience in matters that mattered for presidents. It was Nunn who had the stature to join Jimmy Carter and Colin Powell on their mission to Haiti to negotiate the resignation of General Cedras and avoid war.

Far from challenging Bill Clinton in 1996, Nunn was joining Bradley on the sidelines. He would not seek reelection to a Senate in which divisiveness and partisanship reigned supreme. Voicing some of the same sentiments as Bradley, he was going to withdraw and reassess, take a break. One had the feeling that Nunn too would be back. The question was whether he would be back as a Democrat.

* * *

The Republicans had their share of personalities sitting it out as well, most notably the always enthusiastic Jack Kemp, the hugely popular Colin Powell and the hugely unpopular Newt Gingrich.

Jack Kemp was an attractive political figure, a strong proponent of supply-side economics in the tradition of Ronald Reagan and, along with Bob Dole, a Bush rival for the Republican nomination in 1988. He was also a sports hero. Having won the big one as quarterback of the then AFL Buffalo Bills, he could have won it again in his second career.

Kemp was known as a conservative with a heart, or is it conservative with a conscience? Implicit in the expression is the notion that conservatives have neither. Kemp disproved that theory, exhibiting his social conscience as a member of the Bush cabinet in his work on urban development. He wasn't the only conservative with a social conscience, just one of the relatively few who had managed to develop that image through the media. The combination of strong Republican roots, a perceived sensitivity to issues such as race and the problems of the inner cities and a winning personality should have been sufficient to make Kemp a formidable presidential candidate in 1996.

What happened? Among other things, he didn't seem willing to pay the price a second time, to do what it takes to raise money, to get his jersey dirty. Having made that decision, he must have figured he was through running for political office. Neither he nor anyone else could have anticipated the dramatic change in his plans that would come a few months later.

*   *   *

Colin Powell was an unusual and intriguing personality. For months during 1995, he occupied center stage as the most popular noncandidate. He combined military knowledge with an apparent knack for statesmanship. As a good general should, he maintained calm under pressure.

Two events stood out in my mind concerning Colin Powell: the Gulf War and his mission to Haiti with Jimmy Carter and Sam Nunn. In the former, Powell was impressive not only in fulfilling his military duties, but also in his caution and restraint in the prewar debate. He never seemed comfortable with the civilian call to arms; there was no chest thumping, no rush to battle. When the call came, Powell answered. In Haiti, with the Administration seemingly impatient to start an invasion (nothing like a good war to get you out of a rut), Powell was again thinking clearly and, together with Carter and Nunn, orchestrated the peaceful resignation of General Cedras. For a nation in search of a hero, Powell again was there.

Was Powell the reincarnation of Dwight D. Eisenhower? Not quite. As impressive as Powell's accomplishments were, they didn't exactly rival D-Day. The truth is—and this is not a criticism of Colin Powell—his immense popularity was more a sad commentary on the state of American politics than anything else. He hadn't yet demonstrated that he has the qualities to be president, but he also hadn't disqualified himself, and that was enough to put him at the top of the polls.

It was noteworthy that Powell's ascent in the polls had nothing to do with his actual political views. While his views by and large seemed centrist, that didn't really matter. The most remarkable aspect of Powell's popularity was that it was achieved in the midst of uncertainty and speculation as to whether he was a Democrat or a Republican. Far from hurting him, nonaffiliation seemed to constitute an integral part of his appeal—another sad commentary on the state of American politics in general and the major political parties in particular.

Oh yes, one more point concerning Colin Powell is worth mentioning: he is the first African-American to stand a chance of becoming president of the United States. With all due respect to the reverend, Jesse Jackson is still viewed primarily as a black leader too caught up in his own rhyme and rhetoric. While Jackson was able to garner substantial support in his runs during the 1980s and undoubtedly had a profound effect on the course of Democratic politics, he never had any real chance of being elected president. Not true for Powell, and I have a feeling that fact doesn't sit well with far too many people.

Is race still an issue in America? You bet it is. That's a major reason why Powell's success makes me feel good. I've always been more than a bit embarrassed by the way we hold ourselves out as the model of democracy and forget that sixteen white presidents were sworn in while slavery was legal in this country. Slavery has been illegal for some time, but twenty-six more white presidents have been sworn in without a black person ever having been nominated by either major party. In and of itself, the history we would rather forget is an insufficient reason to hand Powell the keys to the White House. Even the most liberal of our courts never took affirmative action that far. Nevertheless, although Powell had no obligation to play Jackie Robinson, it would have been good for the country if his 1995 book tour had kicked off his campaign rather than merely sold books.

Was it really the case that Powell simply didn't have the fire in the belly necessary to make a run? I doubt it. It would have been an odd way to end months of speculation about his possible candidacy, none of which seemed to have been discouraged by Powell. One normally doesn't need a book tour to discover fire in the belly. You either have it or you don't. If you watched and heard Powell's speech at the Republican National Convention in San Diego, you felt he had it. That leads me to conclude that Powell was balancing the scales during those months, weighing his desire to participate in the process against the ugliness he and his family seemed certain to encounter if he did. At the end of the day, the answer was clear.

Powell's announcement that he wouldn't seek the presidency did not remove him from the political scene. From that moment on, he became the front-runner for the Republican vice-presidential nomination as the experts speculated on how the Republicans could bolster their ticket. The Democrats were hoping Powell's reluctance to run for public office applied equally to both ends of the ticket. A popular African-American joining whoever the Republican presidential nominee would be was their worst nightmare.

* * *

Newt Gingrich was coming off quite a year. He had led the Republican revolution that swept the midterm elections in 1994 and dominated the national political agenda on his way to becoming *Time's* Man of the Year in 1995. We kept hearing during the 1994 congressional campaign what a mistake the Contract with America was. Why would Gingrich want to jeopardize anticipated sizeable Republican gains in Congress with a public relations stunt that could easily backfire? As it turned out, the Contract was either a stroke of genius or dumb luck, depending on your point of view. Either way, you can't argue with success. Gingrich went for broke and came up a winner.

After the elections, Gingrich proceeded to do exactly what he said he would do. Usually, political expediency leads to broken promises. In this case, Gingrich seemed to see value in fulfilling his contract to the letter. He could then distinguish himself from regular politicians and ride his revolution all the way to the top.

Everyone has a theory about what happened to Newt while he was running the country in 1995. It's hard to pinpoint the problem. He didn't help himself with a $4 million book contract that made it seem as if he were capitalizing on his revolution. Perhaps more important, the perception grew that he was moving too fast in implementing a conservative agenda that the country had voted for without reading the fine print. Whatever the reason, the Man of the Year suddenly found himself the most unpopular leading politician in the country, a Republican liability the Democrats would seek to exploit at every opportunity. The transformation goes down as another illustration of the main axiom of American politics: things change quickly. If you don't like the way things are now, just wait. You may not like them any more later, but you can bet they won't be the same.

What was Newt's plan for 1996? After testing the waters for a presidential bid, he realized 1996 would not be his year. Unlike Kemp and Powell, Gingrich didn't give the impression he had backed off for financial or personal reasons associated with the ills of the process. Rather, he appears to have backed off for the best reason of all; he couldn't win.

1996 was to be a terrible year politically for Gingrich, as the Democrats smelled blood and wouldn't let up. The idea was not only to curb the power of the slightly arrogant Speaker of the House, but to extend his rising unpopularity to Dole and the entire Republican Party in a form of political guilt by association. Fairly or unfairly, the "extremist" label stuck to Gingrich, and by extension was beginning to stick to the congressional Republicans he had led in implementing the Contract with America. The man who had spearheaded the shocking Republican victory in the 1994 midterm elections was providing the Democrats with the ammunition they needed to make a rapid comeback, and there was no Contract with America II to bail him out. By year's end, the Speaker appeared to hit rock bottom, admitting to mistakes in providing misleading information to the House Ethics Committee investigating allegations that he had used charitable contributions for political purposes. As in the case of the 1995 edition of Bill Clinton, one was left to wonder how low Newt could go.

Chapter 6

Kickoff

The State of the Union address in an election year is sometimes referred to as the kickoff of the presidential campaign. Coming a few weeks before the first electoral tests, it provides the president with a platform to set the tone, remind the nation who is president and show us who should remain president. This time, the country got a reminder of the extraordinary campaigning talents of Bill Clinton. You recall how comfortable he was on the campaign trail in 1992. He seemed born to run. When he won, he seemed unprepared for the campaign to end. Eventually, Clinton stopped campaigning to endure a rocky three years as President, commencing with his executive order allowing gays in the military and continuing through his state of irrelevancy during most of 1995. The State of the Union address returned him to his comfort zone, and what a return it was. The speech was effective, full of drama and strategically sound. By the time he finished, you could be excused for wondering just whom the Republicans had to do battle with this man.

Remember, Bill Clinton is a Democrat. Admittedly, it's never been entirely clear what that means. The Democratic Party has been home to a wide range of characters, liberal and conservative, with only one thing in common—the desire to win. Even Ronald Reagan and Phil Gramm were once Democrats. Yet it is also true that the Democratic Party has been associated with a left of center ideology, a basic belief in big government as essential to achieve social development. (Reagan and Gramm *did* leave.) In other words, most Democrats have been "liberals," or at least have tended to nominate liberal candidates for president in recent years. By and large, that ideology has been rejected in national elections in thrashings reminiscent of those absorbed by the AFC in recent Super Bowl history.

Since winning is everything, it was only a matter of time for the Democrats to adapt to the country's shift to the right. Centrist themes were stressed in 1992; minority power was curtailed; Jesse Jackson was contained; and the Democratic Convention followed a moderate script with an eye on winning in November rather than midsummer celebration. Something called a New Democrat was invented, presumably to make a clean break with the failed tactics of the past. New Democrats still believe that government can do good, but they are socially moderate and fiscally responsible. They are where they think the country is.

For most of his first term, Bill Clinton the New Democrat looked a lot like the Democrats of old. Things got so bad that Republican David Gergen was invited to do a stint as advisor. But now, entering the election year, Clinton was back on comfortable ground staking out positions that were confounding the Republicans. Suddenly, he was fiscally responsible, defending the people against extremism from the right while the petulant Republicans would either balance the budget their way or shut down the entire federal government.

The State of the Union address left the Republicans staring blankly on national television as the President stole their thunder. Sounding Republican theme after theme, he showed them just how formidable an opponent he would be. Family values, crime, responsibility of the media for decent programming, uniforms for schoolchildren and the end of the era of big government—who was that masked man?

Apart from good strategy, there was good theater. Like other presidents before him, Clinton realized it never hurts to bring in a hero or two. Among his guests was a government worker who went back into the crumbled federal building in Oklahoma City to save three women. A few moments later, the President didn't fail to remind us that our hero couldn't go to work in November because the Republicans had shut down the federal government in the Battle of the Budget.

The tone was also good. Clinton was taking the offensive, but skillfully disguising his attack with language of accommodation. He seemed to sense that the country was as wary of the far right as it was the old liberal establishment and that harsh Republican rhetoric, coupled with Republican overconfidence following the landslide in 1994, left the Republicans vulnerable to charges of "extremism." At the same time, he had to be careful not to open himself up to the same charges from the other side, which required him to distance himself from traditional Democratic liberalism and appear conciliatory amidst the "extremists" in the chamber. Laying the groundwork for the strategy that would carry him through the fall campaign, he positioned himself in the center, arguably to the right of center, and called upon Democrats and Republicans to work together for the good of the country. It sounded presidential, just what people wanted to hear. And what were the Republicans supposed to do? They didn't know, either.

Perhaps the most notable moment was Clinton's praise for his beleaguered wife. She stood, took a bow and absorbed the applause. A touching moment that played well—the President stands by his wife, as she had stood by him before.

* * *

What was Bob Dole thinking when he decided to give the Republican reply to the State of the Union? It should have been easily anticipated that he would suffer badly in comparison with the President on this night. He didn't have a live audience to cheer him on; he couldn't bring in heroes to stir emotions; he couldn't even bring in his wife. Matching up against Bill Clinton is tough enough even when all the props are available. Under the circumstances, discretion would have been the better part of valor.

The speech itself was undisguised partisanship, with hardly a trace of conciliation. Dole's hard message was that there was a time when every leader had to take a stand on principle and this was it. He painted the President as the obstacle to progress, preventing the conservative agenda of America from moving forward. It was a speech some Democratic speechwriter landing behind enemy lines might have written.

Apart from his hard message, Dole's form was poor. He seemed a touch nervous and incapable of taking on Bill Clinton head-to-head, much less leading the country. Once again, image isn't everything, but you don't want to start a tough campaign with your image getting in the way of your message. If Clinton scored a touchdown on his opening drive, Dole's answer was a quick three and out.

The Republican spin doctors (those who explain why your eyes and ears didn't really see or hear what they did) were not out in force after the Dole reply. Most of the air time seemed occupied by his Republican opponents, who seized the opportunity to tear into the front-runner. Our starting pitcher got shelled and it's time to go to the bullpen, was Buchanan's contribution. Alexander went after both Dole and Clinton, the latter for faking a vision, Dole for not being able to. There's that vision thing again. Dole himself made no apologies for his performance, although he did note that fire has a tendency to be extinguished when he delivers a fireside chat. On several other occasions Dole poked fun at himself, including his amusing threat to liven up one gathering by repeating his speech. The negative fallout from the State of the Union reply had given Dole the opportunity to exhibit his renowned sense of humor, but the opportunity cost was too high.

Difficult as it seemed to believe, there was a strategic explanation for Dole's State of the Union reply: he was speaking to Republican voters in the upcoming caucuses and primaries. This apparently conscious decision to use the reply to appeal to the Republican hard core underscored a troubling aspect of the nomination process, namely, the need to cater to the few to have a chance to reach the many. Democrats suffered from this phenomenon for years, as candidates were continually forced to tilt further left to gain the party nomination. Activists from a wide range of minority groups had taken over the Democratic Party and extracted their price from those seeking the nomination—see Jesse Jackson's strength in the 1980s. The same dynamic affects the Republican Party of the 1990s. Right wing philosophy (or what passes as such these days) predominates in the Republican Party and, like left wing philosophy, it does not consider tolerance a virtue.

So Dole, a suspect centrist, still had some convincing to do in his own party. Along the way, he would have to demonstrate a degree of ideological commitment that would not stand him well in the general election. Just as the Democrats had paid dearly in past general elections for positions taken in primary campaigns, Republicans pushing each other further right in their bids to capture the nomination would make it more difficult for them to recapture the presidency. Dole's challenge would be to strike the right balance, to avoid losing the election by winning the nomination. His performance the night of the State of the Union was a bad start. No need to worry; it was only January.

Chapter 7

Let The Games Begin

The slugfests we call primaries and caucuses provide us a close look at the presidential candidates under fire and allow them to hone their campaign skills. When the contests mercifully draw to a conclusion, the battle-tested survivor breaks training camp in top condition for the real contest in the fall. Despite this purported virtue, these preliminaries tend to raise more questions than they provide answers. The questions have to do with whether this unique method of selecting party nominees has outlived its usefulness, and whether it should be scrapped entirely in favor of a process that forces candidates to address issues relevant to the presidency rather than those of principally local concern, doesn't exaggerate the importance of early, small-state contests and develops and rewards presidential qualities rather than campaigning talents. The race for the Republican nomination in 1996 raised all these issues and more in an action-packed six weeks that at once shaped Election '96 and highlighted all that ails American presidential politics.

* * *

In early February, the eyes of the nation were focused on the upcoming Louisiana and Iowa caucuses and the New Hampshire primary. The excitement was building. It was that feeling you get before a big game as the players are ready to come out of the tunnel to the roar of the crowd. Until reality sets in with the first electoral results, everyone talks big; everyone has a chance.

All that excitement, of course, was generated on the Republican side. It is usually the privilege of a first-term president to receive a "bye" in these preliminaries. As in the NFL playoffs, the bye gives you a chance to sit back, heal and watch your opponents bash one another while you get yourself ready for the main event. Only one wild card team has ever won the Super Bowl. The odds are a little better in presidential politics, but the advantage of an incumbent unchallenged in his own party remains substantial. Remember 1992, when George Bush didn't have that luxury? Pat Buchanan's strong second-place showing in the 1992 New Hampshire primary was a setback from which Bush never fully recovered. That's why Bill Clinton's timely return from irrelevancy in 1995 was so important. It eliminated the possibility of a Bradley, a Nunn or even a Gephardt mounting a Buchanan-like challenge; it gave him the bye.

Nevertheless, there was no guarantee of smooth sailing for Bill Clinton. The nature of the game is such that you never know what forces might come into play to prevent a first-termer from sitting back and enjoying the moment. To appreciate the impact of external forces on a campaign, take a look at what happened to Jimmy Carter.

In the last year of his presidency, Carter had to deal with OPEC (in case anyone forgot, that's the Organization of Petroleum Exporting Countries) and its control of world oil prices, on the economic front, and Iran and the hostage crisis, on the political front. We don't like our presidents to appear helpless. And that's exactly what Carter did in 1980. Oil prices were at their peak, apparently headed in a permanently upward direction. It was a time when journalists hounded OPEC ministers in the lobby of the Intercontinental Hotel in Geneva, hanging on every word. Eavesdroppers aplenty sought tidbits of information from casual lobby conversations as rumors emanating from OPEC circles sent the markets into turmoil. With no available wars to fight,

Carter didn't have any answers. While nobody else did either, the President took the blame.

In Iran, defiant demonstrators demonstrated our impotence in dealing with hostage-taking situations. Rather than downplaying the crisis, Carter made it his obsession. The media was only too glad to keep the crisis in our faces. In fact, ABC's hit show "Nightline" was created during that period to follow the crisis. Eventually, Carter attempted to regain control of the situation through a dramatic military rescue. The attempt ended in disaster in the desert and sank the international image of Carter, the presidency and the entire country to its lowest level in memory, lower than the Watergate years. All this and a few lines in his debate with Ronald Reagan proved too much for Carter to overcome. It wouldn't have mattered if he had been spared a fight for his own party's nomination (that was the year of Teddy Kennedy's last hurrah in presidential politics); by election day, the country had had enough.

In Clinton's case, there was at least one offshore problem that could fall into the same category: Bosnia. I didn't know much about Bosnia, just enough to know it was a mess we could not control. Something told me that brutality of the nature and on a scale seen in Bosnia is not easily forgotten by the victims. Sooner or later the victims, whoever they are, become stronger and look for victims of their own. They need a reason to forget. It could be fear; it could be the healing effects of the passage of time, lots of it; it could be a distorted application of the fairness principle, that the misery has been relatively evenly distributed; or it could be religion. Without a reason, the memories remain too vivid to ignore. That's why I worried about Bosnia.

Sergeant Dugan was the first American soldier to die in Bosnia. Clinton took the bad news in stride, reminding us that he had warned of the possibility, even likelihood, of casualties. Since the entire country was a minefield, more casualties were expected. If it happened, it would not only be a tragedy for those who ended up giving their lives for Bosnia; prior warnings aside, it would also ruin Bill Clinton's bye.

Domestic wild cards also had the potential to rock Clinton's boat somewhere along the way to November. Whitewater was at the top of the deck. It was obviously much less serious than Bosnia. Lives were not at stake, just careers. In one respect, though, Whitewater was Clinton's domestic Bosnia, a messy situation essentially beyond his control. The pace of the Whitewater hearings was to be dictated by the Republicans, and they didn't look like they would rest until they either brought Clinton down or brought themselves down trying. In January 1996, the jury was still out as to which way it would go.

Congressional hearings have always played an important role in American public life. That role consists partly of a search for the truth and partly of politics, with a dose of entertainment as an unintended by-product of the process. In modern times, the parts are no longer of equal weight, politics and entertainment having far outdistanced the search for the truth. Consequently, the issues receiving the most congressional attention are those that attract the widest media coverage and pack an explosive political punch. The most memorable hearings of the past 25 years, Watergate, Irangate and the Clarence Thomas hearings, are prime examples.

Not that the issues treated in those hearings were unimportant. We *should* care whether one political party is spying on another; whether the President is inclined to cover up embarrassing misdeeds; whether the President is running undercover operations out of the White House; and whether a justice-to-be of the Supreme Court engaged in sexual harassment. The real question, however, is whether we lose perspective when we make these issues the exclusive focus of our national attention.

Certainly the rest of the world thinks so. Our obsession with Watergate was never understood abroad. The break-in itself was considered clumsy, but hardly surprising. Many assumed that the president was as powerful at home as he was around the world. And around the world, the president of the United States was considered the world's most powerful individual, or at least second to the director of the CIA. When a government fell in the Middle East, Africa, Asia or South America, the change was automatically attributed to CIA maneuvering at the president's behest (and perhaps occasionally on its own). It didn't matter whether the new government was friendly to the United States; signs of unfriendliness were taken as skillful disguise.

This view of the world was comforting in many respects because it gave people the feeling that things were under control regardless of all appearances to the contrary. When things are under control, order prevails, and most people see the need for some sort of order in their lives. Watergate challenged the assumption that things were under control in the United States, the most powerful nation in the world. It made the president seem vulnerable and petty. The president is not supposed to be involved in second-rate burglaries. If he is, surely he would know enough to burn the tapes.

If the international community didn't understand Watergate, it was totally confounded by Irangate. As in the case of Watergate, there was major disappointment. The disappointment was not due to the fact that borderline, if not outright illegal, activities seemed to form an integral part of the Administration's efforts to free the hostages in Iran and help the Nicaraguan Contras; rather, it was due to the rank amateurism shown by the Administration in implementing such an imaginative strategy. To a world accustomed to more polished covert activity, Ollie North and company didn't measure up, even though they may have had good intentions.

Congressional hearings straddled the border of politics and entertainment in the Clarence Thomas nomination. Unlike the others, the Clarence Thomas hearings regarding the Anita Hill allegations were necessarily short and packed with drama. Who could forget the Hill/Thomas confrontation played out on television in a miniseries nobody wanted to miss? I know I wasn't thrilled missing a key episode for a business trip. It was very good for television, very bad for America. That assumes Thomas did what he was accused of doing. Think how much worse it was for Thomas and America if, as I (and those I know who know him) suspect, he didn't.

Whitewater was different, mainly because it had taken so long to clarify what was at issue. There were no burglaries in Whitewater, no easily identifiable crimes and, at least at that stage, no sex. In addition, many people around the world tended to assume that anything taking place in Arkansas more than ten years ago couldn't be important enough to command our national attention, any more than the governor of Arkansas could possibly be prepared for the presidency of the United States. The question they kept asking was: "Don't you have anything good on TV anymore?"

Even the Republicans started to skip over the merits of this one and head straight for the cover-up. Most people can relate to cover-ups and, if one did take place, at least it was within the past decade, an informal statute of limitations on White House scandals. That's why Al D'Amato would make sure we learned more about Hillary Clinton's time records and their whereabouts than we ever cared to know. The hearings seemed destined to continue until Hillary won a showdown with Al or until Al and his colleagues were overshadowed by another story. Could Paula Jones be far behind?

*   *   *

On the Republican side, things were getting interesting as we approached the first caucuses and New Hampshire. The main reason was Steve Forbes. I never thought his candidacy would survive. Then again, I was still getting used to the money thing.

Forbes' spending reached shocking proportions and propelled him into a virtual tie with Dole in early February. The poor souls of Iowa and New Hampshire were subjected to a media blitz the likes of which they had never seen before. Positive ads, negative ads, talk shows. Forbes was everywhere, and the analysts were already congratulating themselves for having accurately predicted the demise of Bob Dole. The general feeling at the time was that if for some reason Dole actually won in Iowa and New Hampshire, the first major tests in which all the candidates would be competing, people would be talking about his *comeback*. All this and not a single vote had yet been cast.

Why were people responding to Steve Forbes? He's likeable, had an optimistic message of "hope, growth and opportunity," struck a chord with his Washington outsider theme and spent his way into everyone's living room. Notwithstanding his success, I sensed, this time correctly, that things were about to change for Forbes. I simply refused to believe that his spending would not eventually catch up to him and become *the* issue. It's one thing to permit Forbes to use his money to send a message to the candidates about your concerns, frustrations, hopes and expectations. It's quite another to allow the nomination to be purchased for hard cash, in public and in your face. Buchanan, always colorful, called Forbes a souffle that would not rise again. It would be a couple of weeks before we found out whether he was right on the money.

* * *

The conservatives had their day in Louisiana on February 6, Ronald Reagan's birthday. The first contests are always important precisely because they are first, which has meant that the Iowa caucus and New Hampshire primary in February always gave people in those states more than their fair share of influence over the selection of the presidential nominees. That's why Louisiana scheduled its 1996 caucus one week earlier than the Iowa caucus. Iowans were upset at Louisiana's attempt to upstage them, so only two of the main candidates showed up in Louisiana: Phil Gramm and Pat Buchanan.

Gramm and Buchanan were conservative with a capital "C." Yet they didn't believe in the same things. Sure, both trashed big government and both believed in "Values." (Who doesn't these days?) But substance was not what bound these conservatives together. What Gramm and Buchanan had most in common was attitude with a capital "A," as exemplified by the vigor with which they attacked the old liberal establishment. It was the tough rhetoric more than anything that stamped them both as conservative.

The conservative candidates had considerably divergent views of the role of the United States in the world. Buchanan wanted to put America first, meaning forget foreign aid, forget foreign adventures and forget foreign trade, at least if it meant international commitments ceding authority to make rules governing what we can and cannot do in this country. You've heard all about the "global economy," which presumably is the economy of the "global village." The terms reflect the thesis that the various peoples of the world have become so interdependent we must start thinking globally, not nationally or parochially. Buchanan thought that was all nonsense.

Gramm, on the other hand, was a free trader, a staunch supporter of NAFTA. Like Bill Bradley, he had debated NAFTA opponents from both the Democratic and Republican sides, usually coming out on top, always prepared. In his view, Buchanan the rightist was a virtual leftist on economic issues; the protectionist message Buchanan was disseminating proceeded from the false premise that Americans cannot compete in the world economy. That mindset was unacceptable to Gramm.

What, then, is a conservative, a rightist, a Republican? Except for Attitude, I've never been sure.

Back in the late '60s and early '70s, conservatives weren't as spooked by big government. Nor were they shy about foreign intervention. The conservative themes of the day were law and order on the home front—would you believe the 1996 Democratic platform says "Today's Democratic Party believes the first responsibility of government is law and order"—and combatting communism abroad. The common thread was a belief that the country was under siege internationally by communists and domestically by hippies, draft dodgers and flag burners. If you loved America, you had to resist the siege, develop an attitude. Suddenly, strapping the flag to the seat of your pants was considered a capital offense. In foreign policy, questioning the assumptions underlying the Vietnam War, or worse, the morality of it, was giving comfort to the enemy and undermining the war effort—treason. The attitude was captured by two expressions: "America, love it or leave it" and "My country, right or wrong." Questioning the government, criticizing it, these were not acceptable options.

So "conservatives," with their serious attitude problem, did not tend to attract intellectuals to their ranks. They did, however, attract an assortment of intolerants, including racists. To those who weren't using law and order as a surrogate for racism, and there were many, it was annoying the way racists and conservatives became identified with each other. While many limousine liberals were closet racists, there was no denying that racists felt more comfortable with conservatives. At times it seemed as if Bill Buckley, Jr., was the lone conservative with a platform—his television show, "Firing Line"—capable of holding his own in an exchange of ideas.

Times changed. Conservatism became fashionable, even on college campuses. By the late 1970s, students appeared more interested in business than revolution. Short hair and suits were in and working on Wall Street became respectable again. In the 1980s, Ronald Reagan had the liberals on the run. As underscored by Clinton's declaration late in Campaign '96 that his positions did not qualify him as a "closet liberal," the liberal retreat continues to this day. Conservatives therefore had good reason to feel good about themselves on February 6. They were celebrating the birthday of their most popular leader with a caucus in Louisiana featuring the two main conservative candidates. Even if the candidates didn't agree on all issues, the Attitude was definitely there.

Pat Buchanan trounced Phil Gramm in Louisiana. It was a major upset since Gramm had expended lots of energy there in an effort to establish himself as the main candidate from the right. Bob Dole, who never considered Buchanan a serious threat for the nomination, seemed pleased that his fellow senator had been slowed if not stopped. Indeed, many assumed Gramm would withdraw following his disappointing showing. Imagine. Years of preparation, months of active campaigning, loads of frequent traveller miles, all those speeches, chicken dinners and handshakes, all that money, and Phil Gramm was expected to bow out because he didn't do as well as expected in the Louisiana caucuses. How would he face his momma if he did that?

*   *   *

On the eve of the Iowa caucuses, Bob Dole, the front-runner/comeback kid, was sitting atop the polls once again. Not without controversy. Iowans claimed to be disgusted with the intensity of the negative campaigning to which they had been subjected. Dole's campaign was accused of particularly dirty pool. A former employee of a Utah firm alleged that his company was phoning Iowans, spreading damaging rumors about Steve Forbes. A new term was injected into the political vocabulary: push poll, where a pollster calls you up and asks something like "Would you still support X if you knew he was a child molester?" The question doesn't actually say X is a child molester, but that's the clear impression it leaves. The underlying assumption is that planting that seed of doubt is sufficient to sway the anti-child-molester vote.

Under different circumstances, disclosures of push polls could have been enough to bring a candidate down. This time, the charges didn't stick. Iowans seemed to be saying that since Steve Forbes wasn't shy about negative campaigning, he got what was coming to him. Lawyers have this doctrine they call "clean hands"; if you want the court to protect you, make sure you come in with your own hands clean.

The most disturbing aspect of the precaucus atmosphere was not the unsavory tactics being used; it was the heaviness of the atmosphere itself. There was simply too much at stake. Almost nine full months before the election and six months before the Republican National Convention in San Diego, a relatively few voters in a small state would have much to say about who the Republican nominee for president would be. Phil Gramm denied saying he would withdraw from the race if he didn't finish in the top three in Iowa. At the same time, he noted that no president had ever failed to do so. While not averse to making history, he understandably preferred the easier road to the White House.

There is something fundamentally wrong with a system that allows so few voters to deliver a knockout punch in the nomination process for the presidency of the United States of America. Five main Republican candidates headed into Iowa, with four additional ones who could attract blocks of votes. Since only around 100,000 votes were expected, a swing of a few thousand votes could easily make the difference between a respectable showing and abject failure. If Phil Gramm lost those few thousand votes in another disappointing night following Louisiana, he would be portrayed as the biggest loser in the biggest game of the season to that point and would feel constrained to withdraw from the race. In that event, he might legitimately question whether he truly got his day in court.

*   *   *

Bob Dole won the Iowa caucuses, garnering only 26 percent of the vote. Somewhat surprising, but not as much as the fourth place showing of Steve Forbes, who didn't quite get his money's worth with only 10 percent. Pat Buchanan, buoyed more than expected by Louisiana, came in second in Iowa with a very impressive 23 percent. Alexander drew a respectable 18 percent for third place. And poor Phil Gramm suffered another disappointment with 9 percent, fifth place and only slightly ahead of Alan Keyes. As expected, the grand total of all votes cast in the Iowa caucuses was approximately 100,000, a small minority of total Iowa Republicans. Exercising their grossly disproportionate voting power, those relatively few Republicans had a profound effect on the course of the race for the nomination.

The Iowa caucuses had significant consequences for each of the major Republican candidates. First, Dole's narrow margin of victory provided more fuel for the theory that he was vulnerable and would eventually fall. Americans enjoy a race, so we tend to root for an underdog to make one. Once the underdog starts doing well and is no longer an underdog, the same people often go back to support the frontrunner, but that's after making him sweat for a while. With a 30-35 percent showing, Dole could have silenced his critics and doubters. With his 3-point victory, he was still there as the front-runner, only now there was no doubt that the race was on and we were going to have some fun.

Buchanan's strong second-place showing firmly established him as the leading candidate from the right, even though we still had trouble distinguishing right from left. All of a sudden, incredulous observers were wondering whether Buchanan had become more than a sideshow, whether he could possibly break out of his talk-show role and be taken as a serious candidate for the nomination. Until now, Buchanan had benefitted from his underdog status.

After Louisiana and Iowa, he would receive the scrutiny—and the cheap shots— normally reserved for serious candidates. The real challenge was to do well without the benefit of underdog status.

Forbes collapsed in Iowa. After rising steadily in the polls to the point where he had begun to shed his underdog status, it all caught up to him—the spending, the backlash from his negative campaigning, his opponents' attacks on him, the impression that he was trying to buy the nomination. Once he fell out of favor, he went into a freefall. In a matter of days he went from a strong second to a weak fourth. According to Forbes, this was part of his 4-3-2-1 strategy, coming in fourth in Iowa, third in New Hampshire, etc. That explanation might have been bought had he not achieved his early success in the polls. However, the basic rule of the game is don't disappoint. Coming in fourth is tolerable if you were expected to come in sixth; it is unacceptable if you were expected to come in second. It's the American version of the revolution of rising expectations.

Alexander established that his campaign strategy— waiting for Dole to fall—was not frivolous. Apart from the premise that Dole would eventually fall, the strategy assumed that no one else was there to pick up the pieces, Buchanan and Gramm being too conservative, Forbes being a flash in the pan (Buchanan's souffle theory) whose popularity would run out long before his money would. Based on his third place finish in Iowa, people no longer scoffed at the Alexander strategy. Alexander had followed the rule; he had done better than expected. That earned him the right to move on to New Hampshire with hope.

Perhaps most significant was the impact of the Iowa caucuses on Phil Gramm. He himself had stressed the importance of finishing in the top three. After losing Louisiana to Buchanan, coming in fifth in Iowa was devastating. Gramm broke the golden rule; he did not live up to expectations.

What confounded pundits and casual observers alike was that those expectations, both in Louisiana and Iowa, had been largely built by Gramm himself. Politicians often prefer to *downplay* their chances, encouraging talk of underdog status. The strategy allows them to claim victory with relatively modest tallies and ride the momentum of such a "victory" to the next fund-raiser. For example, although the Clinton camp was able to celebrate the results of the 1992 New Hampshire primary, Clinton didn't actually win that contest (Paul Tsongas did); it just seemed that way because he had exceeded expectations in the aftermath of the Gennifer Flowers story. And in Iowa itself, the strong second and third place showings of Buchanan and Alexander made them feel better than the contest's "winner"; the nature of the game doesn't allow a front-runner to celebrate a win when the margin of victory is disappointing.

For some reason, Gramm refused to play the expectations game. He did the opposite, virtually imposing upon himself the strict standard of victory in the absolute sense. When the strategy didn't work, the disappointment of his losses was magnified. He had ejected himself from the game. With a touch of humor and grace, Gramm formally withdrew from the race a few days after the Iowa caucuses.

I wasn't at all happy with Phil Gramm's decision. That's not to say I considered him the ideal candidate. It's just that his withdrawal set another bad example that was bound to discourage others. Gramm's withdrawal told us a leading senator with strong ideas and substantial financial backing can be driven away from the process by a few thousand voters in Louisiana and Iowa. With all due respect to those voters, I wondered whether that was in the country's best interests.

* * *

Presidential debates have a long and distinguished tradition in the United States. We all studied the Lincoln-Douglas debates in school. Years from now, it's not likely anyone will be studying the 1996 Republican pre-New Hampshire primary debate.

Nevertheless, the primary warm-up was not without significance. In a true sign of the times, television handled the debate much like an NFL opening day game. There was the half-hour predebate show, with the candidates' prospects being analyzed by experts. A new feature was a dial given to the audience, enabling the listener to turn toward 100 when approving of a speaker and toward zero when disapproving. It wasn't as refined as scoring ice skating or diving, but it was a start. I couldn't wait to see the major advances in TV coverage of the real presidential debates in the fall.

The debate itself was uninspiring and inconclusive, more significant for what did not happen than for what did. With the others ganging up on him, Bob Dole wasn't able to distinguish himself. He missed a golden opportunity to take the high road and establish himself as the only serious Republican candidate. By the same token, none of the others stood out as worthy opponents.

There were some good moments—Buchanan the conservative attacking big business for exporting jobs, Keyes attacking Buchanan the socialist and comparing Forbes' spending of $400 per vote in Iowa to his own $12 investment, Forbes refreshingly admitting that he had made a mistake with his negative campaigning and questioning certain of Alexander's financial deals, Alexander pointing out that flat tax Forbes had not disclosed his tax returns, B-1 Bob imploring the others to observe Reagan's 11th commandment and refrain from attacking fellow Republicans, Taylor blaming the lawyers for the cost of medical insurance and suggesting closing the law schools (presumably in jest). The latter reminded me of Danny DeVito playing an ugly capitalist in *Other People's Money,* telling a roomful of his own lawyers it wouldn't be so bad if the communists took over since the first thing they would do is shoot all the lawyers. Apart from its entertainment value, the debate left the audience doubting whether any of the eight men on stage could handle the White House. The consensus winner? Bill Clinton.

*   *   *

As we edged closer to the New Hampshire primary, Buchanan drew even with Dole in the polls. Buchanan's success was causing panic in the Republican Party. Until then, there had been no need to expend much energy attacking Buchanan and alienating his "brigades" since few thought he could ever win. A Buchanan victory in New Hampshire would change everything. It wouldn't provide him with the nomination; it would just throw the process into a state of chaos from which the Republicans might not recover. Buchanan's challenge to Bush in the 1992 New Hampshire primary had played a major part in Bush's downfall. He was about to gum up the works again, this time looking more intense and not facing any opponent of the unbeatable variety.

The serious efforts to bring Buchanan down began in earnest. Just before the preprimary debate, news broke that Larry Pratt, one of his campaign cochairmen, had hung around with white supremacist groups. Pratt defended himself against the charges, saying he didn't know all the people at the gatherings where he made speeches and denying he shared their views. He took a leave of absence from the campaign. Buchanan, however, refused to fire him and devoted his closing statement in the preprimary debate to standing by his friend.

It was an unusual tactic by an unusual candidate. Having slid through the entire debate without being confronted with the issue—surprisingly, the others had laid off—Buchanan didn't have to turn to it at the end. He did anyway. Never one to back down from a fight, Buchanan made a point of loyalty, friendship and opportunity to defend oneself against unfair attacks. Although admirable, it was a tactical mistake, a sign of his difficulty in distinguishing between a presidential primary debate, where confrontation is not always appreciated, and "Crossfire," where it is the essence of the show.

We soon heard that a Buchanan campaign leader in Florida was fired because of her connections with the National Association for the Advancement of White People. Apparently, Buchanan didn't even know her. His counterattack was to hint that he was being victimized by dirty tricks. Given the allegations of "push polls" surfacing prior to the Iowa caucuses, that suggestion could not be lightly dismissed. Nevertheless, as if to make sure reporters took him seriously, Buchanan reminded them he was a graduate of the Richard Nixon school of politics and could therefore recognize what was happening, that the attacks against him were being orchestrated. Check your sources, he urged.

Not much was made of Buchanan's lighthearted reference to his credentials. Still, I thought it was another tactical mistake, this time of the more spontaneous variety. What was Buchanan suggesting, that he was schooled in dirty tricks when he worked in the White House under Tricky Dick? If so, I questioned the wisdom of highlighting that part of his resume. Buchanan apparently wasn't thinking in those terms. He was frustrated by the dirty tricks he felt the establishment had been practicing on him, and the one-liner about his experience seemed designed to give him the sort of credibility he needed to turn reporters away from the damaging stories.

One by one, the voices of the Republican establishment were coming out against Buchanan. Gingrich stressed the need to distance the Party from racists; Dornan suggested that Haley Barbour, Republican Party Chairman, consider options to stop Pat. Buchanan took the criticism in stride. Demonstrating his "Crossfire" experience, he did not allow insults other politicians would have found infuriating to throw him off balance. Opponents from all sides seemed to be scrutinizing every word he said in search of the expression that might validate the charges of extremism levelled against him. When he didn't cooperate, the insults came faster and louder, as if repetition and volume created fact.

Allegations of racism and anti-Semitism against Pat Buchanan never rang true with me. Until proven otherwise, I preferred to think of him as an honest, decent street fighter who stubbornly stood up for his beliefs and stood by his friends. Unfortunately, his populist beliefs on free trade, immigration and the unpatriotic multinationals tended to attract extremists from the right, including racists, in much the same manner as the law and order philosophy of the '60s and early '70s. To make matters worse, his confrontational style and rhetoric did little to discourage the extremism. Buchanan's strength, therefore, was also his weakness. On the one hand, the force of his ideas and personality attracted a substantial block of voters more passionate than the supporters of any other candidate. On the other hand, that force would rally opposition to him around another candidate, Dole, Alexander or someone else, in a stop Buchanan movement.

* * *

With the "someone else" nowhere to be found, Phil Gramm really had no choice. He could see Dole's campaign reeling under the attacks from all sides. As a consequence of the millions of dollars spent against Dole, the repeated allegations of a vision deficit and the media's long-standing assumption that he would fall, the man with the most distinguished record of public service in the group had been cut down to size. Instead of a cakewalk to the nomination, Dole was struggling to hang on, taking blows from Alan Keyes and Morry Taylor as well as the stronger candidates and allowing Pat Buchanan and Lamar Alexander to challenge for the lead. Gramm himself bore some responsibility for Dole's predicament since he had earlier led the chorus in the refrain that Dole couldn't beat Clinton. Of course, at the time Gramm must have felt certain he, rather than Pat Buchanan, would emerge as the true candidate from the right.

Gramm realized that if he were to have any say in shaping the race, the time to do it was before the New Hampshire primary, when Dole needed him the most. And there really was never any doubt Dole would be the man who would get his support. So Gramm came up to New Hampshire and signaled to the Republican establishment that it could still shore up Bob Dole. Gramm said no other candidate could unite the social and economic conservatives of the party, a goal he had once set for himself. What he was really saying was the fun was over, now let's get back to basics and rally around the only serious candidate we got.

* * *

How did Bill Clinton occupy himself during this period? He had the luxury of doing what every first-term president with a bye likes to do. Campaign unofficially, act presidential, stay above the fray. Thus, without officially announcing his candidacy, he made an appearance in Iowa, unopposed. Another right move for a guy who seemed to make all the right moves during a campaign. It gave him the opportunity to draw a sharp contrast between the togetherness that characterized the Democratic side and a heated Republican campaign getting dirtier by the hour. It also provided us another reminder of the force with which the eventual Republican winner would have to reckon.

No doubt enjoying himself as he hadn't since the end of the 1992 campaign, Clinton continued his unofficial campaign in New Hampshire, drawing another large crowd and again contrasting sharply with the Republican mess on the other side of the fence. The Democrats could hardly contain themselves. In recent history, more often than not they had torn one another apart in the primaries as the Republicans watched in glee. This time the roles were reversed and the Democrats didn't mind either soaking it up or rubbing it in. You could see that look of contentment on George Stephanopoulos' face as he appeared on television commenting on the less than illuminating Republican debate.

Clinton wasn't content to sit by passively. He was out there staking out territory. Like the State of the Union address, much of what he said sounded Republican. By the time the Republicans would be ready to take him on, he would claim the middle ground on taxes, spending and the changing role of government. On social issues, he would be talking about the V-chip, allowing parents to block out what they considered to be objectionable television programming, and pushing the concept of uniforms for schoolchildren. Clinton's new middle ground looked a lot like conservative positions of the past as he attempted to push the Republicans further right into extremist territory. If they claimed to be to the right of the conservative positions espoused by the President, where would that put them? If they embraced the same positions, their argument for change would be diluted. Interesting strategy. Was this the work product of top Clinton strategist Dick Morris, who previously had worked for Republican politicians? Whoever was responsible, on the eve of the New Hampshire primary the strategy seemed to be working.

What about Clinton's problems, the ones that were out of his control? Whitewater hadn't yet heated up, and just when Bosnia appeared about to, a summit of the presidents of Bosnia, Serbia and Croatia was held in Rome. After 25 hours of meetings, Assistant Secretary of State Richard Holbrooke was able to announce, "In Rome we have avoided a crisis." In the long run, it meant nothing. At the time, it meant Clinton was looking good.

* * *

Every Republican to win a presidential election in the past 50 years had won the New Hampshire primary. That was the bad news confronting Bob Dole as Pat Buchanan beat him by a nose in New Hampshire, 27-26. Alexander once again came in a strong third at 23 percent, while Steve Forbes could only manage four field goals.

In practical terms, Buchanan's victory meant uncertainty, the prospect of extended Republican playoff rounds and a longer rest for Bill Clinton. The uncertainty didn't concern Buchanan's chances—most agreed they were as slim as Democrat Jesse Jackson's in the 1980s. Rather, uncertainty persisted over which candidate would rally the anti-Buchanan vote, Dole or Alexander. With his many party endorsements and his organization, Dole was still the favorite. Alexander, having money problems, needed more than merely another strong showing to overtake Dole. It's that expectations thing. Once you exceed them, they keep rising until you can't get away with a victory speech unless you actually win. After New Hampshire, third place for Alexander would look like just that.

All deliriousness over Buchanan's victory aside, the White House clearly would have preferred a further slide by Dole in New Hampshire. A third place finish could have finished him off and paved the way for Alexander. When it didn't happen, everyone began to suspect Alexander would not hold up. Thus far, his principal contributions to the race had been a 100-mile walk across New Hampshire in plaid shirts and incessant attacks on Dole's negative campaigning and lack of vision or ideas.

Alexander's problem was twofold: first, his attacks on Dole's negative campaigning were looking a little too much like negative campaigning themselves; second, people were starting to recall Democrat Walter Mondale's famous 1984 question to Gary Hart: "Where's the beef?" In addition, the Clinton camp must have believed that the questions surrounding Alexander's financial dealings in Tennessee would neutralize Whitewater as an election issue. Reportedly, among those dealings was a $1.00 option that brought even greater returns than Hillary Clinton's commodities investments.

Dole, on the other hand, still had the opportunity to come out of the primaries in decent shape. While he may not have been inspiring, few Republicans and few Americans had fundamental objections to him. With a compressed primary season, it remained possible that the race would be decided in a few weeks, leaving seven full months to focus on Bill Clinton. In presidential politics, that's an eternity, as evidenced by the swing in Clinton's own popularity during the same period in 1995. And the wild cards were still out there.

Chapter 8

A Break in the Action

After New Hampshire, the country was out of breath keeping up with the Republican race. There was no rest for the weary, as events were packed into a front-loaded schedule that would decide the winner: Delaware, February 24; the Dakotas and Arizona, February 27; South Carolina, March 2; "Junior Tuesday," March 5; New York, March 9; and "Super Tuesday," March 12. Nevertheless, there's only one opening day in any season, and New Hampshire was it.

With no more opening day jitters to cloud my thinking, it was time to assess what had transpired and compile my preliminary list of beefs with the proceedings to date.

Money. I'm not sure the Supreme Court was technically wrong in the *Buckley* case. In any event, judging from its June 1996 decision in *Colorado Republican Federal Campaign Committee v. Federal Election Commission*, the Court doesn't appear ready to retreat from *Buckley*. If Justice Thomas gets his way (see his forceful concurrence), the Court might eventually abandon its difficult distinction between spending and contribution limits and hold both unconstitutional. Indeed, it will be interesting to see how the Court reacts to the fund-raising scandals that arose after the *Colorado Republican Committee* case, and whether it will find more persuasive the following statement from Justice

Stevens, who didn't seem overly impressed with money's debate-enriching qualities: "It is quite wrong to assume that the net effect of limits on contributions and expenditures—which tend to protect equal access to the political arena, to free candidates and their staffs from the interminable burden of fund-raising, and to diminish the importance of repetitive 30-second commercials—will be adverse to the interest in informed debate protected by the First Amendment."

Regardless of the future direction the Court takes, the personal wealth spent on recent campaigns is hard to stomach even for the staunchest of capitalists. Steve Forbes and Ross Perot may indicate a new trend in American politics, wealthy and successful businessmen turning political. While there's nothing wrong with that per se, it's not a comfortable feeling knowing that money makes it all possible.

Of course, money can also be a curse in politics if it is not spent wisely. Steve Forbes proved that point. When the message sank in that he was in the process of spending his way to the nomination, voters in Iowa and New Hampshire told him the nomination would not be for sale. An argument can therefore be made that there is no need to place any limitations on campaign spending since voters are perfectly capable of placing those limits on their own. In case of doubt, the adversary system of politics will help the voters along. If there is value in having a pitched battle among opponents in the primaries, it is that we can rely on each of them to expose the others' weaknesses. And if the adversaries don't do it, the press acts as a safety net preventing candidates from spending their way to the nomination without scrutiny. So we should, I suppose, feel fairly comfortable that excessive spending will sooner or later catch up to a candidate and backfire, unless the message is so powerful it transcends the money.

However, that comfort just isn't enough. Even assuming that the system ultimately rejects the money, a lot of damage can be done in the process. In this case, the damage was done to Bob Dole, the object of much of the monetary attack. While Forbes' anti-Dole spending may have generated voter resentment of his own candidacy, the consensus seemed to be he was also quite successful in bringing Dole back to the pack. In so doing, he could have shaped the 1996 presidential election as much as Ross Perot did that of 1992. It was Dole's relatively poor showings in Iowa (not winning big) and New Hampshire (not winning) that threw the nomination temporarily up for grabs. And many believe Forbes' spending was the proximate cause of both.

We often are faced with the necessity of reconciling two conflicting principles. Here we have the freedom to spend, a close relative of freedom of speech, on the one hand, and a combination of principles of fair play and integrity of the electoral process, on the other. Notwithstanding the fact that strong policy arguments can be made on both sides, this kind of debate more often than not winds up on the side of the First Amendment. You know that business about slippery slopes, difficulties in drawing lines, fine art versus pure pornography and taking pains to avoid accepting simplistic solutions. Accepting all that, there still seems to be something fundamentally wrong with a set of rules that permits a person to acquire political power or otherwise distort the system with money.

That's why I would prefer to see a compromise to reconcile the conflicting principles on this issue, one that takes account of the changes in American society and political life over the past fifty years, particularly the predominant role of the media in political campaigns. Precisely what the compromise should be would be a fruitful object of our national attention, perhaps a few more congressional hearings. The scandals that unfolded late in the campaign concerning "soft money" and foreign contributions ensured that the new Congress' attention would indeed be focused on at least those aspects of campaign finance reform. My concern is that attacking the problem from the fund-raising angle is essentially a losing proposition, even if Congress could structure a statute that would withstand constitutional scrutiny. The last time Congress tried it, the seeds were sown for the travesty of 1996. I think I'd rather place my money on the other side of the equation and start by contemplating—investigation won't be necessary—what they're doing with all that money. From my perspective, I would be happy with the measure outlined below, regardless of the amount of soft money or hard cash raised or spent in a campaign and regardless of its source.

Campaign Commercials. Ban them. Don't limit or censor them; just ban them. If that is done, money won't be the problem it is.

There is precedent for banning certain types of television commercials. Years ago, cigarette commercials were taken off the air. Remember the Marlboro Man, the picture of health moving to the tune of the *Magnificent Seven?* I guess society came to the conclusion that freedom of speech did not include freedom to pollute the airwaves, with or without the appropriate warnings. The commercials didn't tell the whole story. Since cigarettes are dangerous and the power of television is virtually irresistible, the public interest outweighed the right to spend.

It could be argued, I suppose, that cigarette commercials should be allowed provided they contain appropriate warnings as to the health hazards of smoking. It is also true that antismoking commercials can effectively present the antismoking point of view. So why not compromise and accommodate the competing interests?

First, as Dole said in his State of the Union reply, there's a time when compromise must end and we must stand on principle—too bad he wasn't talking about cigarette commercials.

Second is the sheer power of television. If a picture says a thousand words, what kind of impression is made by moving pictures coming into your living room and bedroom every day and every night? They actually have awards for the best commercials, with good reason. Who could forget Mean Joe Greene's soda piece or "I can't believe I ate the whole thing"? They and others were sometimes more entertaining and usually more memorable than the shows they sponsored. You didn't have to concentrate for the message to sink in. It made a difference when you headed to the supermarket. And cigarette commercials were among the best; that's why they stick in our minds after all this time.

If the balance was tipped in favor of protecting the public from cigarette commercials, *a fortiori* we should be liberated from this vice in political campaigns. Professional campaigners shouldn't be allowed to blow smoke on the airwaves when so much is at stake. I can't get too upset about Pepsi battling Coke in 30-second skits that ask us to believe a little too much about the power of a soda can. Nor am I too troubled about an oil company talking about tigers in tanks. And so what if a bar of soap doesn't make me smell like the green outdoors? Perhaps we can accept an application of the no harm, no foul rule to those cases. In the case of political commercials, the foul should be called.

The harm I'm referring to is not merely the damage caused by the negative ads so commonly criticized. Positive ads are just as troublesome. Consider for a moment the two main purposes purportedly served by positive TV commercials in a presidential campaign: conveying an image of the personality and character of the candidate and presenting positions on the issues. If the subject of a commercial is a candidate's character, you know we won't be seeing clips of infidelity, wife beating or cheating on exams. I'm not suggesting any such conduct has occurred, only that if it has, we won't be hearing about it in commercials. Nor are we likely on the issues to see or hear anyone proudly proclaiming support for a weak national defense, weak economy, high crime rate or high taxes.

More importantly, even if one could count on an uncommon degree of integrity and objectivity from our candidates, the fact remains that the issues on which the elections should turn are far too complicated for treatment in commercials. Entire seminars could be conducted on any of those issues and you would have only scratched the surface. Are we to believe that the workings of the global economy, the intricacies of international affairs or the impact of complex legislation or court decisions few will ever read can be explained adequately in a few seconds on television, or that any of the above can be understood on the basis of information or arguments conveyed in that format? Only an extraordinary amount of hubris could yield an affirmative answer to those questions. Then again, who cares? The object of the exercise isn't to explain or inform; it is to persuade. In that context, we shouldn't be surprised to see the same techniques used to sell soda and soap (and formerly cigarettes), rather than the boring stuff of seminars.

The entire debate over negativism in political ads is a waste of time, and that assumes it is always possible to distinguish clearly between positive and negative ads, obviously an inaccurate assumption. Is there any real difference between an ad that says "Vote for X because X is the candidate who stands for family values" and one warning "Don't vote for Y because Y is a dirtbag"? The first may deliver the message in a positive format and grant the candidate political license to claim the high ground. In the end, however, both are the same. Instead of applauding the candidate with the proper form, we should be rejecting both forms in Peter Finch's cry from *Network:* We're mad as hell and we're not gonna take it anymore.

In short, negativism is simply not the issue when it comes to political commercials. It's the nature of the medium that is the problem. It plays fast and loose with the truth, whether in a positive or negative format, and that's dangerous when it involves the primary source of information for voters selecting the leader of the strongest nation on earth. Since campaign commercials have no redeeming value, I say ban them before it's too late.

Ballgames. I'm a frustrated jock myself and therefore appreciate the atmosphere surrounding the campaigns, but I'm beginning to wonder whether we've overdone it. Once again, television is responsible, as only television can broadcast every local political contest into everyone's home in the form of a sporting event.

As in the case of real sports, the bigger the event, the greater is its entertainment value; it's hard to sell tickets to meaningless preseason games. The natural consequence of the application of this basic principle to TV coverage of a presidential campaign is gross exaggeration of the importance of the early, small-state primaries, according them the status of regular season games and, in some cases, elevating them to virtual playoff status. In regular sports, they warn against getting too high after individual victories and too low after defeats. In the game of presidential politics, you get blown out in Iowa and New Hampshire and you can forget about finishing the season. That's what made Iowa and New Hampshire so exciting, not the prospect of substantive debate of the issues facing the nation. Without the incessant media coverage, Iowa and New Hampshire might not be quite as important as they are; they might only be as important as they should be.

In recent years, we've taken the sporting aspect of politics further than ever before. It's a product of advanced technology. The camera follows a candidate's every move. The audience's reactions are instantly gauged. Statistics you never imagined are compiled. And we are constantly pummelled with information of the useless as well as useful variety.

Why does TV cover political campaigns as if they were sports events? It's not enough to simply say "ratings." The real question is why is all this good for ratings? The answer, I think, lies in our never-ending search for entertainment, the kind of entertainment we normally receive from the worlds of sports and Hollywood. We like close races, drama, vicariously experiencing the thrill of victory and the agony of defeat. And because we prefer our entertainment in doses, *Lethal Weapon* rather than *War and Peace*, we like to see quick results and move on to new games. Hence the proliferation of primaries, a series of games to be analyzed, broken down and won or lost.

Putting aside the substantial entertainment value of the primaries, it seems clear that the atmosphere surrounding them is not conducive to a full and intelligent discussion of the issues of the day. They contribute to our fascination with the process and tell us something about ourselves, about what we want out of our politics, but they are not the ideal mechanism for selecting presidential candidates. Opening day is for Yankee Stadium, and speculation about the chances of an underdog belongs on the back pages of the local newspaper. We cannot, and probably should not, prevent these sports world images from crossing over into the world of politics. It's when we allow the sporting aspect to take over the process that we get into trouble. And lately, it seems we've had nothing but trouble in the political process.

Primary Debates. I'll reserve judgment on the real debates until later. For now, suffice it to say that the pre-New Hampshire debate was not illuminating. Rather, it was another illustration of the sport presidential politics has become.

The format of the show put on by the eight candidates in New Hampshire was clearly flawed. For starters, eight men cannot intelligently discuss anything in 90 minutes, much less the entire spectrum of issues on which a presidential election should turn. This is particularly true when their interventions come in 60- and 90-second bursts. When you force the candidates into that kind of a setting, you put a premium on acting, placing form over substance.

Ronald Reagan usually did well in those settings. He was comfortable on camera and had his lines well mastered. It was never clear to me whether Reagan would have been able to shine in an intensive intellectual exchange where he would have to stand and defend each position before moving on to the next burst of thought. The debating format with both Carter and Mondale didn't call upon Reagan (or the others) to do that. He therefore always seemed to enjoy a great advantage over his opponents as a consequence of his Hollywood training, the same advantage he had in delivering speeches on television from the Oval Office. Were we really voting for Ronald Reagan, or for Reagan playing the role of presidential candidate? My worry is that the latter is closer to the truth. Although a case can be made that Reagan was the greatest American president of the past half-century, it remains somewhat disturbing that part of his greatness may have been attributable to his ability to play a great president.

If we want to learn more about the candidates' views and thought processes, we will need to see them in settings that call for a more rigorous intellectual exchange. An example might be a free-flowing, 60-minute discussion (no commercial interruptions) of the budget, in which a candidate would be questioned by three or four top reporters specialized in the field as to whether it is necessary to balance the budget and, if so, why, when and how? Ditto for social security, health care, the environment and other issues about which few of us know enough to fully understand (my apologies to anyone who actually read the Clinton health plan). Of course, such serious shows won't educate us sufficiently to make a truly informed decision. What they will do is tell us more about the candidates and the issues than the pre-New Hampshire primary debate.

Should we ban debates? Well, I guess they aren't the menace commercials are. And it's true they're a lot more entertaining than a serious presentation of political issues on television. We can enjoy debates without learning anything from them because they tend to have winners and losers, with analysts always present to help us determine which was which. We also cannot discard the possibility that some useful information may emerge as a by-product of the entertainment, even if it is nothing more than a glimpse of the temperament of the candidates. On the whole, however, we need to recognize the limited utility of modern television debates as a means of providing us with a basis for selection and continue the search for a more effective means of utilizing the media available.

The Field. I don't think I'm the only one who was a touch disappointed in the field of candidates starting the race in 1996. There's that question again: why does such an attractive job attract so few attractive applicants?

On the Democratic side, Bill Clinton stood unopposed. Someone must have been watching over this guy. Four years earlier he won the nomination when bigger names stayed away in the face of Bush's awesome approval ratings. Now, after three lackluster years as President, including one in which he was relegated to the role of bystander in the processes of government, he somehow found himself the undisputed leader of the Democratic Party. Not to denigrate his considerable political skill, the fact was that, as in 1992, he was in the right place at the right time.

Part of Clinton's good fortune could be attributed to the ugliness surrounding modern American politics, the same ugliness that seemed to have influenced Bradley and Nunn to retire from the Senate and Kemp and Powell not to seek the presidency in 1996. However, there had to be another force at work here as well, one that could explain the absence of competition even from thick-skinned politicians raised on a steady diet of dirty campaigns. That was the force of incumbency: you don't challenge a president in your own party unless you don't care about the election in November. It's the feeling I got from Republicans in 1992. Many were not upset at the prospect of Bush losing, so they didn't lose sleep over Buchanan's challenge. The 1996 Democrats wanted to win and, whatever they thought of Bill Clinton personally, they believed he had the best chance. This meant we might not have seen Bradley, Nunn or any of the other Democrats who might have been worth listening to even if they hadn't been turned off by the process, and we definitely wouldn't see any of the lesser Democratic lights searching for an opportunity to shine on the national stage.

The Republican mess was more difficult to fathom. There competition was expected. Without an incumbent or an unbeatable front-runner, the field should have been wide open for Kemp, Powell (once he announced he was a Republican) and others. Instead, Bob Dole and Phil Gramm were the only expected names to announce their candidacy, and Gramm didn't even make it to New Hampshire. None of the seven others would have been considered a serious candidate a year earlier.

It's nice to see Alan Keyes, B-1 Bob and Morry Taylor run for president. It gives us the feeling that the United States is truly the land of opportunity where anyone has a chance. The thing is, they didn't have a chance and their presence in the race only confused the issue. On the one hand, the field seemed crowded with nine Republican candidates. On the other, the question we should have been asking all along is why so few real candidates decided to participate.

*   *   *

As I reflect on all these problems, I naturally find myself searching for contractual solutions, a la Gingrich's Contract with America. Constitutional and other legal obstacles can discourage the most well-meaning of reformers from addressing the pressing problems posed by the combination of money, media and a system so susceptible to manipulation. Taking on the First Amendment, one of the constitutional barriers to campaign finance reform, is an uphill battle under any circumstances, even when pornography is the enemy. When big money joins forces with civil liberties groups, both wrapping themselves in the First Amendment to defend our right to raise and spend money freely, reformers could be excused for losing heart.

So maybe the next time around there should be a Contract with Voters, complete with representations (as to history, qualifications and vices), covenants (what the candidate promises to do and, as importantly, not to do) and remedies (what we can do if the candidate reneges), that would bypass the legislative process, setting forth the bare minimum we expect out of our politicians and the rules by which we expect them to play. WHEREAS, Candidate seeks the support of Voters; WHEREAS, having been repeatedly hosed in the past, Voters are understandably reluctant to place their trust in anyone, much less someone affirmatively seeking it; and WHEREAS, Voters haven't got the time, resources or inclination to gather sufficient information to make an informed decision; NOW, THEREFORE, under penalty of public humiliation and forfeiture of office and financial consideration received, Candidate hereby represents and covenants as follows: . . . You fill in the rest. There's plenty of time for negotiation before Election 2000.

Chapter 9
The Republican Dilemma

The Republicans had a dilemma on their hands after New Hampshire. Party leaders were growing increasingly angry over the prospect of Pat Buchanan causing irreparable harm to the Republican image and were anxious to stop him before he gathered more momentum. At the same time, there was reluctance to turn up the decibel level of attacks on Buchanan for fear of permanently alienating him and his substantial block of supporters.

Increasingly, a parallel was being drawn between Buchanan and Jesse Jackson. Jackson could do well in Democratic primaries involving several candidates because the support he had was committed; in a two-candidate race, he couldn't win. Buchanan was much the same.

One difference making Buchanan potentially more dangerous was that his support would not necessarily go to the Republican nominee. Jackson had his bluff called in 1992. He was not accorded the respect to which he had become accustomed in Democratic politics. But where were he and his followers to go— George Bush, Ross Perot? Of course not. Jackson and his Rainbow Coalition would swallow their pride, stay Democrats and support Bill Clinton, understanding that half a loaf was better than nothing.

Buchanan, on the other hand, was not too pleased with the personal attacks on him by members of his own party and had other options undoubtedly looking more attractive with each additional low blow he absorbed. Unlike Jackson, who for the longest time was accorded free passage in Democratic politics because of his race (a sort of affirmative action for political candidates), Buchanan didn't get a break from his Republican colleagues and had to be wondering whether he really wanted to be a member of this Republican club. His message in any event was sounding less and less Republican as time passed, and even if he stayed in the party and supported the nominee, it was not at all clear his followers would follow suit. If Ross Perot played, at least those responding to Buchanan's economic populism and protectionism would likely be lost. Once again, Perot would be in a position to cause damage to the Republicans.

Nevertheless, although attacks on Buchanan could carry a high price down the road, he was costing the party a lot in the early going. After New Hampshire, he was ahead in the delegate count and seemed to be setting the agenda for the entire campaign. While it was widely assumed he could not win a two-candidate contest, the longer he stayed on top the more comfortable he looked and the shakier that assumption became. Moreover, we didn't have a two-man race at the time and it looked as if it might be some time before we did. Forbes vowed to continue the fight and had the money to back up his threat. Alexander, who had yet to win anything, boldly called upon Dole to withdraw and leave Buchanan to him.

As the Republicans were figuring out how to deal with Buchanan, the rhetoric escalated. Buchanan still seemed much quicker on his feet than his detractors, energetically defending his positions on TV and jousting with reporters intent on bringing him down with the incisive question. However, he was hurt by the constant battering, politically if not emotionally. He was also hurt by the lineup of people expressing sympathy for him, from former Ku Klux Klan leader David Duke in Louisiana, who tried to put his arm around him at one gathering, to Russian ultranationalist Vladimir Zhirinovsky, who called Buchanan a comrade and brother-in-arms. Both were rejected in strong terms by Buchanan, who pointed out he had no control over who decided to throw support his way. (Isn't that what Larry Pratt said about the people attending gatherings at which he spoke?)

On the substance, it was becoming clearer with each passing speech and interview that there was a wide chasm between Buchanan and the other Republican candidates on what was shaping up as the major issue of the primary campaign—job security, its relationship to the international trade policy of the Republican establishment and big business, and its relationship to immigration, legal as well as illegal. Buchanan's positions on all these matters were easy to understand and had tremendous popular appeal. He believed that trade policy had been an instrument of the giant multi-nationals, allowing them to export jobs to countries with cheap labor, which then manufactured goods to be shipped to the United States. He further believed that illegal immigrants had been draining additional jobs and economic resources and placing American culture under siege. Not even legal immigration was spared; we shouldn't keep the gates wide open when we're having trouble taking care of our own.

You didn't have to be an expert to sense that those positions were flawed. Life just isn't that simple. Whenever someone tries to make it sound simple by identifying culprits—big government, big corporations, big immigration—and talks about building walls and erecting barriers, an alarm should go off that forces us to stop and examine with care. I'm not an economist or a trade expert, but the experience I do have does not support Buchanan's assertions. In my business, I've witnessed substantial changes in the quantity and nature of jobs over the past twenty years. Virtually every slot eliminated has been due to advances in technology. On the other hand, other often higher paying jobs have been created, many of which are directly or indirectly linked to the "global economy" for which Buchanan has so little use. I'm not suggesting law is a typical business, but that experience is hardly unique.

Buchanan's positions also do not adequately account for the fact that many jobs lost abroad to cheap labor would be lost with or without trade deals. Movement of American capital abroad has in the past been hampered by nationalistic and protectionist policies of host countries, not patriotism of the American multinational. These barriers are being torn down as countries all over the world compete for capital. Latin America, formerly hostile to foreign investment, perhaps most of all U.S. investment, now views foreign investment as a key to economic development. A prime example is Mexico. Most people don't seem to realize that in the years leading up to NAFTA, Mexico had dramatically altered its policy on foreign investment, radically changing the regulations that had previously prevented foreigners from owning more than 49 percent of enterprises to allow up to 100 percent foreign ownership in most sectors. What were we supposed to do, ask them to close their economy to U.S. corporations so that we wouldn't export jobs there?

A more plausible alternative would seem to be eliminating the hurdles impeding the flow of American *goods*, rather than jobs, abroad. Free trade agreements are designed to do just that. By reducing tariffs, they help compensate for the unavoidable loss of jobs experienced as a consequence of the changes around us by opening up new export markets and creating new jobs in the United States. According to Phil Gramm, if you believe in American competitiveness, you take a chance on the validity of that theory.

Unfortunately, Gramm was no longer around to meet Buchanan in an exchange of ideas, and the other candidates weren't quite up to it. Dole characterized the Buchanan struggle as a fight for the heart and soul of the Republican Party, but he seemed to be ceding the mind of the party to Buchanan. Alexander's favorite line was that Dole had no ideas, Buchanan had the wrong ideas and he was the only viable candidate with the right ideas. His failure to explain precisely why Buchanan's ideas were the wrong ideas and his ideas, whatever they were, were the right ideas was a major reason why his campaign reached its peak without a single victory. Forbes, who probably was best equipped to debate Buchanan on the merits, blew his opportunity with the heavy-handed tactics he used in Iowa and New Hampshire.

So the Republican dilemma continued.

*   *   *

Less than a week after the New Hampshire primary, there was a primary in Delaware. Not too many people noticed. Only Steve Forbes showed up to campaign, the others staying away apparently out of respect for New Hampshire—see Louisiana, which scheduled its caucuses ahead of Iowa and had only Gramm and Buchanan show up. Attracting a grand total of fewer than 9,000 votes, Forbes won his first contest in Delaware, a few percentage points ahead of Dole. Buchanan and Alexander ran third and fourth, respectively. It wasn't the opening day atmosphere of New Hampshire, but it was a regular season game with consequences.

Forbes' victory kept him in the race (he was, believe it or not, second to Buchanan in delegate count at that stage). Since he was the only campaigner in the state, a Forbes loss, certainly another third or fourth place showing, would have sent another loud message of rejection. Delaware allowed him to tell himself he was not wasting his money by hanging around.

Second place was no cause for a Dole celebration. However, Dole didn't violate the principle of meeting expectations. Having skipped the Delaware primary campaign, victory— at least in the sense of coming in first—was not anticipated. The real objective was to avoid another loss to Buchanan or, worse, Alexander.

Perhaps the most significant consequence of the Delaware primary was Alexander's poor fourth place finish. Like Dole and Buchanan, he hadn't campaigned in Delaware and did not have great expectations. Still, another contest had passed with Alexander not finishing in the top two, and most observers agreed he needed a victory more than any other candidate. In that sense, Delaware represented another missed opportunity for Alexander to validate his theory that Dole would fall and he should be the one to pick up the pieces. After Delaware, the theory was looking a little too much like wishful thinking.

Chapter 10

The Cuban Minicrisis

On the day of the Delaware primary, the big news came from off the coast of Cuba, where Cuban MIGs shot down two small civilian aircraft run by Brothers to the Rescue, an organization of Cuban-Americans regularly flying missions off the coast of Cuba to spot rafters and occasionally dropping leaflets over Havana. The Brothers had ignored warnings to stay away. For some reason, Cuba decided this time warnings weren't enough. To make matters worse, all indications were that the downing of the aircraft took place in international waters. The stage was set for a flurry of activity that highlighted the interrelationship between domestic and international politics and severely taxed the patience of an international community shaken by the inconsistency and volatility of our foreign policy.

Clinton immediately condemned the action and had his advisors draw up a list of options. There was talk of military action and a blockade. The next day Secretary of State Warren Christopher announced that U.N. Ambassador Madeleine Albright would press the case for international action in the Security Council. The Republican candidates had their opportunities to comment on the situation, but the bottom line is there's only one president and he gets center stage in a crisis.

Lost in the crisis was any kind of serious discussion of the broader Cuban issue. With the downing of the aircraft, everyone assumed that the U.S. trade embargo on Cuba had been validated and that there was no longer any chance of reevaluating the effectiveness or wisdom of that policy. Far from the loosening of the embargo rumored to be under consideration by the Administration, a significant tightening now became the primary option.

The logic of the trade embargo goes something like this: A, the Castro regime is bad; B, we should not deal with it. There's a missing link in that chain, even if a deeper analysis would lead to the same conclusion. I've never fully understood why we couldn't trade with Cuba, a small island of 11 million people, when we had no difficulty dealing with what Ronald Reagan termed the Evil Empire, not to mention our extensive trade relations with the People's Republic of China—by mid-1996 our trade deficit with China actually surpassed the deficit with Japan. Nobody ever argued that the human rights records of the communist giants were better than that of Castro. Nor did anyone ever consider Castro, whose military power was totally dependent on the Soviet Union, a greater threat to U.S. national security than the Soviet Union or China. They were *Soviet* missiles that caused the Cuban missile crisis in 1962 and it was China, not Cuba, that kept our military on edge in 1996. If we thought engagement in commerce and cultural and political dialogue was appropriate for our principal adversaries, why has it been inappropriate for Cuba? That's not to endorse either an open policy toward Cuba or an embargo of all our declared enemies; it's just to say there's an incongruity here that cries out for explanation.

Then again, when has congruity been a feature of U.S. foreign policy? Aggression in the Persian Gulf could not be allowed to stand, yet aggression in Bosnia was for the longest time met only with words. Human rights violations are intolerable in some parts of the world; in others genocide goes unchecked and almost unnoticed. We are prepared to go to war for democracy in Haiti, but it's OK for the CIA to undermine it in Chile. Did Cuba under Castro ever remotely resemble Cambodia under Pol Pot? None of this means Castro's a good guy, any more than the leaders of the many brutal regimes we have in the past supported and installed around the world. I'm just wondering what it is about Castro that causes us not to be able to think clearly.

Another issue I would have liked to have seen addressed in the broader Cuba discussion is the effectiveness of the embargo. As someone who would probably benefit from a lifting of the embargo, I know at least one category of people hurt by it. That's not the annoying part. What is bothersome is standing by and watching others, including our closest allies, take advantage of our absence. You don't have to listen that carefully to hear the giant sucking sound to which Ross Perot referred. It's just that it wasn't coming from where he thought it was. The one clear point about unilaterally imposed trade sanctions is that while they may or may not hurt the target country, they definitely hurt nationals of the sanctioning country who are prevented from trading and they definitely benefit competitors in other countries who become free to trade without competition. Every time we unilaterally impose sanctions on foreign countries, people in board rooms across Canada, Europe, Japan and other parts of the world with businesses welcoming an edge let out a Marv Albert-like "Yessssss!"

Apart from the damage to U.S. business (meaning U.S. jobs), the embargo does create hardships for Cubans. Of course, the Cubans hurt the most are the ones we are supposed to be assisting, not the ones causing all the grief. Think about it. If sacrifices have to be made due to the embargo, who do you think will have to make them, the government or the people? It should come as no surprise that the innocent bear the brunt of the hardship and, in the process, develop an intense animosity toward the perceived cause of their suffering—us. All of this tends to suit the target government just fine.

Ironically, while unilaterally imposed sanctions are generally ineffective in bringing about political change, I'm not as convinced about the outcome of a full-scale trading relationship. Can you imagine what Cuba would be like with Yankees crawling all over it? Something tells me Castro is not as anxious to see that prospect materialize as American business is. In fact, many feel he precipitated the February crisis precisely in order to forestall advances in U.S./Cuba relations and tighten his own grip on power in Cuba. There's nothing like an external crisis to divert a public's attention from its domestic woes and relieve pressure on an unpopular regime.

The international community has always been both bemused and worried by our treatment of these issues. On the one hand, it is amusing to watch the big cowboy swing into action like something out of a bad western. On the other hand, you can only get so amused when you're watching a 700-pound gorilla up close. And in the new world order still taking shape after the fall of the Iron Curtain, we are unquestionably the 700-pound gorilla. So if we want Iraq out of Kuwait, it will get out, one way or another; if we want the Serbs to ease off Sarajevo, they'll ease off, one way or another; and if we want Aristide back in Haiti, he'll go back, even if it takes an army to reinstall him. That's why when we talk, people listen.

Unfortunately, too often in recent years, what people hear when they listen is nonsense. The art of diplomacy seems to have given way to a kind of caricature diplomacy straight out of Hollywood. Presidents and other high officials have taken to calling other heads of state all sorts of funny names and shooting from the hip, as around the world people watch and cringe. I half expected Bill Clinton to call a press conference and dare Castro to make a move, Dirty Harry style—"Go ahead, make my day." Once his day was made, presumably he would cap it off with an "Hasta la vista, baby."

This time, it was Madeleine Albright's turn to find new ways to turn serious business into a caricature of diplomacy. The United States proposed a Security Council resolution condemning Cuba for its downing of the aircraft. The Council, however, would only strongly "deplore" the action. Although Albright expressed satisfaction with the resolution, arguing that the difference in wording was inconsequential, she couldn't have been entirely pleased. At least my dictionary shows an important distinction between "deplore" and "condemn" that couldn't have escaped the Council. "Deplore" involves regret, but not necessarily blame. By contrast, "condemn" is the term denoting "censure" and "blame," and that obviously was what Albright was looking for.

Later, the tough-talking Albright showed the kind of stuff that is the trademark of modern diplomacy, cleverness at the expense of substance, attention-grabbing one-liners in substitution for serious discussion—the stuff that was later to make her the obvious choice to succeed Warren Christopher as secretary of state. As a vast television audience watched in disbelief, Albright stressed that the Cuban action showed "cowardice," not "cojones." I wondered what the Spanish-speaking world thought of that language lesson, and what the rest of the world thought when "cojones" was translated into who knows how many languages. One thought I'll bet went around was "They don't make 'em like they used to."

Whatever the international reaction, a tightening of the U.S. embargo on Cuba was inevitable. Before the incident, legislation had already been pending to that effect. There were two bills under consideration, the House version going further than the Senate's by subjecting companies and individuals from third countries doing business in Cuba to suit in the United States if they dealt with confiscated property formerly owned by U.S. nationals. Until the downing of the aircraft, it was widely anticipated that the final legislation would be much closer to the Senate's more moderate bill. If for some strange reason the Senate agreed to compromise by approaching the House version, the President seemed certain to veto the bill. After all, the State Department had publicly stated that the bill "would be very difficult to defend under international law, harm U.S. businesses exposed to copycat legislation in other countries, create friction with our allies, fail to provide an effective remedy for U.S. claimants and seriously damage the interests of [Foreign Claims Settlement Commission] certified claimants. . . . The civil remedy created by the . . . bill would represent an unprecedented extra-territorial application of U.S. law that flies in the face of important U.S. interests." It didn't sound like the tougher House bill would receive strong support from the executive branch of government.

The downing of the planes changed everything. Without missing a beat, the President immediately dropped his opposition and sent a letter to Congress urging passage of what we had to presume had somehow been magically transformed into a sound piece of legislation perfectly consistent with international law and essential for the protection of U.S. interests. The request met little resistance in Congress. All traces of moderation had been cast aside as both houses of Congress were caught up in a get-tough frenzy, rushing to send the President a bill incorporating the features that had virtually no chance of passage only a few days earlier. Foreign Relations Committee Chairman Senator Jesse Helms was among the most satisfied of the legislators as he mugged for the TV cameras and sent Castro a simple message: "Farewell Fidel." The final legislation, commonly known as the Helms-Burton Act (the formal name is the Cuban Liberty and Democratic Solidarity (Libertad Act) of 1996), passed both houses by wide margins.

Passing the legislation may have made Jesse Helms' day, but it was not Congress' finest hour. In fact, it was nothing short of a disgrace, an embarrassment to the U.S. government and, of course, a bonanza for lawyers. Even before passage, law firms were busily at work billing time analyzing the bizarre provisions of the legislation, journeying into intricate areas of international and constitutional law worthy of law school seminars. After passage, the work escalated, as lawyers grappled with the extraordinary problems presented and readied themselves for the lawsuits that were expected to flood the courts once the grace period established in the law expired (trafficking in confiscated property on or after November 1, 1996, was made actionable—the idea was to allow the offenders time to wind down their offending activities). Helms-Burton was in the process of becoming the International Lawyers' Full Employment Act.

What made the Helms-Burton Act so controversial internationally was its Titles III and IV. For the most part, previous anti-Cuba legislation and regulations adopted by executive order had caused harm only to the Cuban people (if not the Cuban government) and U.S. business, pretty much a bilateral affair. This time, in Titles III and IV, Congress was directly attacking third countries, including our treaty partners and close allies, who don't share our views as to how best to deal with the Castro regime.

Under Title III, any U.S. national holding a claim to confiscated property in Cuba may sue any person, Canadian, Mexican,

Spanish, English, French or whatever, if that person "traffics" in the confiscated property. Trafficking, by the way, isn't merely buying and selling. According to the *simple* definition set forth in the statute, one can traffic by knowingly and intentionally selling, transferring, distributing, dispensing, brokering, managing or otherwise disposing of confiscated property, purchasing, leasing, receiving, possessing, obtaining control of, managing, using or otherwise holding an interest in confiscated property, engaging in a commercial activity using or otherwise benefitting from confiscated property, causing, directing, participating in or profiting from trafficking by another person, or otherwise engaging in trafficking through another person, without the authorization of the U.S. national who holds a claim to the property.

Does one "traffic" by smoking a Cuban cigar or putting sugar traceable to Cuba in a cup of coffee in a Viennese cafe (assuming, for the moment, that such egregious conduct was performed knowingly and intentionally)? Most people would be shocked at the amount of money spent analyzing these and other esoteric issues under the statute. Those spending the money weren't engaged in an academic exercise. For good measure, Title III provided for treble damages against the traffickers. If the treble damages were to be assessed based on the value of the confiscated property plus interest over a period of more than 35 years, potential defendants from countries all over the world could be looking at billions of dollars in claims. No matter what they say about Cuban cigars, that's an expensive smoke.

If that weren't sufficient to turn our allies' collective stomachs, traffickers, including corporate officers, principals and controlling shareholders of traffickers (as well as their respective spouses and minor children), were supposed to be denied entry visas to the United States under Title IV of Helms-Burton. These weren't criminals we were talking about; they were businessmen and their families from friendly countries who happened to work for companies legally doing business in Cuba. Presumably, conservatives had something else in mind when speaking of the need for immigration reform.

What was to be expected from the Helms-Burton Act? A lot of

hectic diplomatic activity; heavy criticism and retaliation from our allies; legal challenges under NAFTA and GATT; rhetoric from politicians trashing GATT and NAFTA for infringing on our sovereignty—this legislation makes the case that a little infringement every now and then might not be so bad; and, barring suspension or repeal of the legislation, a flood of lawsuits burdening the already crowded federal court dockets and generating millions of dollars in legal fees. One other by-product of an ironic nature: an extension of the life of the very regime we were trying to bring down in Cuba.

The Helms-Burton Act is a prime illustration of the dangers of legislating in response to a crisis in an election year. What happened to the politicians on Capitol Hill who must have known just how bad the legislation was and yet rushed to vote in favor of passage? To be fair, there were a few, such as Democratic Congressmen Rangel and Hamilton, who weren't caught up in the frenzy. And Senator Chris Dodd, Democratic Party National Chairman, did have the courage to question the legislation on the floor of the Senate: "While the events of a week ago Saturday [the downing of the planes] were tragic and senseless, Mr. President, they do not in any way change the fact that title III is contrary to the interests of our country, of the United States, and inconsistent, as I have tried to point out, with international law. . . . Mr. President, I have said on numerous occasions, when we consider foreign policy legislation of this nature—and I said at the outset—we have to ask ourselves two very basic questions: Is what is being proposed in the best interest of our own country, and is it likely to achieve the stated goals in the country to which it is directed? . . . In the case of the pending legislation, I think the answer to both of these questions is a resounding no."

There was a third question that Senator Dodd didn't ask: is the legislation politically expedient in an election year, no matter how foolish it may otherwise be? The answer to that question was a resounding yes.

Chapter 11

The Republicans Begin Sorting Things Out

Back home, three primaries were held on February 27: North Dakota, South Dakota and Arizona. They provided another opportunity for the Republicans to put some order in what had become their house of chaos. The key question was whether Bob Dole would be able to stop the bleeding and become a front-runner on the way up rather than a front-runner just hanging on. In delegate count, he stood third going into the Dakotas, behind Steve Forbes (following his victory in Delaware) and Pat Buchanan. A couple more bad outings and people would look to tag the name front-runner on someone else.

The February 27 contests settled little. Dole did win North and South Dakota by significant margins. They were victories he sorely needed. He had been expected to do well and couldn't afford to disappoint again. Forget expectations, with his losses in New Hampshire and Delaware, he couldn't afford to suffer a hat trick in the three primaries taking place on this night. The victories gave him a chance to take a deep breath and continue credibly to lay claim to the status of front-runner. By avoiding disaster, he had taken an important step toward the day when he would finally break out of the pack.

The Dakotas were also significant for the other principal candidates, particularly Pat Buchanan and Lamar Alexander. A pattern was clearly emerging from the second-place showing of Buchanan in both states. With each passing primary, it became more apparent that Buchanan's strength was limited and had dim prospects for improvement. Slowly, the theory that Buchanan could not win a two-man race with any of the main candidates was being validated. Lamar Alexander suffered perhaps more significantly from the Dakotas. He had very low expectations in either state, conceding both to Dole long before. Nevertheless, mere compliance with the expectations rule could no longer suppress the growing perception that he too had peaked in New Hampshire. His fourth place showings were not what he needed to raise money for the rest of his campaign.

Arizona was a different story. It was there that the souffle rose again. This wasn't Delaware. All the candidates campaigned in Arizona. That's what made Steve Forbes' victory in Arizona so astonishing.

How could someone so devastated by Iowa and New Hampshire have made such a startling comeback? Was it the force of his magnetic personality or the strength of his ideas? I think Forbes would concede it wasn't the former, but he did seem to think his ideas were the source of his renewed strength. While I didn't in the least bit underestimate his ideas, there's no getting around the money thing. Forbes spent another bundle in Arizona and that put him temporarily back in the race. Whereas Phil Gramm felt he had to withdraw after poor showings in two caucuses, not even one primary, Forbes apparently never gave it a second thought. What did he have that Gramm didn't? Money, or the lack of concern that the money would dry up. It was his.

Forbes' victory in Arizona was further proof that the system does not have sufficient checks and balances of its own to withstand the distortive effects of money. Sure, unwise spending was recognized and ultimately rejected in Iowa and New Hampshire. Even there, however, the spending had its distortive effect. Just ask Bob Dole. Now it was starting over, with Iowa and New Hampshire seemingly forgotten.

In Forbes' defense, not every wealthy person is capable of stepping up and winning the Arizona primary. A message of some sort is necessary and Forbes' message of hope, growth and opportunity spurred by flat taxes clearly struck a chord in the desert. Unfortunately, that defense doesn't lead to the conclusion that message outweighs money, or that money is not an indispensable ingredient of political success. The fact remains that other people with ideas and presidential qualities can't afford to spend $4 million on the Arizona primary. You don't have to be a socialist to sense something is wrong with that picture.

Bob Dole's second place finish in Arizona again prevented him from silencing his critics, but it was not the serious blow it could have been. Unlike Gramm in Iowa, Dole had played the expectations game well, setting goals for himself he would almost surely attain—winning two (the Dakotas) out of three. Beating out Buchanan (despite exit polls placing Buchanan ahead) was also significant since Buchanan had made a big push in Arizona, making fiery speeches in cowboy dress. With Forbes spending so much against Dole and drawing much of Dole's support, Buchanan's failure to finish at least second was a setback that deepened the suspicion he had peaked in New Hampshire.

Lamar Alexander did nothing to help himself in Arizona. Another fourth place finish left him looking to the upcoming southern states for a rescue that seemed further and further away. The scenario envisioned by his campaign—the collapse of Dole—was taking too long to play out. Worse, his waiting in the wings made him seem a hollow alternative and could actually have been rallying the support Dole needed to keep that scenario from becoming a reality. The clearer it became that Alexander was not a viable candidate, the less likely Republicans would be to prophecize doom for Dole and the more likely they would be to see the point made by Gramm in endorsing Dole prior to the New Hampshire primary. It was a vicious circle; fewer prophecies of doom for Dole and greater appreciation of the Gramm point rendered the Alexander campaign, which lacked any positive energy of its own, pointless. Unlike the case of Forbes, the money wouldn't be there to fuel Alexander's campaign engine much longer.

* * *

Given the state of the race at the end of February, South Carolina's primary on March 2 assumed great importance. Dole was supported by the Republican establishment there, including popular Governor David Beasely, former Governor Carroll Campbell and still strong Senator Strom Thurmond, a formidable lineup for "outsiders" Buchanan and Forbes to face. Buchanan expected strong support from the social conservatives, although the increase in export-generated jobs experienced by South Carolina didn't make it fertile territory for his protectionist message. Forbes, fresh off his victory in Arizona, didn't expect to win in South Carolina, just to show enough to send him into the New York primary five days later on an optimistic note. In the spotlight as the lone primary state on March 2, South Carolina shaped up as the turning point in the Republican race. As the primary approached, there was a sense that something major was about to happen.

The message delivered by South Carolina was loud and clear: Bob Dole was not about to fall. The long-awaited convincing victory—he received 45 percent of the votes—left no doubt he was in command. Whereas the party establishment had failed to pull off the victory in New Hampshire, it carried the day in South Carolina. No outsider was going to come in and take over there. You could tell that from the look on 93-year-old Strom Thurmond's face as he stood behind Dole applauding after the primary. All business.

Buchanan came in second in South Carolina with a disappointing 29 percent. He had been desperately trying to break out and prove he was more than a minority candidate, that he could be the leader of a reshaped Republican Party. That position, formerly held by Barry Goldwater (who supported Dole in Arizona, calling Buchanan a good Democrat) and Ronald Reagan, Buchanan saw as vacant and up for grabs. He and his movement were laying claim to it.

The Republican establishment, however, didn't see the need for reshaping under new leadership. In only the previous election the party had taken control of both houses of Congress. Newt Gingrich had lots of ideas and provided more than enough energy. If he needed any help, he had those militant Republican freshmen to keep him on his toes. What was needed was the steady hand of an experienced leader to oversee the Republican Revolution from the White House. With the president and Congress working together, the derailed reforms embodied in the Contract with America would get back on track. In short, the Republicans didn't feel they needed another revolutionary. Bob Dole would do just fine. That was the real message delivered by South Carolina.

For Lamar Alexander, South Carolina was for all practical purposes the end of the line. The South would not rise for him. With only three more days to Junior Tuesday, there was little to be lost by staying in until then, but the handwriting was on the wall. He wanted to see Dole back leading the Senate, Buchanan back on "Crossfire" and himself in the White House. After South Carolina, only two of those wishes had a chance to be fulfilled.

Chapter 12

The Middle East Heats Up

It wasn't all fun and games for Bill Clinton while the Republicans were sorting things out. The events beyond his control were making his life difficult. Simultaneously with the Cuban crisis, the Middle East was acting up. Israel was hit by a series of four suicide bombing attacks by militant Palestinians within a span of only nine days, killing dozens and wounding many more. The scenes were grizzly, with flesh and body parts everywhere. Israel declared war on Hamas, the group apparently behind the attacks. Although Yasir Arafat and his new Palestinian Authority condemned (understanding the difference between condemned and deplored) the attack, the peace process was listed among the casualties.

The Middle East has always been on the edge of disaster. Other long-standing conflicts exist around the world, but this region touches us more than most because of our special relationship with Israel and the strategic importance of the entire area, including its vast oil reserves. That wasn't the case with Bosnia—Clinton made Bosnia a potential problem for himself when he sent troops there. By contrast, the Middle East was a problem he couldn't escape. He therefore called Warren Cristopher back from a Latin American trip and instructed his team to draw up a list of steps he could take. The result was a decision to send bomb detection equipment to Israel and provide technical assistance and training to improve coordination with the Palestinian Authority. An international campaign would also be launched to bring those responsible to justice.

In the aftermath of the wave of bombings in Israel, we seemed far removed from that scene on the White House lawn in 1993. Yitzhak Rabin was gone, assassinated by an Israeli at a peace rally in Jerusalem. Many questioned whether Shimon Peres and Yasir Arafat would be on the scene much longer. Peres faced an election of his own in May and the opposition Likud Party, almost broken after the Rabin assassination, became the favorite absent another dramatic turn of events in the short time remaining before the elections. Without his partners in the peace process, Arafat the survivor would be out in the cold.

At least that was the conventional wisdom. I didn't buy it. Shimon Peres didn't look to me like a guy about to fade away, and the international community was bound to make every effort to make sure he, rather than hard-liner Benjamin Netanyahu, would lead Israel into the end game of the Middle East peace process. As for Arafat, let's just say the experts had been writing him off for the past twenty-five years, only to see him come back each time stronger than ever. We say Bill Clinton has an uncanny ability to rebound from adversity, but that's only in the context of U.S. politics. When our universe is expanded beyond our borders, we find people like Arafat giving a whole new meaning to the term comeback.

I also had difficulty with the hasty diagnoses of the state of the peace process. Sure, things were going to slow down for a while. Meetings between Syria and Israel were cancelled; Palestinians were closed off in the West Bank and Gaza; and there was plenty of tough talk coming out of Israel. Nevertheless, the United States (and the rest of the world) had too much at stake to allow the process to be permanently reversed. With Peres committed to staying the course and the international community as a whole backing him in that policy, the prospects for both his recovery and a relatively rapid resumption of progress seemed good. If there was to be a Netanyahu victory in May, it would be only a matter of time before the pieces fell into place.

Not that we could dictate whatever we wanted in the Middle East, but there's no doubt that since World War II, the United States has been the primary player in the area, including throughout the Cold War. I learned that at an early stage, having attended high school in Beirut, where my father had taken up a post with the United Nations. This was well before Lebanon's bloody civil war, a time when Beirut was the place to be—beautiful, at peace, exciting, with beaches, mountains and a wonderful mix of the modern and the traditional. While everyone knew what my father did for a living, the same wasn't true for some others, who were busy playing James Bond. If you don't know what I mean, read the books on it or listen to anyone from the Middle East discuss politics and the exploits of the CIA. Those were the days when the CIA earned its reputation.

More recently, the United States has practiced a less subtle form of persuasion in the Middle East, the deployment of half a million troops and the use of carpet bombing on a scale never before seen. It was enough to make many yearn for the good old days of covert activity.

With the collapse of the Soviet Union, there wasn't even another pretender in the area to challenge U.S. influence. The only question was how we would use it. Many felt that a second Bush term would have brought enormous pressure on Israel to make concessions for peace. Having gone to war against the largest Arab army of the region, Bush and Secretary of State Baker had established whatever credibility they needed to make demands of Israel and, if they had the political will to make those demands, it wasn't likely that they would be ignored given the dependence of Israel on U.S. support. We didn't get to see that scenario materialize, but something was cooking. One by one, Arab countries were conceding that Israel had a place in the Middle East. For its part, Israel was slowly accommodating itself to the reality that Palestinians had to be given a homeland and self-determination, that no matter what label was put on it the homeland would eventually become a state, and that withdrawal from the Golan Heights was the key to peace with Syria.

So why does it seem to be taking so long to get from the

scene on the White House lawn to the final settlement? I think it has something to do with unrealistic expectations. We saw that when Anwar Sadat made his historic trip to Jerusalem. Our desire for instant gratification and happy endings Hollywood-style imposed unrealistic expectations on the process. The people of the area, including Egyptians, weren't quite ready for a full acceptance of Israel after decades of war. A hero to the West, Sadat's bold step left him a target at home.

Yitzhak Rabin also raised Western expectations with bold steps. Not that long ago he had led Israel in war, and even more recently he had incurred the wrath of Palestinians through his harsh measures against the Intifadah, the Palestinian uprising in the West Bank and Gaza Strip. Then, sensing the time was right, he and Peres together broke new ground leading to the White House. No longer was Arafat called a terrorist. Suddenly, he was a full partner in the peace process. Mayor Rudy Giuliani may have found it politically expedient to embarrass Arafat in New York at the U.N.'s 50th anniversary ceremonies, but Rabin and Peres found him more attractive than the alternative. The trouble was, while experienced politicians like Rabin and Peres were able to adjust their perceptions of Arafat from terrorist to partner, others were not as ready to accept such a dramatic shift. As in the case of Sadat, Rabin became a target at home.

The fact is that the governments of the area are all out in front on the peace process, and there is only so far they can go without broader acceptance of a settlement by the people. The real question is not why the governments are taking so long to make peace, but whether we are pushing them too hard too fast.

This point underscores a common error—one of many—in analyses of Middle East politics, namely, the erroneous conclusion long drawn from the erroneous premise that democracy is the prescription for peace, that if only the governments would get out of the way of the people the problem would be solved. My experience in the area doesn't bear out that theory. On the contrary, democracy and peace are on the verge of becoming virtually irreconcilable objectives throughout the area. My feeling is we would have a tough time accepting the outcome of a truly democratic vote in Iraq today, just as the West was stunned by the Islamic victory in the electoral process in Algeria a few years ago.

If we want to see more progress in the region, progress that has some reasonable chance of surviving any particular regime, we'd better start paying more substantive attention to the forces at work at the popular level. Showmanship, theater, public relations, these are instruments of policy that do not bridge the gap created when your audience is operating on a different wavelength. Without bridging that gap, long-term stability in the region will remain an elusive goal. Sooner or later, we'll find a way to do that. It's just not likely to happen in an election year.

Chapter 13

Super Junior Tuesday

Still overshadowed by the news from the Middle East, eight more primaries and two caucuses took place on Junior Tuesday, March 5. It was the biggest day of the season. In total, 259 delegates were at stake, a little more than a quarter of the amount required for the Republican nomination in San Diego.

As Bob Dole said, Junior Tuesday was "super to us." He swept the eight primaries in a dramatic turn of events that essentially decided the race. Only one primary, Georgia, was reasonably close. It was the largest of the bunch and Buchanan had hoped to make a breakthrough there with social conservative support. This time, close wasn't good enough.

Just prior to Junior Tuesday, Lamar Alexander had indicated he would withdraw from the race after Super Tuesday if he did not win in Florida. Most observers wondered why he was prolonging the agony. He apparently agreed with them after the beating he suffered in the eight primaries, in which he could not record a single finish higher than fourth place. The next day he formally announced his withdrawal. The waiting for Dole to fall had finally come to an end. Now Alexander would join the rest of the Republican establishment in supporting the man he had claimed had no vision, no ideas.

Richard Lugar also ended his campaign immediately after the Junior Tuesday results. He had staked the remainder of his campaign on victory in Vermont. When he lost there, he followed through on his promise and withdrew. For whom did he plan to vote? Bob Dole.

Dole ended his near perfect day with another major endorsement. This time it was George W. Bush, governor of delegate-rich Texas and son of the former president. The former president himself was very complimentary of his 1988 rival, noting that Dole had great "credentials" for the job. This from a man who knew about credentials. Like Dole, he never had much charisma, but his resume read as if he'd been training for the presidency his entire adult life.

Buchanan and Forbes? They vowed to march on. In fact, Buchanan became somewhat testy as he reluctantly conceded that Dole's nomination seemed inevitable. Buchanan had come to believe he deserved to win and was being robbed by the Republican establishment, which was, as he described it, carrying Dole across the goal line. After campaigning hard in Arizona, he had fallen short due to Steve Forbes' free-spending there. In South Carolina, he couldn't overcome the support thrown Dole's way by powerful and popular local Party regulars. And he did well in Georgia, just not well enough to break through. A believer in momentum, Buchanan thought about the small margin separating him from Dole. One break was all he needed to regain momentum. Fate was not on his side, and he seemed to have difficulty dealing with that.

Unfortunately, Buchanan was correct when he talked about momentum. He was accurately and honestly summing up one of the key factors that drive the process. I say unfortunate because I'm not comfortable with the idea that the outcome of our presidential election process could turn on a fumbled line, an intercepted communication or a sack by some journalist. Big Mo' does have a way of turning around sporting events for reasons that are difficult to explain. It has something to do with emotion, adrenaline, psychology. Everyone searches for it. That's why football teams spend high draft choices on players who can deliver momentum-shifting types of plays. None of that is troublesome when we're talking about the world of sports. But the thought that the Republican nomination could have turned, as

Buchanan perceived, on one or two breaks in Arizona and South Carolina is nothing short of frightening. If nothing else, it is another loud warning that we'd better pay more attention to the "sportification" of our politics.

Forbes was sounding positive notes after Junior Tuesday. He attributed the results of the day to a general feeling that it was necessary to stop Buchanan. The Dole vote was largely a negative vote, he reasoned. Now that Buchanan didn't seem to be the threat he was only a week earlier, the voters could vote for positive ideas, and those belonged to him. Wednesday morning, word came that Forbes would make a major announcement later in the day, prompting speculation that he, like Alexander and Lugar, would withdraw. The announcement was big all right: Jack Kemp, oblivious to the dramatic turn his own life would take just a few months later, would endorse Forbes.

Kemp's endorsement of Forbes was hardly surprising in view of the fact that he was much closer to Forbes than to Dole on the issue of tax policy. Kemp had long advocated a Republican strategy of making taxes, or tax cuts, the focal point of the 1996 campaign, and the Forbes positions criticized by Dole were essentially Kemp guiding principles. What was difficult to explain was the timing of the announcement. Although the primaries were not technically over, Kemp was clearly raining on Dole's parade. It wasn't enough to ruin Dole's splendid day, but many thought the endorsement burned all bridges between Kemp and the Republican establishment. If so, the real surprise announcement concerning Jack Kemp that came later in the campaign demonstrated that even badly burnt political bridges can be repaired in short order when an election is on the line.

* * *

For a brief moment, I wondered whether New Yorkers would be crazy enough to shock the country and prolong the process. Forbes had spent another bundle, a good portion of it in a legal battle to get on the ballot in the New York primary. Perhaps New Yorkers, who don't appreciate being told what to do, would send a message not to take anything for granted. After all, we hadn't even reached Super Tuesday or heard from any of the other big-delegate states, including California, Texas and Florida. New Yorker Jack Kemp had just reminded us the race was not over. And what about that burning desire for entertainment?

New York didn't seem to be in the mood for excitement on March 7. Instead, it gave Dole his expected victory, unofficially crowning him with the Republican nomination. Dole had again been backed by the Republican establishment. This, however, was a very different group of Republicans: Governor George Pataki, the new star who retired Mario Cuomo; Al D'Amato, leader of the charge against the Clintons on Whitewater; Susan Molinari, one of the energetic young Republicans in Congress and someone who looked like she had a bright future in politics (before she surprised everyone with the announcement of her intention to move to television); and Mayor Rudy Guiliani, who managed to remain in the party despite having supported Mario Cuomo in the gubernatorial race against George Pataki. By and large, these guys believed in traditional Republican values: more private enterprise, less big government, a balanced budget, lower taxes and free trade. On social issues, they weren't quite as conservative. New York was saying Bob Dole was the only guy who could unite all wings of the party under one banner.

The New York victory allowed Dole to concentrate on the real race, the one against Bill Clinton. In one short month, he had gone from faltering front-runner to virtually certain nominee. We'd seen the rise and fall of Steve Forbes, and we'd seen him rise again to hang around with the help of lots of his own money—more than $30 million of it. We'd seen Buchanan emerge as a force, actually threatening to take the nomination, and then settling back into a comfortable minority position. We'd seen Lamar Alexander making a plaid fashion statement that didn't catch on and revert to jacket and tie. It had been everything we wanted out of a political drama, and it didn't drag on.

The Democrats enjoyed watching the Republicans sort things out. Yet there was a sense of disappointment that the Republican internecine strife didn't last. All things considered, it was mild compared to the Democratic battles of the past. Sure, there were plenty of clips to be used against Dole on the vision thing. Democrats would be able to say don't take our word for it, just listen to what his friends in the Republican Party have to say. But the party appeared firmly united behind Dole and there were still seven months until Election Day.

*   *   *

Super Tuesday was anticlimactic. Dole won all seven states handily. The biggest chunks of delegates came from Texas, where Dole had received Governor Bush's endorsement, and Florida, where the Cuban vote was strong. As impressive as the victories were, they were expected, and therefore not as exciting as the earlier primaries. The race had already been decided and the candidates were just playing out the string.

Two days after Super Tuesday, Steve Forbes finally returned to fiscal conservatism and withdrew from the race. A good Republican, he threw his full support to Bob Dole. He had disagreements with Dole, particularly with Dole's emphasis on a balanced budget rather than tax reform. In the end, Forbes is a Republican, much closer in spirit to Dole than to Bill Clinton. There would be no talk of a third party candidacy for Forbes, no sour grapes. He would come back to the fold and be welcomed with open arms, notwithstanding the serious misgivings about Forbes' unbridled spending during the campaign.

The same wasn't true for Pat Buchanan, who vowed to continue to the Convention in San Diego. Buchanan hadn't come all this way simply to become one of the guys. He wasn't spending much money and he was leading a movement, enjoying himself in the process. If he just gave up, what would it get him? Respect? That was something the Republican establishment would not hold out for him. It had nothing else to offer.

Chapter 14

The Minefield Abroad

As Dole was cruising through Super Tuesday, international events dominated the news once again. No longer could Clinton sit back and relax as the Republicans tore one another apart. Dole had overcome his opposition earlier than the Democrats had hoped and was setting his sights on the real opposition, Bill Clinton. Meanwhile, Clinton had his hands full with international crises that, on the one hand, afforded him additional opportunities to act presidential and, on the other hand, represented a minefield he would have to cross to attain reelection—nobody likes a president who bungles a crisis.

The Helms-Burton Act was signed into law on Super Tuesday. With that stroke of the pen, we, not Cuba, became the object of international reprobation. Our friends around the world were outraged at the arrogant extension of U.S. jurisdiction. Canada immediately instituted "consultation" proceedings under NAFTA, a prelude to adversarial arbitration. Mexico joined the proceedings. The Europeans, led by our close friends the British, threatened retaliatory legislation. The State Department was busy at work figuring out whom it was supposed to exclude from the United States under the new legislation and how. It was a predictable mess. None of this caused anyone in the Administration or any Republican candidate to question publicly the wisdom or legality of what Congress had done. There would be plenty of time to worry about that when the campaign was over. In the meantime, the checks and balances built into the system were suspended. The President was not about to risk his lofty perch in the polls with an unpopular veto, particularly since he had already gone on record urging Congress to pass the legislation.

That same day, Clinton took off for a summit of world leaders in Sharm el-Sheikh, Egypt, which he had hastily arranged in the wake of the bombings in Israel. It was an impressive gathering, with Arab leaders showing support and sympathy for Israel in a manner that would have been out of the question a short time before. It was also a gamble, as everyone recognized that another bombing during the summit would have had enormous consequences and given Clinton the same helpless look Jimmy Carter wore in 1980. But there was to be no such interruption. Clinton had managed to steer his way through another crisis.

While Cuba and the Middle East struck sensitive political nerves in the United States, a third crisis of potentially far greater import was brewing in March. China was displeased with independence noises coming out of Taiwan, which was getting ready for presidential elections of its own on March 23. China has this thing about Taiwan; it considers Taiwan a renegade province that eventually will be brought back to the fold, perhaps with a little help from the motherland. Patience is a Chinese virtue, but apparently not when the renegade province takes steps to make the separation permanent.

China conducted war games in the Straits of Taiwan, firing missiles, flexing muscles and generally scaring the heck out of everyone. The Administration was both cautious and uneasy in its response. The Taiwan Relations Act, passed by Congress to emphasize and clarify our commitment to Taiwan in spite of the one-China (the big one) policy, didn't do much to clarify the situation. The Act's declaration of purposes states that it was designed to "help maintain peace, security, and stability in the Western Pacific" and to authorize the "continuation of commercial, cultural, and other relations between the people of the United States and the people on Taiwan." In other words, because there are a billion people in the big China and it is potentially the most powerful nation in the Far East, we had to recognize it and deal with it, notwithstanding our fundamental disagreement with everything it stands for. That recognition, and the consequent severance of diplomatic relations with Taiwan, shouldn't be interpreted as rejection of Taiwan, with which we want to maintain relations. Isn't all that clear?

The Taiwan Relations Act doesn't quite provide the answer to the question of what to do in case of a military conflict. In its declaration of policy, always an interesting part of foreign relations acts (check out the nonsense in both the Cuban Democracy Act of 1992 and the Helms-Burton Act), it states that our policy is, inter alia, "to maintain the capacity of the United States to resist any resort to force or other forms of coercion that would jeopardize the security, or the social or economic system, of the people on Taiwan." I suspect most people assume we "maintain the capacity" to do that and will continue to do so for as long as we can, with or without a statute declaring it to be our national policy. The real question is what are we supposed to do with that capacity, not whether to have or maintain it.

More nonsense follows in the implementation of policy section of the Taiwan Relations Act. Its enlightening language calls upon the President "to inform the Congress promptly of any threat to the security or the social or economic system of the people on Taiwan and any danger to the interests of the United States arising therefrom. The President and the Congress shall determine, in accordance with constitutional processes, appropriate action by the United States in response to any such danger." Translation: we should be ready, willing and able to use force to defend a state we don't recognize against a state we do, but we don't have to if we don't want to.

It was obvious that the Administration was trying (for once) to avoid escalating the crisis through Rambo rhetoric. This wasn't Haiti; it wasn't even Cuba. So questions of whether we would use force if China invaded or simply misfired one of its test missiles were dodged. At the same time, two carrier groups, the nuclear-powered *Nimitz* and the *Independence*, were making their way to the Straits of Taiwan. I was hoping someone knew what they were supposed to do once they got there.

The elections finally came and went without a hitch, with President Lee Teng-hui winning big. The common view was that his victory represented a rejection of China and its tactics of intimidation. The Chinese, however, showed that they too were masters of spin; they interpreted the vote as a rejection of the Taiwan independence movement since one of the political parties in the race was more overtly proindependence than the independent-minded winner. Was this a way of winding down the crisis? The world wished it to be so.

Unlike Cuba and the Middle East, there was no predetermined script to be followed in the China crisis. The President would have to do some real thinking on this one. Not even Jesse Helms was volunteering much assistance. No one was mugging for the camera, proposing "Farewell Deng" legislation, and no one was daring China to make our day. The truth is people were scared that these war games, which seemed a bit too real for comfort, could easily turn into an actual conflict. It didn't happen, of course, and everyone breathed a sigh of relief. But the entire episode was a reminder of just how dangerous a place the post-Cold War world is. I shudder to think how much more dangerous it might have been had the crisis over Taiwan arisen after the election, when China was linked to the fund-raising scandals breaking late in the campaign and when some political consultant might have come up with the bright idea of proving the Administration was not under Chinese influence.

As if the other crises weren't enough to keep him busy, Bosnia required Clinton's constant attention. In mid-March, Warren Christopher unexpectedly called for a meeting with the three sides in Geneva, maintaining pressure on all sides to avoid a renewal of the fighting. Christopher said that a multiethnic society was the solution to the Bosnian problem. The facts on the ground, however, did not portend a multiethnic society. As the Serb forces relinquished control of Sarajevo's suburbs, a Serbian exodus provided little hope that the utopian image of former enemies living side-by-side would ever materialize.

The next couple of weeks did nothing to alleviate the concern over Bosnia. First, we saw film of the killing fields that left little doubt even those with the shortest of memories would take a long time to buy into the multiethnic society concept. Then news broke that the Administration had given its blessing to Iranian arms shipments to Bosnian Muslims, a development Republicans victimized by Irangate were eager to exploit. Finally, a tragic plane accident in Croatia took the lives of Secretary of Commerce Ron Brown and other civil servants and business executives. Recalling the car accident that had claimed the lives of U.S. diplomats several months earlier, one had to wonder whether Bosnia was turning into the nightmare we all feared. The question on everyone's mind was what would happen when (or if) the troops withdrew at the end of the year. Another question on Clinton's mind had to be whether he should have sent them there in the first place.

The flurry of activity on the international front served to highlight the fact that the roles of the president as foreign policy chief and commander-in-chief of the armed forces are clearly among the most important functions of the office. From a political standpoint, it also illustrated how easily international events can sway a presidential election. Handling a crisis well invariably leads to a bump in the president's standing in the polls; bungling one can dissipate a lead in a flash. Small wonder, then, that predicting the outcome of presidential elections months in advance is risky business.

Perhaps most disturbing, the international events underscored another serious shortcoming of the presidential election process, namely, the relative lack of attention paid to foreign policy during the course of the campaign. At no time is this deficiency more clearly evident than during the early phases, when small-state primaries take center stage and issues of more immediate, local concern are at the top of the political agenda. Naturally, voters in those states expect the candidates to address matters of concern to them, which vary from state to state and often are not of an international nature unless war or some other crisis is upon us. This local focus means that not only is a small minority of the electorate selecting the presidential nominees, it is often doing so on the basis of issues that may not be the object of the winning candidate's attention as president. In other words, the primaries are more suited to state-by-state elections of governors, other state officials, senators and congressmen than they are to selecting candidates for the presidency. Politics may be politics, but you don't select your marathon team by timing runners in the 40-yard dash.

To people around the world closely following the presidential campaign, the lack of any serious discussion of international issues in 1996 was confounding and disappointing. They were waiting for the debate on America's world role in the post-Cold War era. Would we keep troops in Bosnia to enforce the peace after December? Where else would we put our troops, and what exactly would be the conditions for their deployment? Troops aside, what embargoes, sanctions or innovative pieces of extraterritorial legislation did we have in mind for imposing our will on other countries and, by the way, what precisely *is* our will? Surely there is some common thread in our foreign policy, something more than a series of disconnected reactions to incidents essentially beyond our control. When you're the only remaining superpower, you're supposed to have the answers to these questions, and you're not supposed to keep everyone guessing.

Maybe you don't buy the notion that we owe anybody outside the United States any explanations. Fair enough. We still owe it to ourselves to answer these questions. While a reasonable argument can be made that the president, whoever he or she may be, won't be able to do much at home to change our daily lives, the same isn't true for foreign affairs, where the president can have an immediate impact, where a single decision can make the difference between war and peace. That was the case in 1991, when George Bush sent our troops into battle in the Persian Gulf. It was obviously a decision that had a profound effect on the lives of people in the area. But its impact in human terms was felt at home as well. As veterans of the Gulf War can attest, you don't have to suffer large numbers of casualties on the battlefield to feel the adverse consequences of war.

Think back to the Vietnam War and the impact of the key

presidential decisions during that period. Even though foreign policy was not as low on the agenda then as it has been in recent years, the campaigns of the '60s left us with a substantial information gap concerning decisions whose impact was far greater than that of Bush's decisions in the Gulf War. Did anyone feel adequately prepared for the escalation of the Vietnam War by President Lyndon Johnson, and did anyone fully understand what candidate Richard Nixon had in mind when he said he had a plan to end the war? The course of history, and millions of American lives, might have been quite different had there been a timely appreciation of the views of the candidates in those elections.

All things considered, I don't think it's too much to request some idea of a candidate's thinking on international affairs before Election Day. Then again, to win an election you've got to get there, and getting there's a lot easier without public exposure of a candidate's thinking on international affairs during the primaries.

Chapter 15

Dole Goes Over The Top

One week after Super Tuesday, four more primaries were held: Illinois, Michigan, Ohio and Wisconsin. Each state had the distinction of having a Republican governor who was on everyone's short list of vice-presidential candidates. Once again, with the help of the governors, Dole swept. This time, at least by some counts, it was enough to put him over the top, although Dole decided to defer the official pronouncement until California a week later.

How did people in California feel? Probably not too well. California had moved its primary up a couple of months in the schedule so it could get in on the action. It wasn't enough. The candidates still spent their time, energy and money in the smaller, earlier contests, correctly sensing that the race would likely be over before even the accelerated California primary rolled around.

Californians had plenty of company. Texas, Florida, Pennsylvania, Illinois, Michigan and other big-delegate states were in the same boat for all practical purposes. Did New Yorkers have much more to say than Californians? Not really. True, many felt the New York primary was the unofficial crowning of Bob Dole as Republican nominee, but the race was largely history before then, when Dole whipped the opposition in South Carolina.

What are we to conclude from a process that allows a Louisiana caucus in which only two candidates compete, an Iowa caucus in which only approximately 100,000 voters participate and primaries in six of the nation's smallest states measured by electoral college vote to determine the Republican nominee? Certainly not that it is designed to reflect a national expression of will. Primaries and caucuses are often mistakenly cited as examples of democracy in action. The phrase retail politics, connoting pure democracy where the candidates are directly in touch with the voters, is used repeatedly during the Iowa and New Hampshire contests. In 1996, as Steve Forbes flooded the airwaves with political commercials, many lamented the demise of retail politics. What they should have been lamenting was what has happened to the entire political process, both wholesale and retail. In a real sense, the system has become undemocratic, robbing the vast majority of Americans of any meaningful say in the selection of their presidential candidates. If people in California and elsewhere across the country were upset, they certainly had good reason.

*   *   *

With Dole over the top, it was a good time to take stock of where the larger contest stood. The consensus was that Dole trailed Clinton badly, by approximately 10 points in a head-to-head race. An impressive lead for the President? Yes. Insurmountable? Definitely not. Michael Dukakis would attest to that. The lead he blew to George Bush in 1988 (with much less time left in the campaign) was considerably larger than the 10 points Clinton held over Dole in late March. No one doubted it could happen again.

One interesting twist linked the issues of Dole's standing vis-à-vis Clinton and his choice of a running mate: Colin Powell's addition to the ticket drew Dole virtually even with Clinton in most polls. Clearly, the choice of running mate would assume great importance in 1996.

Powell's impact on the ticket according to March polls was

truly remarkable and demonstrated the continued uneasiness of voters with both of the major presidential candidates. That's why someone whose views had still not been subjected to intense public scrutiny, but who had a presidential aura about him, could be so popular. For his part, Powell tried to quash talk of his joining the action, publicly reiterating his disinterest in running for any elected office. Notwithstanding his position, he remained the top choice of many Republicans and there was a feeling that he would not be able to turn down a request for help from Dole at crunch time. So Powell would get some of the scrutiny he seemed so intent on avoiding, whether he liked it or not.

To make life more uncomfortable for Powell, Buchanan had made Powell's possible nomination a key issue linked to Buchanan's own refusal to withdraw and support Bob Dole. Buchanan tagged the "Rockefeller Republican" label (referring, of course, to former New York Governor Nelson Rockefeller) on both Powell and New Jersey Governor Christy Whitman, meaning that they were too liberal, principally on social issues. He drew the line on abortion, declaring that his party would remain pro-life or he wouldn't remain in the party—not a position designed to court the African-American vote or the support of women. Just as Powell would have been the first African-American candidate for national office with a chance to win, Whitman would have been the first woman in that category. Because of their positions on abortion, Buchanan indicated he would not be able to support the Republican ticket if either was nominated.

Although it didn't seem to impress Buchanan much, the Rockefeller Republicans weren't exactly in full campaign mode. By the end of March, Whitman had removed her name from contention with a public announcement. She had been flattered by all the talk of her candidacy but had little to gain by waiting to be told later she would not be the choice. This way, she withdrew on her own terms and improved her image back home in New Jersey. Everyone believed her. For some reason, the same wasn't true for Powell. His name would hang around as long as those polls continued to show his impact on the ticket like no other potential vice-presidential candidate.

Powell and Whitman were not the only names dropped in the speculation as to Dole's choice for vice-president. The list seemed to grow daily, crowded with governors whose successes in their own states were viewed as shining examples of the virtue of Washington returning power to the states, a cornerstone of the Dole campaign. Among the governors mentioned were the midwestern quartet: Edgar of Illinois; Engler of Michigan; Voinovich of Ohio; and Thompson of Wisconsin. And what about Merrill of New Hampshire, who did everything he could for Dole on opening day but fell short, and former Governor Campbell of South Carolina, who played a role in delivering that key state to Dole? Even Congressman John Kasich, who had been making a name for himself in the Battle of the Budget, was a possibility, his energy and enthusiasm being elements the Dole campaign sorely lacked. There seemed to be only one prominent Republican name that went unmentioned: Jack Kemp.

Chapter 16

Bad News For Both Sides

Toward the end of March, Clinton and Dole both absorbed blows that shook them up, two on each side.

The Clintons had the misfortune of attending the annual Radio and Television Correspondents' dinner in Washington, normally a fun affair attended by newspersons and politicians alike. Someone came up with the bright idea to invite radio talk show host Don Imus as the main speaker. Walter Cronkite, once the country's most trusted newsman and the epitome of dignity, presented an award. Newt Gingrich then spoke, followed by the President, both in the light spirit of the evening. Gingrich noted there was good and bad news for Pat Buchanan, the good news being he would be speaking on prime time during the Republican Convention, the bad news that he would do his speaking on "Crossfire". He also poked fun at Dole, providing historical examples of the less articulate man winning. Clinton, ironically, alluded to Imus' taking credit for his 1992 victory and jokingly conceded that Imus may have been right. Then came Imus.

If you've ever heard Imus in the morning, you knew that the organizers of the dinner were asking for trouble inviting him to speak. Imus is funny, but often tasteless. One thing you don't want to do is invite him to lampoon those sitting at the table live, especially if they happen to be the President and the First Lady.

Roasting the President and First Lady is always a tricky matter. We like humor and tend to dislike politicians who take themselves too seriously. Nevertheless, as a general proposition, we also tend to dislike direct confrontation and like to think that we maintain some minimum level of respect for the office of the presidency. Relatively little of the ugliness that has been so pervasive in campaigns of recent vintage is seen in direct confrontation. On the contrary, while candidates and their henchmen are often too eager to spread rumors and hurl accusations behind each other's backs, when they appear together a greater sense of civility can be detected.

A prime example was the 1995 televised discussion between Clinton and Gingrich in New Hampshire, where both, especially Gingrich, seemed more intent on demonstrating civility than exploring substance. There was one quasi-substantive agreement to come out of the discussion: the agreement to appoint a commission on campaign finance reform. Subsequent developments, including the failure to appoint the commission and the obvious fund-raising abuses emerging late in the campaign, made apparent that the smiles and famous handshake accompanying the agreement in New Hampshire were more important than the agreement itself. Not that politicians won't go after their opponents; not that they won't raise issues face-to-face. But there is an invisible line they generally don't cross. Where exactly that line is we can't say with precision. What we can say is that when someone crosses it, an alarm goes off.

Imus knows no such bounds. He started by pretending to lose his papers, then produced a folder that he said had just materialized. He continued to poke fun at Hillary and her Whitewater woes, reading mock time sheets. Borderline stuff. Then he turned to the President and, in front of his wife, crudely reminded the audience of his proclivity to mess around. It was embarrassing, and it wasn't funny.

Mike McCurry, the President's press secretary, called C-Span to suggest that it consider whether to proceed with its broadcast of the dinner as originally scheduled. Of course, he couldn't prohibit C-Span from doing so; he was hoping it might censor itself. No way. Probably feeling it could not set a bad precedent by responding to pressure from the White House, C-Span went ahead, with more people, myself included, watching out of curiosity.

In the short run, both Clintons may have gained points by sitting through the painful performance and maintaining their dignity when others felt they would have been justified in walking out. Gingrich and many other Republicans joined in the chorus of sympathy. In the long run, however, the incident was not helpful to the Clinton cause. It was another reminder of the potential for scandal at the top of the Clinton Administration. The Republicans believed that character would be a major issue in the fall, and Imus' remarks made clear Clinton was vulnerable on that issue. It's not that Bob Dole would stand up in a debate and accuse Clinton of sleeping around; nor was he likely to look Clinton in the eye and say at least Elizabeth ain't got no subpoenas. Nevertheless, while Dole wouldn't do it face-to-face, the same couldn't be said for Republican operatives behind the scenes.

The second episode was more of Clinton's own making. He threatened to veto legislation curbing plaintiffs' ability to recover punitive damages in product liability cases. Punitive damages is the term used for the portion of a damage award that exceeds actual, compensatory damages. They send a message to defendants, punishing them for making defective products that place consumers at risk.

The problem with punitive damages is they have gotten out of hand. Juries all over the country have been returning huge verdicts consisting largely of punitive damages, and not just in product liability cases. Examples of a system gone haywire are too numerous to ignore, from a multimillion-dollar award for burns from spilled hot coffee to a 10 billion dollar award against Texaco for allegedly interfering with a Pennzoil business transaction. Are these outrageous verdicts, which are becoming increasingly common, the fault of the lawyers pursuing them? Of course not. The lawyers are just doing their jobs, sometimes so well that the system becomes distorted. (How's that for solidarity with my colleagues?) That's why some sort of legislative reform is needed.

Congress finally approved legislation many felt didn't go far enough. It was limited to product liability cases, leaving untouched a wide range of other suits, including the medical malpractice suits Morry Taylor blamed for the skyrocketing cost of medical insurance. Even in product liability cases, punitive damages were not eliminated, just limited to $250,000, the court retaining the power in each case to raise that limit in its discretion. Proponents of the legislation, including leading Democrats, thought they had a deal with the White House. Now Clinton was changing his tune.

Defenders of Clinton's stance argued that the legislation was the product of pressure by big business, which likes to be able to manufacture and distribute defective products with impunity. The threat of high damage awards keeps them honest, they said. But big business wasn't the only interest group involved in this fight; the trial lawyers have always been quite effective when it comes to protecting their turf from legislative interference. Clinton had a reputation for standing by his fellow lawyers, and it looked like this would be no exception.

Just to prove all lawyers aren't the same, I think the President earned his criticism on this one. Having seen the operation of our legal system at close range, I'm convinced the system is in deep trouble and in need of serious reform. Punitive damages in product liability cases is just one of many areas where corrective action would be in order. Punitive damages in other cases and the high cost of litigation totally apart from the issue of punitive damages are other serious problems that need to be addressed. Litigation should be a civilized means of resolving unavoidable legal disputes, not a threat to bring an opponent to its knees through protracted and abusive court proceedings designed to induce a cash settlement. Unlike in some forums, a plaintiff bringing a frivolous case doesn't have to pay the defendant's legal fees. The lack of that downside, coupled with the lack of sufficient curbs on abuses of the judicial process, makes us by far the most litigious people in the world, not exactly a distinction of honor.

From a political standpoint also, Clinton was on the wrong side of the issue. Notwithstanding Hollywood's current fascination with lawyers, defending lawyers against charges of abuse of the system is a losing proposition. Even though the legislation had nothing to do with ambulance-chasing, Clinton's position gave Republicans the opportunity to identify him with that practice and in the process to deal another blow to the already low image of lawyers. My colleagues in the profession should be grateful Dole was never able to capitalize effectively on the issue, although he did raise it in both presidential debates in October. Recalling a frightening fall he had suffered on the campaign trail, he joked that before he hit the ground his cellular telephone was ringing; it was a trial lawyer telling him I think we got a case here.

* * *

At about the same time as the Democratic fun-busters, two events occurred on the Republican side that couldn't have pleased Bob Dole. As in the case of the Democrats, one headache came from outside government and the other from Congress itself.

A former employee of the Republican Party brought suit claiming she was let go because of her weight and subjected to harassment. To support her allegations, a tape was released that apparently at some point had been used by the GOP for entertainment. The scene replayed many times on national television had a young female job applicant showing her credentials (of the physical kind) to a male boss. I don't know if it would have been funny years ago. It certainly wasn't funny now.

The Republicans said the tape didn't represent their thinking on such sensitive issues as the treatment of women, minorities and homosexuals in the workplace. They planned to defend what they considered to be a frivolous case. The problem they faced was twofold: first, even frivolous cases have a way of turning into costly, damaging affairs these days— legislative reform is not yet upon us; and second, regardless of the merits of this particular case, about which I could not express an opinion, the pictures played repeatedly on national television were not politically helpful. Moreover, just as many believed Imus' portrayal of Clinton's character contained more than a grain of truth, the GOP film revealed an ugly sense of humor many suspected long had Republican written all over it.

Another problem for Dole was a bill passed by the House of Representatives to repeal the ban on assault weapons enacted just a few years earlier. The highlight of the debate on the floor of the House was an exchange between Representative Patrick Kennedy, Democrat from Rhode Island and nephew of JFK and RFK, and Republican Representative Gerald Solomon from a rural part of upstate New York. In an emotional outburst, Kennedy invoked the memory of his slain uncles, arguing that if you haven't had someone killed in your family, you can't appreciate what it does. It's not just the victim, he implored, it's the whole family. In response, Solomon chastised Kennedy for lecturing him and, sounding more agitated than the young Democrat, shouted the purported clincher: five days a week his wife is home alone in upstate New York and she should not be denied her constitutional right to protect herself.

I don't buy the argument that someone close to you has to be murdered for you to understand the argument in favor of gun control, any more than I bought the argument that you had to go to Vietnam to have a valid opinion on the Vietnam War. Solomon's argument, however, was even more difficult to grasp. The image of poor Mrs. Solomon on guard back home, armed with her assault rifle, didn't quite clinch it for me. If that's what it takes to defend ourselves these days, emigration would be a better alternative.

Gun control has always been a difficult issue in American politics. On one side are ultraconservatives who wrap themselves in the constitutional right to bear arms, with one of the most powerful, well-oiled organizations to represent their views, the National Rifle Association. On the other are liberals who often focus on gun control as the means of combatting crime at the expense of other measures. Despite their relative ineffectiveness in getting gun control legislation passed, the liberals have long been in the majority on this one. The very strength of the gun lobby, its consistency and determination in opposing virtually any form of gun control legislation, was turned against it in the fight over the ban on assault weapons. It just became too difficult to argue that the Constitution protected our right to use uzis and AK-47s in the face of police opposition across the country, not to mention common sense. The argument that guns don't commit crimes, people do, lost its force as more people became persuaded that criminals armed with assault weapons are capable of a lot more serious crimes than criminals without them. You don't have to be a liberal to see that logic.

Against the advice of some prominent Republicans who no doubt foresaw the adverse political fallout from the move to repeal the assault weapons ban, the House pressed ahead with the legislation, putting it in Bob Dole's lap. Dole said the legislation was not a priority, meaning it was a colossal headache he didn't need at the time. The President saw the fat pitch coming and couldn't wait to belt it out of the park. He announced he would veto the bill if it passed. Whether or not it did, the Democrats seized the opportunity to hammer home their message that they now represented the center, with the Republicans off somewhere on the extreme right, beholden to extremists who had taken over the party. The world of the 1980s had been turned on its head.

* * *

Bad news for both parties came in the form of rumblings of third, fourth and fifth party candidacies.

Ross Perot appeared on his favorite television show, "Larry King Live," and gave strong indications that he would join the action as the candidate of his Reform Party. He hoped the two main parties would address in a serious manner the problems facing the country, but if they didn't, and it didn't look like they would, then a third party candidacy was inevitable. With this inevitability sinking in, the airwaves were full of speculation as to whom Perot would hurt more if he indeed did decide to run. Democratic and Republican consultants alike tended to feel he would divide the anti-incumbent vote and therefore hurt Dole. Most didn't think he would do as well as he had done in 1992.

Ralph Nader, arguing that Clinton vs. Dole simply didn't offer a meaningful choice, indicated he might be on the ballot in California as the candidate of the Green Party. Even though I was occasionally bothered by his impracticality, I have fond memories of Nader's consumer battles going back to the 1960s. At the time, his idealism seemed infectious, his integrity unassailable. In addition, he stood for something. Not that it seems to matter much in our system, but there is something comforting about a person in public life standing for something, whether or not we agree with it. Nader had always made clear he wasn't in the battle for personal gain of either a political or financial nature. It wasn't clear why he had decided to campaign for office after all these years, but I still felt the same way about him. While his views can be more than a touch off center, the prospect of Nader participating in the fall debates was not good news for the main candidates, particularly Bill Clinton. Unlike in the case of Perot, most assumed that whatever support Nader garnered would be at Clinton's expense.

Finally, there was Pat Buchanan. Still campaigning in the Republican primaries, still claiming he intended to support the Republican nominee, he nonetheless seemed to be positioning himself for a break with the party. He made clear on national television that his support of the party was not unconditional. What exactly were the conditions? At the very least, that the party retain the pro-life plank in its platform at the convention in San Diego. Others might include refraining from nominating a Rockefeller Republican for vice-president. And what about allowing him to speak at the Convention—in prime time and uncensored? If you heard Buchanan's speech about a "cultural war" in America at the 1992 Republican Convention in Houston, you knew how high a price giving him the podium again would be. Buchanan may have been correct in his view that one says something important if people are still talking about it years later, but the Republicans didn't seem to be in the mood for another dose of important thoughts.

The proliferation of candidates outside the mainstream was not fortuitous; it was a sign of the times. The inescapable fact was that a large number of Americans remained dissatisfied with the choices offered by the main political parties. At the same time, it seemed clear that no existing third party satisfied the desire for change. Despite the large, fertile territory represented by the roughly one-third of the electorate that considered itself independent, it was safe to say none of the three potential third party candidates had any chance of rallying the unaffiliated. Did that mean the main political parties could ignore the independents? Not without serious peril. The lack of a candidate didn't imply the lack of a problem. Voter discontent with the main candidates meant the system was in trouble and, sooner or later, frustration was likely to give birth to a more serious third party candidate (did anyone say Bill Bradley or Sam Nunn?) to the regret of both Democrats and Republicans. In the meantime, there was damage to be done in Election '96.

Chapter 17
California Has Its Day

Even if it didn't mean anything, Californians weren't about to cancel their primary. So they went ahead, the most populous state in the nation, knowing that what they did would not have any effect on the only contested nomination in 1996—if you don't count the Reform Party, which didn't hold primaries. That knowledge drained most of the excitement out of the day. To his credit, Dole did what he could to help, delaying his claim to the Republican nomination one week out of respect for California. It didn't help; the suspense was long gone.

The virtual irrelevance of the California primary is hard to square with the notion of a democratic process for the selection of presidential candidates. When you have more votes in the electoral college than any other state, you'd like to think you have more than a ceremonial role in selecting the nominees who would be elegible to receive those votes in November (actually December, when the vote takes place in the electoral college). Yet the meaningless California primary came and went in 1996 without serious discussion of the issue. I didn't detect much concern or recognition of the fact that the primary system had to a large extent disenfranchised Californians and was disappointed neither Californians nor anyone else seemed to be clamoring for the abolition of the primaries. California was one of those late season matchups that looked good on paper but turned out to be devoid of consequence because the pennant had already been wrapped up. When that happens in the world of sports, all we are denied is that extra bit of entertainment only big games can deliver. When it happens in politics, it's time to take a closer look at what our primaries are serving up for us in November, and at how we're getting there.

By the way, Dole won California, as he did Nevada and Washington the same day. He then promptly went about the business of healing the wounds resulting from the primary battles, talking of unity in the party and recognizing the valuable contributions made by his defeated contestants in the form of enriching the debate with important issues. Both Forbes and Buchanan had stressed issues striking sensitive nerves in California. Californians have long been hostile to taxes, one reason Forbes might have mounted a serious challenge there had he stayed in the race. Buchanan was the guy who wanted to build that wall on the border to stop immigration, another popular issue. Californians had voted for Proposition 187, denying benefits to children of illegal aliens, huge numbers of whom populate the state's public school system at enormous cost. Dole rode both issues, as well as the anti-affirmative action sentiment Governor Wilson had hoped would fuel his own presidential campaign.

Success in the California primary couldn't mask the difficulties Dole was likely to encounter there come November. George Bush seemed to concede California to Bill Clinton in 1992, not a strategy on which to build a winning presidential campaign. While Dole wasn't about to follow that strategy, he had to overcome a general lack of excitement about his candidacy in California as well as the liberal social views prevailing there. Among other things, most Californians, although strong fiscal conservatives, are pro-choice. Whatever Buchanan thought of Dole's position on abortion, many others viewed him as pro-life.

There was some speculation that Dole might look to a Californian as a vice-presidential candidate to boost his chances in that state. The problem was that Wilson, the logical choice, had become quite unpopular at home. It may have had something to do with his willingness to abandon the state to pursue his presidential ambitions less than a year after winning the gubernatorial election. Apart from California, Wilson didn't set the rest of the country on fire with his own unexciting and short-lived campaign for the Republican presidential nomination. The second most prominent California Republican, State Attorney General Lungren, was not exactly a household name. Who did help the ticket according to the exit polls? Colin Powell.

Chapter 18

Character

With no further entertainment emanating from the primaries, it was time to reflect on the issues that would shape the real campaign in the fall. The problem was, nobody knew what they would be. Abortion, taxes, affirmative action, the budget, Bosnia, crime, immigration, trade, economic growth, all these and many others would be on the table. But the overriding political theme of the campaign hadn't been established.

As the main political parties have drawn closer to each other in ideology, the controlling issues of the day have kept changing. Candidates and their professional advisors seem to be engaged in a perpetual search for the popular issue that can galvanize a campaign. There is no real philosophical debate in 1990s America as to the virtues of big government, for years the key point of distinction between Democrats and Republicans. All now say, even if they don't fully agree, that the era of big government is over. That's why the Republicans were frowning during the State of the Union.

Whenever you go deep into an election year without having settled on the substantive issues, you can expect character to take center stage. In April, with all the confusion over the distinction between Democrats and Republicans and with many Americans feeling, as Ralph Nader said, that Clinton/Dole simply didn't offer a sufficiently meaningful choice, character was again shaping up as a key issue.

All this seemed tailor-made for the American electorate. In the first instance, the more the campaign focused on character the less ideological it would be. And, as I have come to understand, pragmatism is America's favorite ideology.

Second, the character discussion adds more spice to our politics than any substantive discussion of issues. Economic statistics just don't play as well on television as pictures of Gary Hart on vacation, Bill and Hillary Clinton explaining the state of their marriage or the showdown between Clarence Thomas and Anita Hill at the Senate confirmation hearings. When politics becomes that entertaining, don't expect people to lobby hard for change even if intellectually they know there's something wrong with the system.

Third, as nebulous as the concept is, character is much easier to understand than substantive issues. This, of course, is especially true when we do not have strong, clearly defined ideologies to fall back on. The one nice thing about political ideologies is they provide you with answers to a whole range of questions about which you would otherwise have to think long and hard. Armed with an ideology, you don't have to spend much time pondering individual issues; just learn the internal logic of the ideology and you've got it. If we have to think about whether free trade is good or bad for the economy, perhaps take a few courses, read a few books, engage in a few roundtable discussions, well, it just seems like too much to fit into our daily schedules. And that's only one issue. If any significant number of people devoted the time necessary to digest the full range of substantive issues and formulate informed views on them, the economy would be a shambles.

Under these circumstances, character constitutes an attractive alternative, particularly when there is a perception that one candidate holds an advantage over the other. In this case, without attempting to pass judgment on the character of either Bill Clinton or Bob Dole, the perception certainly existed that this was one area in which Dole enjoyed an advantage. It was therefore to be expected that the Republicans would inject the character issue into the debate at the most strategic time, while the Democrats would make every effort to make the Republicans look like petty mudslingers devoid of substantive ideas.

The film *An American President* contained a most entertaining depiction of precisely such a battle. I saw it at 35,000 feet, where I see a lot of movies, and was sufficiently amused to put down my manuscript for a couple of hours. It was a good, light story—a young, popular, Democratic widower occupying the White House starts dating an environmental lobbyist. The much older Republican adversary, *Bob* Rumson, couldn't wait to tear into the girlfriend and sling mud at the president, who was trying to take the high road and stay on the substantive issues as he sank in the polls. At the end, the president finally strikes back, agreeing to debate the character issue and standing by his girlfriend. The message he came back with redefined character as the will to support the right legislation and pursue the right policies.

While I thoroughly enjoyed *An American President*, I recall becoming somewhat infuriated by the end of the film. Partisan politics seemed to get in the way of the story through a not too subtle attempt to portray the darker Bob Rumson as Bob Dole. The fact is the film would have been more entertaining if the president had been a conservative Republican dating in the White House. But then we wouldn't make the association between Michael Douglas, the substantive president whose character demands he resist the temptation to engage in gutter politics, and Bill Clinton, who would just as soon redefine character the way it was in the film.

Movies aside, character cannot simply be assimilated into the substantive issues of the day. Whatever you think about free trade, gun control or a balanced budget, we can all agree that supporting or opposing it is not what we mean by character. If it were, character wouldn't be an issue separate and distinct from the others.

What then is character? Is it like pornography, difficult to define but you know it when you see it? Something like that. While there doesn't seem to be a clear consensus on any affirmative definition, it is possible to recognize conduct inconsistent with good character, at least if you have your Values straight. In fact, one definition of character is sticking by what we identify as Values. Cheating on your wife or husband, for example, is a no-no; doing it repeatedly is worse. Using public office for personal financial gain is definitely out, even if we're talking about peanuts. Don't abuse women in bars. Don't cheat on exams. Watch which bridges you drive over. Don't get caught paying political operatives to spread rumors about opponents. Show respect for hard work and don't act as if money is everything. Religion would help. In general, show you have a moral compass, some code other than hedonism to guide you. Everyone strays on occasion; just don't make it a habit.

A second definition of character is the inner strength that comes from conviction, knowing what you believe and standing by it regardless of popular opinion. That's not to be confused with stubbornness and inflexibility. We like our leaders to be open-minded and flexible, to be able to recognize and admit mistakes and change their minds based on evidence and persuasive argument. One might say that itself is a manifestation of character. But if your views on an issue depend upon the last person to speak to you or the last poll you're shown, you have a serious character problem.

Is a perceived character shortage enough to bring a president down? Bill Clinton seemed to prove otherwise in 1992, when he overcame both Whitewater and Gennifer Flowers and asked us to believe he didn't inhale. That remarkable precedent made a powerful case against the Republican strategy of campaigning on the character issue again. However, 1992 presented an unusual set of circumstances, including a President who had lost the confidence of his own party, a strong third candidate who severely wounded the President, and the novelty of Bill Clinton and his forceful wife. Even with all that, Clinton won in 1992 with only 43 percent of the popular vote. Election '96 presented a new mix of factors, and there was no guarantee the character issue wouldn't hit home the second time around. Besides, with Bill Clinton moving to the right to co-opt the Republican agenda, the Republicans didn't seem to have any other viable strategy.

Chapter 19

Not Just An American Phenomenon

We're not the only ones who do this election thing. It's happening all over and, not surprisingly, can lead to bizarre behavior abroad as easily as it does at home.

Most of April saw Israel flexing its muscles in Lebanon. Each side blamed the other for starting the hostilities. Hezbollah fired Katyousha rockets into northern Israel. Not limiting its attack to Hezbollah positions, Israel took the air war all the way to Beirut, hitting an important power plant outside the city and causing Lebanese to wonder anew whether their lives would ever return to normal. Several hundred thousand new refugees were created by the attacks as Israel appeared to be following the strategy of making life miserable for all in an attempt to force Lebanon to deal with Hezbollah. Then, in what was termed an unfortunate "mistake," Israeli artillery rained down on a U.N. camp in southern Lebanon, killing more than one hundred civilians and wounding many more. The grizzly scenes were reminiscent of those following the suicide bombings in Israel. The world was momentarily shocked. There were widespread cries for a cease-fire, but no calls for a summit a la Sharm el-Sheikh.

Many suspected that the tough Israeli action had something to do with its upcoming parliamentary elections and the Labor Party's need to show strength after the Hamas bombings. The hard line policies of the opposition Likud Party reflected the mood of much of the Israeli public, and Shimon Peres seemed to be searching for ways to toughen up his image and take some of the steam out of Likud. The renewed hostilities in Lebanon gave him the opportunity to take over the opposition's agenda and counter accusations of softness on security matters, while at the same time maintaining his claim to being the only leader having a chance to make peace. We've seen that principle in operation in many contexts and many places before, including Campaign '96. With Clinton talking conservative during the State of the Union, he set the Republicans back on their heels while maintaining his position as the only candidate able to attract liberal support.

Unfortunately for Lebanon, it was the most convenient place to carry out the strategy. Where else? Having made peace, Jordan was out of the question. Attacking Syria would be too dangerous. The Palestinians were the new partners in the peace process. That left poor little Lebanon, a country that has paid the heaviest price of all for Middle East politics since I was evacuated from Beirut in the 1967 June War.

The U.N. General Assembly condemned Israel for the attacks, but not with the same degree of unanimity that characterized past General Assembly resolutions against Israel. International criticism was generally muted as there seemed to be a broad understanding of the politics behind the fighting, including a consensus that a Likud victory would be a major setback to the peace process. Until the artillery barrage against the U.N. compound, the Clinton Administration seemed to express only sympathy for the Israeli position. Even the attack on the U.N. compound was not met with the same condemnatory language that came from all sides after the March bombings in Israel, or that came from the Administration after the planes were downed off the coast of Cuba.

When the U.N. produced a report that cast serious doubt on the Israeli claim of "mistake," the Administration's official response was to question that judgment and attack the publication of the report. Rushing to judgment and taking hasty action may have been politically acceptable, or required, when Cuba downed the two planes, but it wasn't in the cards here. Imagine for a moment what everyone would have said if British Prime Minister John Major had ordered air strikes on a Catholic residential neighborhood in Belfast in retaliation for bus bombings in London, arguing that IRA sympathizers lived in the neighborhood. Somehow, I don't think either the Administration or the international community would have been as understanding. Neither would Teddy Kennedy and the Irish in Boston.

As has often been the case in the Middle East, the fighting shook things up and created new opportunities for the players to push the game a step forward. Warren Christopher started a round of shuttle diplomacy between Damascus and Jerusalem. Syria was back playing a leading role, having once again demonstrated it held the key to the final settlement that still lay ahead. In the most dramatic political move since the handshakes on the White House lawn, the Palestine National Council voted to amend the PLO Charter to eliminate the provisions that were inconsistent with the concept of peace with Israel, *i.e.*, the clauses referring to the destruction of the State of Israel. Arafat had delivered the most sought after symbolic act in the midst of another wave of Israeli attacks on Lebanon. The next day, Israel's Labor Party reciprocated by eliminating from its platform its opposition to a Palestinian state. Peres also announced that Israel would be withdrawing from Hebron by the end of the first week in May. The expected agreement ending the fighting in Lebanon followed in short order. The peace process, pronounced dead just one month earlier, was alive and well again. So were Peres' chances in the upcoming Israeli elections, or so it seemed.

In spite of the obvious efforts of Clinton and other western leaders to prop up Peres, Benjamin Netanyahu squeezed out a victory in Israel's first direct election of a prime minister. In the short and medium term, Netanyahu's victory meant a likely detour for the peace process as everyone reevaluated the events of the past few years and the best way to move forward. For Clinton, it represented somewhat of a defeat. He had invested much political capital in Peres, perhaps because he genuinely believed

Peres was on the right path, perhaps because he was looking forward to playing up his foreign policy credentials, the president who brought peace to the Middle East after so many years of war and hostility. Now it was clear that, at best, there would be no major breakthroughs prior to November. While the U.S. campaign had not yet focused on international affairs, Netanyahu's victory took one of Clinton's trump cards out of his hand. Depending on Netanyahu's moves during his first six months in office, the possibility existed that further damage lay ahead. In the meantime, the Lebanese wondered why everyone had already forgotten the damage they had suffered in the weeks leading up to this demonstration of democracy in action.

* * *

As this drama was playing out in the Middle East, Clinton inserted himself into another important foreign election. Boris Yeltsin was in the fight of his political life in Russia. Presidential elections were only a couple of months away and much was at stake for Russia, for the United States, for everyone. That's why Burly Boris was pulling out all the stops, literally dancing his heart—and almost his life—away while it was still allowing him to run an American-style campaign. There haven't been many real elections in Russia this (or any other) century, and this one looked as if it could have real consequences. Yeltsin's principal opponent, Gennadi Zyuganov, was an uncharismatic communist who brought back memories of a more secure past that appealed to many Russians, particularly older ones having difficulty coping with the new economic order after the collapse of the Soviet Union. Talk about choices! This wasn't exactly Clinton/Dole.

I've always had difficulty with this aspect of democracy. When there are such fundamental differences in the political and economic philosophies of candidates and their respective parties, elections become heavy stuff, and there's only so much heaviness a society can take. A democratic system of government not only features the people choosing their leaders; it calls for that choice to be made with some frequency, more than once a century. In certain cases, you can't do that without causing a shock to the system. If every four years communism and the Soviet Union are to be dismantled and reassembled, there isn't going to be much time for anything else. This may partially explain why ours is the longest running "democratic" show around; we don't tend to have such dramatic choices. Sure, the candidates will strongly disagree on individual issues. Sure, there will be sharp differences in personality and character. But don't look for the Democrats to call for the nationalization of major industries or the Republicans to scrap the federal government.

The dangers inherent in the Russian elections—talk of the good old days under Stalin and the reestablishment of the Soviet Union—also challenge the assumption that the spread of democracy is necessarily in our national interest. Until relatively recently, promoting democracy was not a priority of our foreign policy; combatting communism was. That left room for an assortment of options, including military dictatorships of the far right and other regimes having little in common with us other than their staunch opposition to the left. With the collapse of the Soviet Union, the focus changed. We thought we could afford the luxury of pushing democracy U.S.-style. However, that policy didn't take account of the fact that democracy isn't easy to grow in places without democratic traditions; nor did it take into account the distinct possibility that we may not be entirely comfortable with the outcome of the democratic process. As the saying goes, be careful what you wish for; you may actually get it.

So this trip to Russia was more than just routine politics. It looked very much like an attempt to shore up Yeltsin, improve his image as an international leader, while at the same time showing off Clinton's developing talents in foreign affairs. Listening to what the two were saying at their joint press conference, it wasn't clear that there was much substantive agreement in Moscow, but there were plenty of smiles, handshakes and other overt signs of friendship. If nothing else, the two shared one objective: winning an election.

Chapter 20

The Republicans Nearly Self-Destruct

By the time Clinton returned home from Moscow, the Republicans were in a funk. Even in the land of constantly changing political fortunes, it is unusual to see such political strength so rapidly dissipated. The polls had Clinton's lead over Dole ballooning to 20 points. While Dole's weakness eventually could have an impact on congressional races as well, there was no sign that the country as a whole was shifting back to the left, which meant that the Republicans were in the process of blowing it all on their own.

It's never easy to allocate blame or responsibility for this kind of political collapse, particularly when things could change in the middle of your analysis. In any event, focusing entirely on the negative wouldn't pay sufficient tribute to the extrordinary political talents of Bill Clinton. The Republican problems could be traced to the resilient President's return from his state of irrelevancy in late 1995. The turning point was the Battle of the Budget. Somehow, notwithstanding traditional Democratic resistance to budget-cutting and the electorate's desire to balance the budget, the Republicans managed to lose the public relations battle. Clinton vetoed the Republican budget, professing agreement with the necessity of cutting spending and casting the Republicans in the role of uncompromising extremists. The public bought it.

Around the same time period, Newt Gingrich was transformed from visionary, revolutionary, and inspirational and popular leader into villain, the most unpopular major political figure in America. It was nothing short of amazing, and it had its effect on Gingrich's psyche. He appeared confused, tired, frustrated and immature—a little boy who didn't get his way, picked up his marbles and went home. Reports that he pouted about a back seat in Air Force One didn't make him look one bit more mature. Gingrich was shaken and appeared to lose confidence in himself. While he was still a big draw at fund-raisers around the country, he had lost his edge and was no longer dictating the agenda. The Democrats, smelling blood, were making Gingrich and the Republican "extremists" in Congress the centerpiece of their campaign. They weren't just running against Bob Dole; they were running against Dole/Gingrich. Whenever the opportunity arose, Gingrich's name or face would be inserted alongside or in front of Dole's, making sure no one forgot that they were part of the same Republican leadership team.

In a televised interview, Gingrich tried to put it all in perspective, pointing out that the Republicans would have plenty of time to get their story out. In the meantime, he took aim at the unions, liberals and trial lawyers. But the fire was clearly missing. The next week, Gingrich tried playing nice guy as substitute host for Larry King with an assortment of animals as the featured guests. It worked for Johnny Carson and Jay Leno; it wasn't the answer to Newt's image problems.

To make matters worse, prominent Republicans began to criticize Dole's campaign, or the lack thereof, publicly. Highly respected former Secretary of Education William Bennett and commentator Bill Kristol led the way. They were impatient with the lack of ideas coming from the Republican side. The campaign was stalled before it had gotten off the ground.

Conventional wisdom had it that the public was not ready for a Republican president to go along with a Republican Congress, any more than it had previously been anxious to elect a Democratic president to go along with a Democratic Congress. It had something to do with checks and balances. I wasn't so sure. After all, wasn't Clinton the same guy who had steered his way into a state of irrelevancy over the first three years of his Administration with unpopular policies? It didn't look then like the country was too happy with a Democrat in the White House; nor were the proponents of the theory of ballot box checks and balances arguing that it would have saved Bill Clinton had the election taken place in 1995. No, there was more to the sorry Republican predicament than a political calculation on the part of the electorate regarding the merits of the two main political parties splitting the legislative and executive functions.

The more relevant point was that Bob Dole was living up to expectations as a poor candidate. He was a poor campaigner caught in a system that placed a premium on campaigning talents, and, as he had demonstrated on State of the Union night, his oratorical skills were no match for those of Bill Clinton. In Buchanan's terms, the Republican establishment had managed to carry Dole to victory in the primaries, but no enthusiasm had been generated and now the party was paying the price. With the main event six months away, the establishment was no longer rallying around Dole; it was publicly bailing out, not unlike the way it had on George Bush privately in 1992. This time the Republicans were giving up before the fight had begun.

The Republican performance was disgraceful. Of course Dole was not the ideal candidate. He wasn't even as inspiring as his opponents in the primaries, none of whom were major political figures. As Republicans everywhere kept saying for more than a year, he was definitely not as "electable" as any number of other potential candidates. However, for reasons we all should spend more time analyzing, most of those other candidates decided to stay on the sidelines, leaving the field to Dole. While the system may be at fault for that, Dole himself hardly deserved blame for being as unexciting a candidate on the campaign trail as everyone knew he would be.

More importantly, there was no reason to bail out so early in the game. The country remained conservative and, although Clinton was doing a great job of taking over the Republican agenda, there were six months left to ask why the country should want a

New Democrat who acts like an old one three out of four years when it could have a plain, old-fashioned Republican instead. A reassessment of strategy was needed, not a prophecy of doom that could easily become self-fulfilling.

Apart from the substance, the character issue, still the Republican trump card, hadn't yet been played. While the Republicans were busy feeling sorry for themselves, the President was giving testimony on videotape from the White House in the Arkansas Whitewater trial of Jim and Susan McDougal and former Arkansas Governor Jim Guy Tucker. People were also asking why, if Hillary Clinton didn't know the whereabouts of her billing records, they bore her fingerprints. At the same time, accusations against Independent Counsel Starr of conflict of interest, political agenda and personal ambition managed to make the rounds. It wasn't quite the all-out war publicly declared much later in the campaign by James Carville, but it gave rise to speculation that trouble lay ahead for the Clintons and that a campaign had been started to taint any action by Starr before it was taken.

Instead of taking the initiative on any of these fronts, the Republicans were doing their best to self-destruct. A prime example was their handling of the abortion issue. In early April, the President had vetoed the so-called Partial Birth Abortion Bill, which banned late-term abortions performed through a procedure that can upset even the staunchest of pro-choicers. Without getting into the gruesome details widely portrayed in the press, suffice it to say that the procedure involves a partial birth that isn't allowed to become complete. The veto received the condemnation of the Vatican, and priests around the country weren't shy about spelling out the details of the horrible procedure in their Sunday homilies. The abortion issue, politically delicate for Republicans, had suddenly been handed to them. However, they just didn't seem interested. Rather than attacking Clinton for an unpopular veto, the prominent pro-choice Republican governors—Wilson, Whitman, Pataki and Weld—opened what appeared to be a concerted attack on the abortion plank in the Republican platform, calling for a fight if necessary on the floor of the Convention. What made this strategy more unfathomable was that, unlike the other Republican self-criticism, which obviously had not been orchestrated by Dole, there was a suspicion that the abortion debate might actually have had his blessing. Three of the governors were on his campaign team.

As the Republican camp disintegrated, talk of third party candidacies became more serious. "Bay" Buchanan, Pat's sister and campaign manager, acknowledged that a third party candidacy remained a possibility since no real overtures had been made to the Buchanan camp. Dole's sinking poll figures were making that decision easier. Meanwhile, Ross Perot must have been gloating. Even though his agenda was modified Republican, for some reason he seemed to find special glee in Republican troubles, much as he did in 1992.

All this was good news for Bill Clinton. Yet the Republicans could take some comfort in the fact that the election was still six months away, and now they had the advantage of the underdog. Dole would at least be able to enter the next phase of the campaign on an optimistic note—there was no place to go but up.

Chapter 21

The White House or Home

The Republicans needed a jolt, and Bob Dole gave it to them in mid-May when he announced his resignation from the Senate. Many had been calling upon him for some time to step aside as majority leader and concentrate on the campaign. Few thought he was listening. Well, he not only listened, he went one giant step further by saying good-bye to Capitol Hill and hello to America. Bob Dole would leave the Senate in June after an illustrious 35-year career in Congress, announcing that the next stop was the White House or home.

It's not likely that leaving his stomping ground was Dole's first choice. More likely, he realized he had no choice. Something had to be done to rescue a campaign that was rapidly headed down the road to nowhere. His dramatic decision didn't quite turn the tide, but at least it stopped the bleeding. A Dole unshackled by his Senate duties would seem less the ultimate Washington insider, more free and relaxed, a regular guy with wit and more fluidity to his speech, and less tied to the fortunes of the Gingrich-led Republican (extremist) Congress. If all that weren't sufficient grounds to support his decision, there was his wife, who seemed frustrated with a campaign dead in the water and anxious to get moving. With him on the campaign trail instead of on the Senate floor wrapped up in the procedural niceties of the legislative process, she could play a larger, more visible role. Given her ability to present the case for her husband far more effectively than he could for himself, the prospect of a larger role for Elizabeth was good news for Bob Dole.

Although the announcement led to a bump in the Dole approval ratings, there was no immediate dent in Clinton's huge lead over Dole. Nevertheless, the announcement had a significant short-term impact that at the time seemed likely eventually to pay dividends: the Republican self-flagellation temporarily ceased and newfound enthusiasm was generated throughout the Republican Party leadership. The only problem was they still hadn't identified the defining issue of the Dole campaign.

The search for a defining issue had been taking on a distinctly desperate look. First came the attack on the 4.3 cent gas tax, a move triggered by the rise in crude oil prices and the consequent rise in gasoline prices at the pump. Somehow, the repeal of this tax, which nobody cared about just a few weeks earlier, became the answer to the middle class squeeze and the key to protecting our presumed constitutional right to cheap gas. The version of the bill that made its way through the House would have repealed the tax until January 1, 1997.

As usual when it comes to taxes, the Democrats were uncomfortable in dealing with the gas tax issue. They recognized the silliness of the debate. Oil prices were indeed higher than they had been recently, but they were still far below their level in OPEC's heyday and drivers in the United States still paid far less for gas than their counterparts in Europe. There was simply no reason for the 4.3 cent tax suddenly to become the focus of the political debate, except that the Democrats, who had pushed the tax in 1993, seemed to have difficulty dealing with Republican demagoguery of the issue. The standard Robin Hood strategy on tax cuts didn't work on this one, as it wasn't a case of taxing the rich to give to the poor. Lots of poor and middle class people, people who drive their own cars, paid as much or more of the gas tax than the rich, and it took a much bigger bite out of their incomes. Without a class attack to fall back on, Democrats would have to attack the Republican initiative on the merits and risk falling into the tax and spend liberal stereotype they were working so diligently to escape.

There was, of course, an alternative for the Democrats: a little demagoguery of their own. The proposal for a 90-cent increase in the minimum wage provided the perfect opportunity. Raising the minimum wage is nearly always popular, as arguing against it is too easily associated with defending the proposition that $4.25 an hour is a good wage. The real issue isn't whether $4.25 an hour is a good wage; it's whether raising the minimum wage would result in layoffs because of the impact on the salary structure of small businesses. The Democrats weren't about to conduct a seminar on that issue, and the Republicans, as anxious to avoid the "party of the rich" label as the Democrats were to shed their reputation on taxes, couldn't put up a serious fight. Assisted by a sufficiently large number of Republicans apparently concerned about their fortunes in November, the Democrats got their minimum wage hike through the House.

The wind taken out of their sails, the Republicans stopped banking on the gas tax. Even before they were upstaged by the minimum wage hike, they knew or should have known the gas tax wasn't going to carry them to victory in November. It was simply too trivial to form the basis of a serious campaign. So the search for a defining issue continued, the Republicans poking in various directions and Clinton frustrating them at every turn. He went to Wisconsin and praised Republican Governor (and leading vice-presidential contender) Tommy Thompson's welfare reform experiment, which seemed to be to the right of federal welfare reform bills Clinton had already vetoed. Clinton also announced he would sign a bill banning gay marriages, thereby preventing Republicans from using that issue to portray him as the social left-winger they claimed he was. The last thing Clinton wanted was a repeat performance of his early gays in the military fiasco to disrupt his overall strategy of co-opting the right while maintaining support from the left.

Nevertheless, although Clinton always seemed to be one step ahead of the Republicans, a marked change was taking place in the tone and pace of the campaign. That change was a positive one for the Republicans. Their campaign was no longer dead in the water. It was moving, though not yet in any particular direction, and there was a sense that throwing darts at the board would eventually hit the bull's eye.

The first sign that Dole was getting to Clinton came in late May when Dole attacked Clinton's veto of the bill banning "partial birth" abortions. On the defensive, Clinton gave an emotional response, talking about protecting the health of the mother and asking why Dole's position was any more moral than his own. He cautioned we should be skeptical of politicians piously proclaiming their morality. For the first time, he seemed off balance, forced to defend a liberal position that did not enjoy wide popularity. And for the first time, Dole was able to take the offensive on the abortion issue, rather than watch the Republicans fight among themselves over the abortion plank in the party platform. The Republicans weren't going to win the election on the abortion issue, but Clinton's veto gave Dole the opportunity to paint Clinton as the "extremist" who supported abortion on demand.

Clinton was still regaining his composure when news broke that his lawyer had cited the Soldiers and Sailors Act, a statute designed to protect military personnel on active duty from lawsuits, in support of his own defense in the Paula Jones case. The suit alleged that Paula Jones was working at a conference Clinton attended while governor of Arkansas, and that he had invited her to a room and exhibited, inter alia, some unpresidential (or ungubernatorial) and offensive behavior. The Republicans put out a strategically placed TV ad that zeroed in on the legal argument made in the Clinton Supreme Court brief and closed with a clip of Clinton in shorts taking a golf swing. I've seen more farfetched arguments than the Soldiers and Sailors Act in a lot of expensive briefs, but this one carried a political cost I'm not sure the President thought he would have to pay.

At around the same time, the Republicans started to get comfortable with the Clinton maneuvering on substantive issues, like a hitter up for his fourth at bat against the same pitcher. Haley Barbour said Clinton's got only one play in his playbook: fake right, run left. Instead of crying over Clinton's newfound taste for the right, the Republicans had apparently decided they could use it to their advantage. Another TV commercial drove the point home by stringing together clips of Clinton stating various positions on balancing the budget—five years, nine years, seven years. No attempt was made at substantive discussion of the appropriate period, of why a balanced budget was necessary at all, or of precisely how it could be attained. That was all beside the point, which was to show Clinton as a campaigner without convictions other than political expediency.

The message was clear: the Republicans intended to play the character card for all it was worth, both sides of it. The Paula Jones commercial hit the Values side of the issue. It reminded the viewers at once of Clinton's lack of military service and of his reputation for extracurricular activity. Haley Barbour's fake right run left line and the budget commercial addressed the issue of core beliefs. The implication was Clinton had none, other than the burning desire to win. If that meant moving to the right during election year, so be it.

The Democrats, meanwhile, were practicing their response to the character attack. Basically, it was the same response provided in *An American President*—the adversary is ideologically bankrupt and therefore can only resort to mudslinging of the lowest kind. It worked in the movie. Whether it would work in real life remained to be seen, especially when the plot didn't involve a single president dating a likeable environmental lobbyist.

It was painful watching this drama unfold. Not that the price of admission was too high. It's just that somehow we had a right to expect more from this race for the world's most powerful office. In Russia, they were about to vote on the direction of their country—on with the market economy or back toward communism. In Israel, they were about to vote on the peace process. What were we supposed to be deciding? Five months before the election, we still weren't sure.

Chapter 22

Guilty

Just as the Republicans were getting their act together, a jury in Arkansas concluded eight days of deliberations and gave the President his worst day of the campaign. All three defendants in the McDougal/Tucker Whitewater trial, Clinton's two friends and business partners and the governor who succeeded him, were convicted on felony counts emanating from a series of allegedly fraudulent loan transactions.

Immediately the Democrats were out in force putting their spin on the unexpected verdicts. Their line was that the President wasn't on trial in Arkansas and the verdicts proved nothing as to him; they were simply irrelevant. From a technical standpoint, they *were* irrelevant. Unfortunately for the President, however, legal technicalities are not the stuff of political campaigns; guilty verdicts are. As various commentators pointed out, had the verdicts in Arkansas been "not guilty," the White House undoubtedly would have found special meaning in the jury's decision.

What stuck in the minds of many people was that Bill Clinton was the only witness for the defense aside from Jim McDougal. His testimony contradicted that of the prosecution witness Hale, who had accused Governor Clinton of pressuring him into making an illegal loan. Some jurors apparently disregarded the testimony of both and based their decision principally on the documentary evidence presented by the prosecution. The fact remained that Clinton's buddies in Arkansas had been convicted, and many were playing the game of guilt by association.

As bad as the day was for the President, it was good for Al D'Amato. Al had been taking it on the chin for his relentless pursuit of phantom crimes and misdemeanors in the Senate hearings on Whitewater. In fact, he had announced that he would wrap up the hearings shortly. As everyone saw it, the Committee would deliver a highly partisan report that would be promptly dismissed as such; D'Amato would have lost his showdown with the Clintons. Now things were looking brighter for D'Amato. In a way, he had been vindicated, or at least could credibly so claim. He wasted no time doing precisely that.

The other big winner was Kenneth Starr. The attacks against him now seemed weak. Starr, a man of some stature, had gone about his job quietly and achieved a victory many had thought unlikely; an Arkansas jury had convicted the governor and two Arkansan friends of Bubba Clinton. It was the expectations game again. The verdicts had impact because many assumed the jury wouldn't convict, part of the fallout of the O.J. case.

Perhaps the worst news for the President was that Starr would now go on with other trials, full of confidence and without having to feel the sting of Democratic criticism for wasting the taxpayers' money. On deck was another Arkansas trial in which the President was again expected to testify. Two bankers were accused of illegally contributing to his last gubernatorial campaign in Arkansas. It was expected that Starr eventually would work his way to the White House itself, turning to the two Washington events that appeared the most disturbing: the materializing of Hillary Clinton's billing records and her role in Travelgate. Both were recent. Both were relatively easy to understand.

It was still too early to measure the full impact of the guilty verdicts on the course of the campaign. It wasn't too early to tell that the verdicts, combined with the brief submitted on the President's behalf in the Paula Jones case and the development of a Republican strategy for dealing with Clinton's newfound conservatism, had energized the Dole campaign. The race was on.

Chapter 23

A Tearful Farewell

Bob Dole's Senate farewell speech may not have been great, but it sure beat his State of the Union reply. This was Dole at his best, on his home court, not playing a role, just playing Bob Dole. It was one of those rare occasions when a challenger gets to make a major campaign speech without it being labeled a campaign speech. The setting created an unfair advantage for the retiring Senator, almost as unfair as the President's advantage on State of the Union night.

Dole's stroll down memory lane recalled the bitter debate over cutting off funding for the Vietnam War, which he felt was wrong. It sounded not only like a highlight of Dole's career, but a contrast with Clinton's own record with respect to the Vietnam War as well. There was also a proud reference to Dole's leading role in passing the Americans with Disabilities Act. Once again, the contrast between his sacrifice and Clinton's lack of military service was drawn without any mention of the President.

Other highlights included Dole's praise for Democratic senators with whom he had collaborated and jousted over the years. Most remarkable were his kind comments about George McGovern, the venerable liberal Democratic candidate for president thrashed by Richard Nixon in 1972. Dole recalled his days working with McGovern on programs for the poor. This from the same tough conservative who had no use for compromise on State of the Union night.

Dole's form was also better than average. Although he read uneasily from his notebook at times, it didn't seem unnatural. On the contrary, a slick speech would have been out of character and left the audience with the uncomfortable feeling of watching the genuine article turn fake before their very eyes. At several points, Dole showed the sense of humor that had served him well in the past. And this time, unlike State of the Union night, he had a friendly live audience encouraging him, laughing at his jokes, cheering him on. It was a performance as good as his State of the Union reply was bad.

*   *   *

Even though the second week of June belonged to Bob Dole, it wasn't completely smooth sailing. The Republicans continued their intramural fighting over the abortion issue. What confounded the experts was that it was Dole himself who kept the issue alive.

The debate raging for weeks between the pro-choice Republican governors and pro-lifers had apparently led to a compromise in the form of a Declaration of Tolerance, a recognition that people can have different views and still be Republicans. While both sides had reservations about the proposed solution, it seemed to work. The Republicans had faced the divisive abortion issue months before their Convention in San Diego and seemingly avoided the prospect of a politically damaging fight on the Convention floor.

For some reason, that scenario wasn't satisfactory to Dole. He surprised everyone with the announcement that the Declaration of Tolerance would not be in the platform's preamble, as anticipated, but in the abortion plank itself. What's more, Dole wasn't merely expressing an opinion; he was in effect saying I'm the nominee and that's the way it's gonna be. The conservatives didn't like it one bit. It was the same language Ronald Reagan had lived with in 1980, but in 1996 it represented somewhat of a retreat at a time when they thought the battle had already been won.

To many, the precise location of the Declaration was much ado about nothing. In the first instance, not too many voters read party platforms. Were it not for the flap over the abortion plank played out on TV and in the newspapers, few would even know what language was at issue. People don't read party platforms for a good reason: they generally don't matter. Absent some sort of Contract with Voters, they have no binding force and are quickly forgotten once the election is over. Candidates themselves typically pay little attention to the platforms unless and until they wish to send a political message for campaign purposes. That, apparently, is precisely what Bob Dole had in mind.

If the substance of the language had meant anything, it is difficult to see how pro-choice Republicans would have been pleased with the Dole solution. The abortion plank would not be substantively different from the pro-life position it had embodied since 1980; it would simply acknowledge that it was possible for others to hold different views. Was that supposed to comfort those who firmly believed in a woman's absolute right of choice? No. More likely, it was designed to send a message that the conservatives were not going to dictate the platform. In effect, the liberals should be content with the mere fact that the conservatives were discontented.

From the conservative perspective, the pro-lifers might have been excused for wondering why it was necessary to compromise on such a fundamental issue. If you believe life begins at conception and abortion is tantamount to murder, you might have difficulty acknowledging respectable opposing views. That, after all, is what distinguishes the abortion issue from taxes, free trade and all others.

Yet Dole, a committed pro-lifer (except in the case of rape, incest and threat to the life of the mother), was more interested in symbolism than purity of thought. Even if he himself opposed abortion, he wanted to end once and for all the notion that the Republican Party had no room for pro-choice Republicans, a notion that was costing him dearly in the polls. Besides, where were the pro-lifers going, to Bill Clinton? In case anyone needed a reminder of where the Democrats stood, Clinton had just vetoed the Partial Birth Abortion Bill. Simply put, if the choice was between Bob Dole and Bill Clinton, and between the Republican abortion plank, with the Declaration of Tolerance in it, and the Democratic platform, there really wasn't any doubt where the conservative vote would go. Dole's only serious concern on that score was a third party run by Pat Buchanan, a prospect that was looking less and less likely.

* * *

At around the same time that Dole was shifting positions on abortion, he seemed also to shift slightly on affirmative action. He didn't seem as firmly opposed to it as he was during the primaries. Some saw this as an accommodation to Colin Powell, still the favorite noncandidate for vice-president. In addition to being pro-choice, Powell supported affirmative action.

While Dole's mellowing may have pleased Powell, it was more likely designed to have broader appeal. True, the country had shifted dramatically to the right on the affirmative action issue. There was little doubt affirmative action was on the way out—the fate of controversial California Proposition 209 in November was to underscore that point. But Dole had already established his right-wing credentials and they didn't appear to be serving him well enough in the broader electorate. He still trailed Clinton by as much as 22 points in some polls.

There may have been something else bothering Dole, as it was many of us. The battle against racial preferences was leading to some ugly consequences. Racism seemed to be on the rise and, in a manner reminiscent of the '60s and early '70s, the line between legitimate conservatism and racism was becoming blurred. What drove this point home was the rash of black church burnings across the South, an ugly development that hadn't been seen for some time. Although conservative leaders spoke out, perhaps more than they had in the past, and the Republican Congress took up legislation to facilitate the investigation of the fires, one had a nagging feeling that the rhetoric coming out of some conservative camps had gotten a little too hot and contributed to racial tensions across the country.

It's hard to defend affirmative action from a logical standpoint. No matter what the justification for a preference, you can't get there in a straight line if you're starting from the concept that we're all equal in the eyes of the law. Apart from logic, affirmative action can have the effect of exacerbating racial tensions through the proliferation of the kind of damaging anectodotal evidence that finds such a receptive ear in some conservative circles. Doesn't everyone have a story about how one person or another was unfairly favored in school admissions, in job applications or in job promotions? How many times have you heard that he or she never would have made it if it weren't for affirmative action, or for the fear that denial of admission, employment or promotion would result in a lawsuit?

Nevertheless, the ills of affirmative action do not remotely approach the adverse effects of racism. That's why Dole's mellowing on affirmative action made sense. Even if it is time to get rid of affirmative action, playing up the issue in the heat of a political campaign was neither in the interests of the country nor in the interests of Bob Dole the candidate. As in the case of abortion, the right would support Dole over Clinton any day. The problem for Dole was the center, where the election would be won or lost and where he had thus far failed to make inroads.

Was Dole guilty of a reverse Clinton strategy, faking left and running right? Maybe. However, whereas in Clinton's case the positions he was either faking or taking represented a substantive shift to the right, Dole's shifting had more to do with form than substance. As is often the case with conservatives, form is important. It's the Attitude thing; the bigger the Attitude, the more conservative the candidate. Dole was changing his Attitude, not his positions. In so doing, he was beginning to win his share of the center so dominated until then by Clinton.

Sound political strategy. The only thing needed to top it off was a nice, juicy scandal.

Chapter 24

Another Gate

They didn't have to wait long for a scandal to develop. The Travelgate investigation uncovered the fact that the White House had been requesting and receiving from the FBI its files on several hundred past holders of White House security clearance. The names of the subjects included many low level officials and a few notables, such as former Secretary of State James Baker and former Reagan Chief of Staff Ken Duberstein. The excuse given for requesting the files was the need to update the list of those with White House clearance. To Republicans, it smacked of an enemies list reminiscent of the Nixon Watergate days.

An embarrassed White House immediately apologized for what was termed an innocent mistake, a bureaucratic snafu (situation normal all f___ed up), stressing that the list had not been put to any ill use. But the damage had been done. FBI Director Freeh, who would have preferred to soak in the accolades emanating from the peaceful resolution of the Freemen showdown in Montana, was busy explaining how the FBI had managed to deliver hundreds of confidential files to the White House without question, and his explanations weren't entirely satisfactory—the FBI was "victimized" by the White House. Dole and the Republicans were having a field day with the new scandal, not buying the innocent mistake routine. Congressman Clinger, whose House Government Reform and Oversight Committee discovered the "bureaucratic snafu," planned to hold immediate hearings on the FBI files affair.

Whether or not the scandal escalated, the White House was obviously facing a serious problem due to the cumulative effect of a lot of bad news generated in a relatively short period of time. Less than a month earlier, the Clinton buddies had been convicted in Arkansas. In mid-June, the Arkansas trial of the two bankers accused of illegal contributions to Clinton's 1990 gubernatorial campaign got under way. White House Deputy Counsel and close Clinton aide Bruce Lindsey was named as an unindicted coconspirator. Another set of convictions following more videotaped testimony from the White House would be tough to brush aside.

As the second Arkansas trial opened, Al D'Amato's Senate Committee on Whitewater issued its strongly worded report pointing the finger at the First Lady in White House cover-ups relating to her billing records and the files in former White House Counsel Vince Foster's office. It was a highly partisan report following a highly partisan hearing. The Democrats were understandably angry at this blatant politicization of the congressional hearing process. However, in the midst of the chaos created by the Arkansas guilty verdicts, the FBI files scandal and the new Arkansas trial, their denials sounded as partisan as D'Amato's accusations. Had the Committee's report been issued just one month earlier, it would have been dismissed as a feeble attempt to justify the protracted hearings and caused more damage to the Republicans than to the Clintons. In mid-June, the report was still seen as partisan, but it could no longer simply be dismissed.

Would it all blow over? Yes—if it ended there. The problem was there was no certainty it would in fact end. There was now serious concern, almost an expectation, that more bad news lay ahead. It might be further developments concerning "Filegate." It might be another guilty verdict or more high profile indictments by Independent Counsel Starr, perhaps of the First Lady herself. Fortunately for the President, the Supreme Court wasn't scheduled to tell us what it thought of that brief in the Paula Jones case until after the election.

Chapter 25

Seesaw

What the public was making of all this remained a mystery. At the end of Dole's week of glory, a CNN/*Time* poll showed the huge gap between the candidates had narrowed to six points. While each of the previous two elections had featured remarkable collapses—Dukakis in '88 and Bush in '92—this one, if true, was truly shocking. The very next week, the polls showed Clinton's lead back up to the 19-20 point range, causing everyone to wonder what the heck was going on. With more than four months left in the campaign, the best advice was to fasten seat belts.

The conventional explanation for the seesaw motion of poll results was that Dole had received a boost from the pomp and circumstance surrounding his departure from the Senate—something like the boost candidates normally receive from the summer conventions. There was also speculation that Dole's sudden rise may have been partly attributable to his stand on the Declaration of Tolerance. And, of course, Clinton's mounting troubles undoubtedly contributed to some degree. All these explanations were beside the point. The real issue, the issue receiving the least attention, was WHY—why did the extensive coverage of Dole's emotional farewell and the accompanying developments give him a 16-point boost, and why did Clinton make such a rapid recovery, reestablishing his huge lead only one week after he had lost it. No new substantive debate had taken place. No new substantive issue had arisen. In fact, the seemingly endless search for the defining issue of the campaign had yet to yield any results.

One couldn't help but wonder whether there were any new defining issues to be found, whether American politics had become the epitome of form over substance, whether substance had become simply irrelevant to the process. If the candidates had to work so hard to invent an issue that would capture the public's imagination, maybe it wasn't the candidates' fault; maybe it was us. If we had the same passion for issues as we do for process, it would be hard to imagine such wild swings in the polls. When you have a predominant substantive issue—consider the one Russian voters faced in their June presidential election—you're not likely to see so many people change their minds twice in two weeks. You have to be very confused indeed to swing from communism to capitalism and back to communism, even if your period of reference is two entire decades. No, only in a nonsubstantive environment is this kind of political schizophrenia possible.

And in a nonsubstantive environment, style is always at a premium. A Ronald Reagan does well; a Barry Goldwater doesn't. A Bill Clinton thrives; a Paul Tsongas falters. A Kennedy, any of them, can win; a Eugene McCarthy can't. In the context of Election '96, this was bad news for Bob Dole, as he had little style. The most remarkable story of the first half of 1996 was how it came to pass that Dole became the Republican nominee in spite of his serious style deficiency. Now this lack of style was catching up to him, manifesting itself in his inability to capitalize on Clinton's mounting difficulties. The contrast between the smooth Clinton and the awkward Dole was painful. It was beginning to look like the only thing that could stop Bill Clinton was Bill Clinton.

*   *   *

The general frustration felt by Republicans and independents alike with Dole's inability to provide direction was exacerbated by the tobacco flap. Dole raised questions about the addictive qualities of tobacco, not a smart move in today's virulently anti-smoking society. Suddenly, the evils of tobacco became the focal point of the campaign. Democrats pointed out that huge sums of tobacco money supported Republican campaigns, implying that Dole's statement on the addictiveness of tobacco was made because he was beholden to tobacco interests.

Dole fought back with film of Al Gore, who had led the charge against Dole on the tobacco issue, speaking to a tobacco audience with more than a bit of enthusiasm. Although he had claimed to have reformed his thinking after the death of his sister from lung cancer, Gore, who had long represented a tobacco state, was obviously having difficulty with the issue. His widely quoted protobacco speech came in 1988, several years after his sister's death. The delayed reaction had many wondering whether Gore's current position was the product of an actual transformation or sheer hypocrisy.

But Dole was clearly suffering the most. He hadn't said smoking was good or that it wasn't harmful to your health. He'd merely said it wasn't addictive in the same manner for everyone. Nevertheless, even if some people may be able to control their smoking more than others, his comments *sounded* pro-smoking, a little too much like something the powerful tobacco lobby might argue. To an increasingly antismoking public, they struck the wrong chord. It didn't help that Dole decided to take his frustrations out on popular "Today" show co-host Katie Couric when she questioned him about his tobacco statements on the air.

Most importantly, Dole was not only losing the battle over the tobacco issue, he was missing yet another opportunity to establish a positive agenda for the campaign. Like it or not, the presidency was Clinton's to lose. Battling to a draw would not win it back for the Republicans. They had to give people a reason for change—we can do as well as Clinton wasn't going to get the job done.

Publicly, everyone hoped the reason would be positive—perhaps embodied in a Contract with America II. The tobacco flap told us that if the Republicans were to come up with a reason, it was more likely to be negative. That wouldn't be the high road, but it would be the easier one. It would also be the road most suited to Dole. In this game, with no midseason trades allowed, your game plan better conform to your candidate's talents.

*   *   *

As Dole wasted his time grappling with the tobacco issue, international events again took over the news. A truck bomb in Saudi Arabia destroyed a building housing U.S. personnel, killing 19 and wounding many more. Clinton was about to begin a G-7 summit in France, a meeting designed to focus on economic issues. He managed to shift the focus of the meeting to combatting terrorism, emerging as the clear leader of the group. Returning home after the summit, he attended services for the fallen Americans, receiving plenty of additional positive airtime.

Clinton's presidential performance was remarkable on several counts. First, he showed his international political skills rivaled his ability to maneuver at home, exercising leadership that seemed to be readily accepted by the other summit participants. Second, Clinton struck the right chord, as he usually did, consoling both the families of the victims and the country as a whole during a time of grief, another important presidential function. It was precisely that kind of performance in the aftermath of the Oklahoma City tragedy that many feel sparked his comeback from a political state of irrelevancy in 1995. Third, his performance at the G-7 summit served to defuse our allies' harsh criticism of legislation aimed at extraterritorial enforcement of U.S. embargoes, including the Helms-Burton Act, about which the Canadians were livid, and legislation making its way through Congress providing for sanctions against companies investing in Iran and Libya, which had the Europeans as upset as the Canadians were over Helms-Burton. It would have been unseemly for our allies to press their case in the wake of the bombing in Saudi Arabia with the President speaking out so strongly. Put in a corner, they had to ease up, and they did.

The events raised a lot of serious questions. The simple ones concerned the security arrangements for U.S. personnel in Saudi Arabia. Why was the security fence so close to the building? Why was the FBI not allowed to interrogate four Saudis convicted of an earlier attack before they were beheaded? Did Secretary of Defense William Perry properly carry out his duties in pressing the case for security for U.S. personnel with the Saudis? More difficult questions concerned the purpose of keeping U.S. personnel in Saudi Arabia, defining what our interests there were and precisely what we were prepared to do to protect them. Presumably, the security of Saudi oil fields was in our national interest, at least to the extent threatened by outside forces. Although George Bush struggled mightily to articulate the reasons for the Gulf War, most people assumed oil had played at least some role in his decision. But what if the threat were to come from inside—would we go to the same lengths to protect those same interests? Answering such questions required not only an in-depth analysis of our relationship with Saudi Arabia and the entire region, but also a deeper understanding of what we were facing. In other words, to borrow a line from Hollywood, who are those guys—and why are they blowing up our buildings?

Congressional hearings were planned to look into all these issues, but not much was expected to come of them. Even if security was lax, it would be hard to pin the blame for the attack on the Administration's security lapses. Procedures would change, as they do after every tragedy. There would undoubtedly be a higher degree of alertness, and an officer or two might be reprimanded or lose a promotion. That would be it. As for the substantive questions, the heat of a political campaign was not the right atmosphere for a fundamental policy reassessment. Neither candidate would be offering any answers.

The problem for Dole was that Clinton didn't have to offer any answers. Far ahead in the polls, he didn't have to take risks.

Dole, on the other hand, was going nowhere. The boost he had received from Senate resignation week wasn't strong enough to propel him into a permanently upward motion. He was back on earth being Bob Dole, ineffective candidate, desperately needing another major boost from somewhere. Coincidentally, the end of the July 4th weekend brought Clinton's second round of videotaped testimony from the White House, this time in the trial dealing with illegal contributions to his last gubernatorial campaign. With four whole months to go, it wasn't over yet.

Chapter 26

He's Back!

The lack of enthusiasm for the Dole candidacy, coupled with a nagging feeling that Clinton's lofty position was actually quite shaky, provided a strong incentive for political mavericks to test the third party waters. On July 9, former Colorado Governor Richard Lamm, once a Democrat, announced he would do just that. He would seek the nomination of the Reform Party founded by Ross Perot. It was hard to imagine anyone other than Perot as the Reform Party candidate, but Perot himself had repeatedly stated the movement was not personal.

Lamm was an attractive fellow with a sense of humor and political experience no less impressive than Bill Clinton's in 1992. If he could solve the problem of how to fund his campaign and gain access to the fall debates, he could be a disruptive wild card. As of the date of his announcement, however, he remained a sideshow. The next day he found out just how personal the Reform Party nomination was. The announcement of Lamm's candidacy seemed to push Perot over the line. If anyone was going to be the Reform Party nominee, it wasn't going to be a Perot challenger. It would be Perot's nominee, and what better Perot nominee was there than Ross himself. Lamm's moment in the spotlight had barely ended when Perot confirmed he in fact would run again. He immediately became the favorite to win the Reform Party's nomination.

Polls following Perot's announcement showed his support at around 13 percent, drawn evenly from Clinton and Dole supporters. Considering that Perot had drawn only 19 percent of the popular vote when he was the talk of the town in 1992, 13 percent was not unimpressive. The election remained almost an eternity away and there was a feeling that the Reform Party Convention, to be held on two Sundays sandwiching the Republican Convention in August, might provide him with a springboard to vault into the fall campaign.

Republicans were unhappy with the developments. Conventional wisdom for some time had been that Perot would hurt Dole more than Clinton by dividing the anti-incumbent vote. The Clinton people apparently subscribed to that theory as they welcomed Perot's entry into the race, taking the opportunity to highlight the issue void in the Republican campaign—the party line was whatever would help focus the campaign on the important issues facing the American people was good.

One couldn't help admiring the confident manner in which the White House handled the Perot announcement, particularly in contrast with the frustration emanating from the Republican camp. Nevertheless, there had to be some trepidation behind the scenes. In 1992, Perot had played a major role in bringing down George Bush. While Perot's feelings toward Bush appeared a little too personal, Bush was the logical focal point of criticism since it was his presidency that all challengers presumably wanted to change.

In 1996, Perot still seemed more interested in frustrating the Republicans than winning the presidency, but if he went too far in that direction, his mean streak could well finish the job Al Gore had started in the NAFTA debate some three years earlier. In addition, Perot had a score to settle with both Clinton and Gore as a result of that same debate. So there was at least some chance Perot would turn his attention, and his considerable resources, to Bill Clinton. A revved up Perot picking on Clinton's personal problems would not be a pretty sight and would make Dole the unlikely beneficiary of the Perot candidacy. Once again, Perot had the opportunity to be a kingmaker, or a spoiler, depending on your point of view.

Chapter 27

The Battle of the Platforms

The preconvention maneuvering intensified in early July as Democrats and Republicans alike were eager to avoid platform battles at their respective conventions. Declarations of tolerance became the order of the day, with both parties playing a game of can you top this.

On the Democratic side, there was a new sensitivity to anti-abortionists. The party remained firmly pro-choice, but language would be included in the platform respecting "the individual conscience of each American on this difficult issue." Other controversial issues—gay marriages and gays in the military—weren't tackled head on. In addition, big government was trashed and law and order labeled the "first responsibility" of government. It was a remarkable performance that helped dispel the notion that the Democrats were too liberal.

The Republicans were busy drafting their own tolerance language, which for weeks had been the subject of so much public debate. A month earlier, Dole had purportedly ended the debate on the location of the tolerance language in the Republican platform by declaring it would be right in the abortion plank. Now he was backtracking, settling for an undiluted anti-abortion plank and a separate, fairly elaborate tolerance plank which recognized that members of the Republican Party "have deeply held and sometimes differing views on issues of personal conscience like abortion and capital punishment." It went on to depict this diversity as a "source of strength, not as a sign of weakness," to "welcome" Americans holding differing positions "on these and other issues" and to recognize that "tolerance is a virtue."

I had some difficulty understanding precisely what it meant to say in a party platform that you recognize and respect differing views in your party. Not that tolerance isn't a virtue. It's just that the primary purpose of a party platform in a society in which political ideology is at all relevant is to state the party's position, not to see how many differing views can fit under the same tent. Tolerance is not a position; it is, as the Republicans were saying, a virtue. For a list of virtues, most people refer to documents other than political platforms.

Of course, it's easy to chide the parties for their platform performances. It's also a bit unfair. Party platforms are not serious documents in American politics. Since we are somewhat wary of political ideologies, we don't insist on clear ideological expositions in platforms as a condition to lending our support to individual candidates; if and when ideology manages to slip in, we don't hold our politicians to it once elected. One lesson of past elections is that the stronger the ideology, the more dangerous a platform is to a party's political fortunes.

In 1996, both of the main parties fought hard to avoid the "extremist" label. Essentially, however, this was a battle that had the Democrats on the offensive and the Republicans shakily on the defensive. For years Republicans had succeeded in using the same tactic, only they didn't need to use the word "extremist." "Liberal" did just fine. It connoted everything that had led to a series of Republican landslides in presidential elections and the 1994 Republican takeover of Congress—big government, high taxes, welfare and laissez-faire morality. When the Democrats finally learned their lesson, they changed their rhetoric. They were now comfortably echoing Clinton's State of the Union conservatism. For emphasis, the party platform proclaimed right in its introduction that the Democratic Party offered "the end of the era of big government." (Of course, immediately following were the hardly noticed words "and a final rejection of the misguided call to leave our citizens to fend for themselves.")

As the Democrats (except for diehard Teddy Kennedy and some other long-standing members of Congress) succeeded in shedding the liberal label, they sought to give the Republicans a taste of their own medicine. "Conservative" not being a dirty word since Ronald Reagan first took office, "extremist" became the label of choice. At first, it was used to characterize the religious right, then the economic right, then anyone to the right of the new Democratic right. Accusations of Republican extremism seemed to form part of virtually every interview with virtually every Democrat on virtually any subject. For effect, the name of the remarkably unpopular Gingrich was often used in conjunction with the label, as in Gingrich and the Republican extremists in Congress. The Republicans were too cocky to pay attention, until they found themselves dropping in the polls like a lead balloon. Suddenly, they acquired a sensitivity to the accusations of extremism, going out of their way to proclaim their moderation. One way to do that, both parties apparently believed, was to declare their "tolerance" at every opportunity.

This kind of political maneuvering wasn't attractive to a public fed up with the antics of the main political parties. Both looked silly. But the Democrats were clearly out-tolerating the Republicans, keeping them on the defensive. Unlike the unruly Democrats of the past, the 1996 edition of the party was determined to put on a show of solidarity at the upcoming Democratic National Convention in Chicago, the site of the party's worst performance back in 1968. The Republicans, on the other hand, gave every indication that their internecine struggle would continue. Although some expressed satisfaction with the platform compromise, the Buchanan camp wasn't happy. Pro-choice Republicans were also displeased with Dole's mild retreat, even though the position from which he was retreating was itself unsatisfactory to them. When the damage was assessed, the Democrats had clearly come out ahead.

* * *

It wasn't the only game the Republicans were losing in early July. The Senate finally passed the 90 cent increase in the hourly minimum wage, after yet another failed attempt by some stubborn Republicans to modify it by exempting certain small businesses. The Republican attitude not only proved futile on the minimum wage issue, it also inured to the benefit of the Democrats in the larger battle. They were siding with the people against those extremists who wanted to deny the poor an extra 90 cents an hour so the rich could continue to line their pockets. Robin Hood lives! No matter how demagogic was the Democratic position, and no matter how sincere (or correct) the Republican opposition, it should have been obvious to all that there was no tolerance for serious debate on the issue in the middle of a campaign. The public was on the side of the minimum wage hike and the stubborn refusal of Republicans to concede the issue wasn't doing much for their image.

The Republican image sank even further when Dole turned down an invitation to speak to the NAACP, citing a scheduling conflict. The conflict, which turned out to be Major League Baseball's All-Star Game, was a poor excuse for the obvious slight, the kind of move one campaigning on race might make. That wasn't the message Bob Dole was trying to send to the African-American community; nor was it indicative of his actual record on civil rights. When the heat was turned up by the press, Dole compounded the error by indicating he was being set up by NAACP leader Kweisi Mfume, a liberal Democrat. As might have been expected, that exhibition of paranoia only exacerbated the problem.

Embarrassed at this new level of campaign incompetence, the Republicans resumed the self-destructive behavior that had preceded Dole's announcement of his resignation from the Senate. The short-lived enthusiasm accompanying the announcement had already become ancient history, and the campaign was disintegrating. Some deeply disappointed and impatient conservatives actually suggested that Dole step aside and open up the Convention in San Diego. Even those officially involved in the campaign, such as Al D'Amato, publicly exhibited their impatience with Dole's dismal performance.

What does the modern American politician do when faced with such dire circumstances? What is the single most effective move a presidential candidate can make to stop the bleeding? "Larry King Live!" Dole made another appearance, this time with his wife, Elizabeth. They addressed the tobacco fiasco, the NAACP snub, the mistakes of the campaign. Despite Elizabeth's tendency to overmanage, they appeared honest, sincere and ready for a fresh start. No good television show is complete without a touch of drama, and this episode of This Is My Political Career was no exception. Dole announced that Susan Molinari, the thirty-eight-year-old popular Republican Congresswoman from New York, would be the keynote speaker at the Republican Convention. Of course, it wasn't enough just to make the announcement. In the spirit of TV talk and game shows, Dole noted that Susan hadn't yet been made aware of the honor. Later, she called in live and showed the audience the qualities that made her the choice. Bright, articulate, young, female, a new mother, Catholic, pro-choice—Susan Molinari didn't fit the stereotype of the modern Republican. The next day, the headline of the New York Post read: SUSAN TO THE RESCUE.

Selecting Molinari as keynote speaker was indeed a bold move for the soon to be 73-year-old candidate. It was obvious that a lot of thought had gone into the decision. Dole trailed badly among women, including the so-called "soccer moms" of suburbia, who should have been part of the Republican base. He had also just agreed to the platform compromise that left the tolerance language out of the abortion plank. He needed at once to expand his base and energize the campaign. Newt Gingrich was still a public relations disaster, the Republican governors heading the list of potential candidates for vice-president were too much of a men's club, Colin Powell didn't look as if he wanted the responsibility and Christy Whitman hadn't supported the Partial Birth Abortion Bill. Although it may have been asking too much of Molinari, there was a political logic to the choice.

From another perspective, however, the episode made no sense at all. It was embarrassing watching this game played out on live television. What if Susan had lost her nerve and called in with a polite thanks, but no thanks? Can you imagine how painful that would have been? The good news was Dole was honest enough to have been telling the truth about not knowing her answer before the show; the bad news was he was willing to risk being branded as the greatest campaign bumbler of all time in front of an international television audience.

Given the popularity of the Larry King show in the many countries reached by CNN, the interview with the Doles presented a unique opportunity for the world to see what has become of the American electoral process. It wasn't a pretty sight, this candidate of a major political party struggling to resuscitate a failing campaign with gimmicks, still uncertain of the main points of the program he wished to sell. Were it not for the enormous impact of the U.S. presidential election on people all over the world, they might have been more inclined to appreciate the good television. After all, if the O.J. trial was a hit abroad for an entire year, a presidential election must be good for some entertainment. Under the circumstances, I had a feeling they were hoping for a little more.

Chapter 28

Helms-Burton Comes Into Effect

On July 10, the State Department notified nine individuals affiliated with Sherritt International, a Canadian mining company, that they were no longer welcome in the United States courtesy of Title IV of the Helms-Burton Act. All indications were that executives and principal shareholders of a Mexican company and an Italian company investing in the Cuban telecommunications industry were next on the list. What had these suddenly undesirable individuals done? Held positions or interests in companies doing business in Cuba, *legally*. The mini-trade war with our own allies based on the anti-Castro legislation passed in March had begun in earnest.

While third countries affected by the legislation uniformly denounced it, none seemed to know quite what to do. The 700-pound gorilla had swung into action and everybody seemed to be standing by, waiting for the gorilla to calm down. There was heated activity in the Organization of American States, the United States coming under heavy attack for attempting to dictate the business relationships of other countries. The Europeans were furious and threatened retaliation. Mainly, however, everyone was hoping that somehow the President would come to his senses and exercise his authority under Section 306 of the statute to suspend the effective date of the onerous liability provisions of Title

III, the ones allowing former owners of Cuban-confiscated property to sue anyone who "traffics" in the property for treble damages. The effective date was August 1, 1996, but Section 306 gave the President the right to suspend it for a six-month period (and thereafter to continue the suspension in effect for successive six-month periods) by notifying Congress at least 15 days in advance that suspension was in the national interest and would assist a transition to democracy in Cuba. Suspension would have been significant because it would have had the effect of extending the statute's grace period beyond November 1, 1996, the time period originally allotted to traffickers to wind down their Cuban business without risk of liability under Title III. Without the suspension of the effective date, companies trafficking in confiscated property on or after November 1 could be subject to such enormous liability that they might, as a practical matter, be forced to choose between abandoning their investments in Cuba or ceasing all activity in the United States. For companies with hundreds of millions of legally invested dollars at stake, that wasn't much of a choice.

As July 16 approached, word spread that the White House, under intense external pressure, was strongly considering suspension of the effective date. It was wishful thinking. A basic reassessment of U.S. foreign policy anywhere, much less Cuba, was simply not in the cards during an election year, not unless desperate circumstances existed. That wasn't the case for Bill Clinton in mid-July. Moreover, Helms-Burton was not merely a policy; it was a law, passed only four months earlier with the President's backing. Although Congress had left open the possibility of suspension purportedly in recognition of the President's leading role in foreign affairs and the need for flexibility in that area, Section 306 amounted to a trap for the President. Everyone knew he would be tempted to suspend rather than defend the statute to a very upset group of friends abroad. Yet suspension would have seriously weakened Clinton in two states having substantial blocks of electoral votes in November, Florida and New Jersey, where the Cuban-American vote is strong. Nor would the damage have been limited to those two states. The Republicans would be sure to point to the move as another example of Clinton's flip-flopping on issues, his inconsistency in foreign policy and his lack of character. Bob Dole, needing all the help he could get, could not have passed up the opportunity to go on the offensive, even if he did (and one can only hope he did) understand that suspension was the right move.

Against this background, it was clear no suspension of the effective date was forthcoming. Bill Clinton had earned every bit of his reputation as an extraordinary campaigner. He wasn't going to blow it all on an issue of which relatively few voters (other than those who would disagree with the suspension) had taken notice. Nevertheless, the legislation had put him in a jam he would eventually have to face, assuming he would in fact be able to renew his White House lease in November. If he took no action at all, the troublesome Title III lawsuits were virtually certain to begin on November 1, just four days before the elections. It wasn't a good idea to have to face that music as the first order of post-election business. In addition, in the event (however remote the possibility appeared at the time) of his losing, it wouldn't have been appropriate to place that burden on his successor. Something had to be done.

In an unexpected move sold as a means of stepping up the pressure on Cuba and making the legislation more effective, the President exercised his right under another provision of the same statute to suspend the *right to sue* for six months (with the possibility of consecutive six-month extensions to follow), the right to sue being a separate and distinct issue from the effectiveness of the statute itself. The net result of the action was to place persons from third party countries in the uncertain position of accruing liabilities due to the statute's coming into force, but getting a temporary reprieve lasting until the lifting of the suspension of the right to sue. If their governments cooperated in putting pressure on the Castro regime, the reprieve just might stay in effect indefinitely; if they didn't, maybe it wouldn't.

The uniquely Clintonesque compromise didn't please anyone. Anti-Castro groups focused on the suspension of the right to bring suit, accusing the Administration of going soft on Castro in spite of its decision to allow the legislation to come into effect. The international community remained stunned, dissatisfied with the limited suspension and fully appreciating the adverse long-term consequences of the decision to allow the statute to come into force. There was no longer light at the end of the tunnel, absent congressional action to repeal the legislation or the advent of a democratically elected government in Cuba. Since neither of those developments seemed imminent, it looked as if Helms-Burton was destined to fulfill its promise of trouble and chaos on the international front. In Canada, two imaginative members of Parliament proposed legislation that would allow several million Canadians to claim compensation for the seizure of U.S. lands of their ancestors during the American revolution. It wasn't entirely clear they were joking.

As negative as the international ramifications of the legislation coming into force were, and as likely as the situation was to deteriorate eventually, one overriding fact stood out: the news came and went, together with the accompanying criticism, in mid-July. By the time the Olympics would be concluded, the news would be forgotten, maybe not in Canada, Mexico or Europe, but certainly in the United States. Clinton had made his move early and it was confusing enough to defuse Republican criticism, especially since it was clear that whatever he had done did not sit well with the international community. If it hadn't gone down well there, it would be dangerous for the Republicans to make his decision the centerpiece of a soft-on-Cuba campaign at home. The bottom line was, while Clinton hadn't solved the problem, he had managed to defer it. With any luck, the deferral would last through November, after which a way would be found to take care of business.

Not long after the election, it became apparent that Clinton would take care of business by indefinitely continuing in effect the suspension of the Helms-Burton Act. He really didn't have a choice. Were it to be lifted for even a moment, there was a risk that the Title III claims would flood the federal courts, wreaking international havoc. To complicate matters, another section of the statute provided that, once filed, a claim could not be suspended by a subsequent suspension of the statute by the President. It was therefore hardly surprising that the reelected President would make sure to keep that window shut. In January, prior to the expiration of the first six-month suspension of the right to sue under the Helms-Burton Act, the suspension was quietly renewed.

By April 1997, the United States and the European Union were entering into an "Understanding" in which the United States "reiterate[d] its presumption of continued suspension of Title III during the remainder of the President's term so long as the EU and other allies continue their stepped up efforts to promote democracy in Cuba." Those stepped up efforts didn't look like much to a lot of people. The President, however, had set the stage for the disappearance of Helms-Burton, at least until he himself was no longer on the scene. And Congress, so agitated about Cuba only a year earlier, didn't seem to mind one bit.

Chapter 29

Halftime

It was supposed to be a glorious halftime show, a much-needed break from politics as the United States, courtesy of Atlanta, hosted the Summer Olympic Games. Everyone would be filled with the Olympic spirit, the United States would win lots of medals, Bill Clinton would ride the euphoria and Bob Dole would lose another couple of weeks he needed to get his campaign on track. That's what had been predicted for weeks prior to the opening of the Games. It didn't happen that way.

Shortly before the Olympics opened, TWA flight 800 to Paris out of New York's JFK Airport was blown out of the sky, killing all 230 aboard. Although the FBI was later to announce that mechanical failure was the likely cause, at the time everyone suspected a terrorist attack. The Olympic spirit had clearly been broken. Little more than a week later, terrorism struck directly at the Olympics. A pipe bomb exploded in a crowded Centennial Park in the early morning hours, just after a concert had ended. Two more died and many others were injured by the blast. The Olympics went on; there were some remarkable performances and a lot of talk about how we wouldn't let any of this get us down—it's not the American way, was the White House line. Plainly, however, the country was in a state of shock. Coming on the heels of the bombing in Saudi Arabia, and with Oklahoma

City and the World Trade Center attacks still a vivid memory, the new tragedies seemed to drive home the point that the horror for years confined to the rest of the world had now reached the United States. The threat was a combination of international and homegrown terrorism, concerted acts of organized groups and random acts of disgruntled individuals, and no one seemed to have any answers.

By the second week of the Olympics, things started happening on the political front. It wasn't full-fledged campaigning, but politics was definitely in the air. The "do-nothing" Congress rushed through significant and historic legislation, including health care and welfare reform. In the case of health care, the legislation was not radical in the sense of the failed Hillary Clinton health plan; it provided for "portability" of health insurance and limited the ability of carriers to deny coverage for preexisting conditions, but there would still be millions of Americans outside the system. Welfare reform *was* radical and thus more controversial. The tough legislation that made its way through Congress imposed relatively strict time limits on welfare benefits and cut off aid for needy children. The message to welfare recipients was unambiguous: get a job!

Bill Clinton had long advocated ending welfare "as we know it." It wasn't entirely clear what that meant, the "as we know it" part. Did it mean ending welfare, or just ending the version we have and substituting a new form of it? The phrase was both catchy and convenient; it signaled a desire for change toward the right, while simultaneously allowing room to preserve whatever concepts underlying the welfare system were necessary to maintain support from the left. "As we know it" was the perfect political expression for a "New Democrat." Now, however, Clinton had to give substance to the expression in the context of the most radical legislative overhaul of traditional Democratic policy in 60 years. Only another presidential veto blocked the way.

The pressure to veto the legislation, as Clinton had two earlier versions passed by the Republican Congress, was intense. Standing 20 points ahead in the polls, Clinton might have been able to withstand the political heat resulting from a veto. In addition, he had been enjoying remarkable success fending off Republican attacks with accusations of extremism that consistently seemed to find the mark. But Clinton apparently sensed danger in pushing that strategy too far. The Republicans had been desperately searching for an issue to carry them into the fall campaign, and a large part of Clinton's comfortable lead was attributable to their lack of success. No matter how low the image of Newt Gingrich and the Republican Congress had sunk, and no matter how irrelevant Bob Dole and his presidential campaign had become, there was no denying the country's right wing tendencies. A veto of welfare reform had the potential to wake up sleeping dogs and restore hope to what was rapidly deteriorating into a lost Republican cause. Politically, it was much more important to be on the "right" side of the welfare debate than the right side of the tobacco debate. So Clinton, in true Clintonesque fashion, somberly announced he would sign the bill, stressing to his liberal constituency that he wasn't completely happy about it. In other words, although he felt their pain (has any president ever done that better?) which was more than could be said for Bob Dole, Newt Gingrich and the Republican extremists in Congress, it was important not to miss the historic opportunity to change a failed system. Extremism had been curbed by his earlier vetoes and the bill was now good enough to sign.

The drama surrounding Clinton's deliberation on whether to sign the welfare bill was another vivid illustration of what's wrong with American politics and how dangerous our political system has become. Even if Bill Clinton was a New Democrat, a theory that had been largely discredited his first three years in office, most observers were convinced his endorsement of the welfare "reform" came more out of politics than conviction, the desire to deny the Republicans an issue for the fall and the fear of being tagged as just another tax and spend *liberal*. If that was the explanation, his endorsement, coming less than a year prior to his dedication of the new FDR Memorial in Washington, was a sorry way to end 60 years of liberalism.

Not that the Democratic experts in the field, such as the venerable Senator Daniel Patrick Moynihan, were correct in condemning the legislation or that the Republican Congress was wrong in belatedly fulfilling an important obligation undertaken in the 1994 Contract with America; it's just that most of us would like to have a higher degree of confidence that if such sweeping changes are to be made without extensive and informed public debate, at least the outcome isn't turning on its anticipated impact on the political campaign. And if reelection is be the predominant motive in major policy decisions, couldn't we at least be a little less offensive in covering it up? In an unusually honest explanation of Democratic congressional support for the welfare bill, one Democratic Congressman from New York was quoted as saying, "This is a bad bill but a good strategy. . . . Sometimes in order to make progress and move ahead, you have to stand up and do the wrong thing. If we take back the House, we can fix this bill and take out some of the Draconian parts." How comforting it is that we have leaders with the courage *to stand up and do the wrong thing.*

With health care and welfare seemingly put to bed, the Democratic strategy looked annoyingly effective. Even if you recognized what was happening, you had to admire the skill with which the strategy was being implemented. A little luck didn't hurt. The second Olympic week finally brought a verdict in the second Arkansas trial. Unlike the first trial, the long wait resulted in not guilty verdicts on some counts and deadlock on others. Not without sweat. The jury had earlier indicated it could not reach a verdict, but the judge had instructed it to keep trying. Considering the other events dominating the news at the time, it's understandable that the trial didn't receive quite the same publicity as the guilty verdicts in the McDougal case. Yet a reasonable case could be made that, from a purely political standpoint, the new verdicts were the most significant happening of the eventful week—perhaps of the entire campaign. Their significance did not lie in any positive impact on the campaign, but in the fact that had the originally hung jury veered toward guilty when instructed to persevere the verdicts would have dealt Clinton another serious blow and recharged the character issue for the second half. As it was, we didn't hear much about the setback to Kenneth

Starr. The Republicans couldn't do anything with the verdicts and the Democrats, far from celebrating, seemed content to count their lucky stars.

All this left Dole empty-handed. Since no issue was about to be handed to him, he would have to generate one internally. Ordinarily, that shouldn't have been too heavy a burden on an experienced politician seeking the presidency. In this case, Dole had yet to prove he was up to the task, and it was getting late, three months until the elections and only a week before the Republicans gathered in San Diego. The Olympic distraction hadn't really hurt Dole. If anything, it seemed to help. While he hadn't gained any ground in the polls, he was no longer in a freefall. Moreover, there was a sense that Clinton was walking a tightrope, that he was vulnerable on too many fronts, if only the Republicans could get their heads into the campaign. Something had to be done quickly.

Chapter 30

The Gamble

It was the day after the Olympics closed when Dole finally unveiled his economic plan, the one they called the Gamble. The highlights were a 15 percent across-the-board tax cut, a $500 per child tax credit for low and middle income families, a 50 percent cut in the capital gains tax and the repeal of a 1993 tax increase on certain social security benefits. Total estimated cost: $548 billion over six years. To pay for it all, Dole proposed eliminating two cabinet departments, Energy and Commerce. The rest would come mainly from increased revenues generated from the economic growth resulting from the tax cuts. SUPPLY SIDE.

What made the proposal a gamble was that this was Bob Dole, long-time deficit hawk, speaking. Dole had long been associated with the drive to balance the budget, highly skeptical of supply side economics. He had helped Reagan get his tax reduction program through in 1981, but he had also made clear his disapproval of tax cuts as a means of balancing the budget, his basic distrust of the supply side theory that the economic growth spurred by tax cuts would generate additional revenue more than offsetting the lost revenue directly resulting from the cuts.

The Democrats were well aware of this history and started their counterattack even before the speech, maintaining their reputation under Bill Clinton as the fastest political guns in the country. Dole was accused of winning the gold medal of flip-flop. Old clips showed him asserting he was not one of those recommending across-the-board tax cuts. How could a man who had made a career out of balancing the budget, who had joked that the bad news when a supply side bus went over a cliff was that three seats were empty, so suddenly cast away his core principles for political gain?

As impressive as the Democratic rapid response machine was, there was a touch of Democratic nervousness in the air. The long search for a defining Republican issue had ended. Republicans had stumbled and bumbled their way from liberal judges to the gas tax to tobacco, wasting time and falling further and further behind. Now Dole had settled on the single most dangerous issue for Democrats. Clinton certainly couldn't propose deeper tax cuts, and his opposition to the Dole program, however sound, ran the risk of appearing too liberal. There was, in the minds of many, a fine line between opposing tax relief and supporting big government, big spending and big taxes, the era of which was supposedly gone forever. The Democratic counterattack would have to be steered carefully away from the stereotype of modern liberalism, concentrating on the dangers to the economy of a ballooning deficit and the lack of character evidenced by Dole's flip-flop. That approach was also dangerous, however, as it played into Dole's strength on the issues of character and trust. When Dole claimed deficit reduction was in his blood and a balanced budget would be his legacy to America, he enjoyed a measure of credibility he had earned through the same history the Democrats were trying to use against him. If anyone could simultaneously cut taxes and balance the budget, it was Bob Dole.

Dole had also made sure to attack both sides of the tax issue. Not content merely to address the amount of taxes, he promised a frontal assault on the complexity of the tax code and the power of the IRS, music to the ears of voters across the political spectrum. Jack Kemp and Steve Forbes, who had been urging Dole to base his campaign on an aggressive program of tax relief and overhaul, had been vindicated. Borrowing an expression from

Clinton, Dole said he would eliminate the IRS "as we know it." As in the case of Clinton's promise to end welfare "as we know it," it wasn't entirely clear what the new IRS we didn't know would look like, but it sounded good. The Democrats certainly were not about to defend the IRS we all know and love.

Personally, I found the proposal quite attractive (not surprising for someone who found the flat tax appealing). Nevertheless, there was something very disturbing about it. Not on the merits. This isn't the place to argue the merits of supply side economics—whether it is possible to cut taxes and balance the budget at the same time, whether economic growth and the consequent increase in tax revenues would offset the effect of the decrease in tax rates, whether the deficit explosion in the Reagan era was the consequence of tax reduction or a Democratic Congress unable to control spending. I'll leave that to the economists and historians. What was immediately disturbing was what the program told us about the political process.

Only a few months earlier, nine candidates had been vying for the Republican nomination in the primaries. Steve Forbes, who had captured the imagination of a large segment of the Republican Party with his flat tax message, had been beaten back by Dole, who ended up winning with no tax message at all. Think for a moment what Dole would have said about the same economic plan he was counting on to revive his campaign had it been proposed by any of the other eight candidates during the primaries. If he would have treated the plan with anything like the disdain he had long exhibited for supply siders, it wouldn't have been pretty.

There is ample precedent in American politics for changing one's mind on important issues, even changing political parties, and going on to enjoy spectacular electoral success. However, while consistency of thought isn't consistently demanded, a sense of timing is, and it is bad timing to change colors right in the middle of a presidential campaign, particularly when the change comes as a result of a publicly announced period of deep reflection designed to produce an economic plan for the nation. Were we to conclude that Dole's prior positions on economic policy were the product of a lack of thought and that the first time he had sat down to think seriously about the issue was the end of his long political career, when he would conclude the time was right for a change?

Apart from this bad timing in the larger sense, a serious issue of timing was raised in the narrower context of the Republican race for the presidential nomination. Assuming that the primaries would serve a salutary purpose if the candidates were to present us at that time with a menu of policies from which to choose, a questionable assumption under any circumstances, there clearly is no point to a process in which the real substance is deferred until long after the outcome is determined. That simple proposition is as true for the primaries as it is for the election itself—unless you're very big on surprises. Bob Dole didn't exactly clean up in the pre-New Hampshire primary Republican debate. Imagine how much worse he might have done if he had said I really don't know what the right economic policy for the nation is, but don't worry, when this is all over and I get a chance to think about it I'll come up with something. It'll either be more of the same or it'll be this tax thing my buddies Kemp and Forbes have been blithering about.

The biggest problem with the Gamble was what it told us about the effect of the process on candidates, not just any candidate, but all candidates, including one with as distinguished a record as Bob Dole's. The Gamble seemed to indicate that Dole, whose only advantage over Clinton in the polls consisted of the public perception of his character and integrity, had bought into the winning is everything philosophy. In this respect, he had taken a page from Clinton's book. Clinton had little difficulty putting on a conservative face when necessary. Now Dole was following through on his offer to be another Ronald Reagan if that's what the people wanted him to be. Not only were the substantive messages of the two drawing closer together; the two were projecting one common message to the American people and the world, namely, that in case of a conflict between principle and political expediency, the former must give way.

Was it Dole's fault that he appeared to have succumbed to

the pressures of the process in adopting his economic plan? Not entirely, even if that's what happened. True, Dole had been unable to articulate a theme for his presidential campaign, a reason to vote for him other than the unstated claim that he had earned it through his experience in government. Yet it is equally true that there is something very wrong in the way we select our presidential candidates and the way we elect our president. Rather than passing harsh judgment on Dole, holding him to standards few meet, I would prefer to treat his conversion as a huge red flag, another in a series of unheeded warnings that this process, which induces and promotes such bizarre moves as the Gamble, requires some serious attention. If the argument that the process made him do it sounds a little liberal, so be it. Remember, it's still legal in America.

* * *

Before anyone had a chance to digest Dole's most important speech of the campaign, news broke that Dole had again changed his mind on the Declaration of Tolerance in the Republican Party platform and agreed to eliminate any specific link between that "virtue" and abortion. Pro-choice Pete Wilson threatened a floor fight, and it sounded like the Republicans were getting ready for a meltdown on national television. The bonus for the Democrats was that the platform fight, rather than Dole's economic plan, got most of the attention during pre-Convention week.

Fortunately for Dole, it didn't last. A strange compromise was worked out whereby the platform language would remain pure and the rejected minority views on abortion and other issues would be compiled in an appendix to the platform for all to see. The idea was to make clear that the Republican Party is diverse, the "big tent" theory. If Republicans with minority opinions (by definition rejected opinions) exist, then the Republican Party must have room for the people holding those opinions. You might call it the modern American version of "I think; therefore I am." Somehow, the large but largely disorganized pro-choice contingent, including the prominent gubernatorial quartet of Wilson, Pataki, Whitman and Weld, was satisfied. The spotlight had been removed from Dole's economic plan for a couple of days, but a floor fight had been averted and it now appeared that Dole would have a smooth Convention. Everyone except Bay Buchanan, who was busy declaring victory in the platform battle, seemed anxious to get past the issue and move on to the one unifying issue on which the Democrats were vulnerable: taxes.

Bay Buchanan was right. The pro-lifers had won the day, maintaining an undiluted, absolutist plank against abortion and in favor of a constitutional amendment (one of seven called for by the platform) banning it. From another standpoint, however, she was grossly mistaken. Her brother, who gave Dole and the Republican leadership all they could handle during the early primaries, was not even allotted time to speak at the Convention. While pro-choice Governors Weld and Wilson also weren't going to speak (Weld declining because he had been asked to speak about economic matters rather than abortion and Wilson apparently disinvited), that was due more to the general desire to avoid further controversy than a desire to focus attention on the abortion plank. In fact, what seemed to allow the compromise to occur was the knowledge that the platform simply didn't mean anything. Dole himself hadn't changed his own position on abortion, which would allow exceptions in the case of rape, incest or threat to the life of the mother, and had made clear that he didn't feel bound by the platform—reportedly, he hadn't even read it. No one expected Bob Dole to introduce the constitutional amendment called for by the platform his first day in office.

With all the turmoil surrounding the party platform, Dole was unable to cut into Clinton's enormous lead in the polls during the days following the unveiling of his economic program. Yet there was a different feeling in the air, a feeling that the Republicans had found something to carry them and turn the tide. There was also a feeling that an even bigger announcement was coming.

Chapter 31
The Choice

I had been wondering why no one was talking about Jack Kemp when word leaked that he was high on the list of possible vice-presidential candidates. What better spokesman was there for supply side economics than the football hero who had led the Buffalo Bills to back-to-back AFL titles in the 1960s (before they had Super Bowls), the man who followed in the intellectual footsteps of the actor-turned-President, Ronald Reagan, and the man whose jersey number, 15, matched the magic number of the tax plan. Just ask him a question about the supply side (or anything else) and watch him get revved up with his optimistic message of economic growth, which we would have in abundance if only we would give ourselves the tax break we richly deserved.

The problem was precisely that; Kemp had always been on the other side of Dole in the great Republican economic debate, highly critical of Dole's emphasis on a balanced budget. For his part, Dole had long had unkind things to say about the quarterback who needed hairspray and maybe had taken a few too many hits. When Kemp almost ruined Dole's super Junior Tuesday by endorsing Forbes and his version of the "hope, growth and opportunity" message, most assumed Kemp had written himself out of consideration as a possible running mate. It didn't seem that unwise a move at the time, as his long-standing rivalry with Dole made Kemp a most unlikely choice in any event.

Yet one had to wonder, after Dole's dramatic, perhaps desperate leap to the supply side, whether another surprise was in the air. Although Dole and Kemp had on occasion gotten a little too clever in seeking an edge in their debate on economic policy, personal animosity was not readily apparent. During the primaries in 1988, Dole had seemed genuinely disturbed by George Bush and bitterly accused him of distorting and lying about Dole's record. It didn't appear to be the same with Kemp, despite his untimely and awkward endorsement of Forbes in 1996.

Moreover, Kemp was a popular and widely respected Republican. He was pro-life and strong on Values, but still viewed as a social moderate both within and outside the party. He wasn't too thrilled with the harsh Republican positions on affirmative action and immigration—in fact, a somewhat ungracious Pete Wilson suggested Kemp should not accept the nomination unless he was prepared to modify his positions on those issues. Nevertheless, if anyone could lend credibility to the plan Dole had chosen to make the centerpiece of his campaign, it was Jack Kemp.

The bubbly Kemp brought something else to the ticket: enthusiasm. Everyone was talking about it—Jack's enthusiasm, Dole's enthusiasm, the party's enthusiasm. There was enough enthusiasm to make you sick. And if the enthusiasm didn't get you, the sports metaphors would. (*See, e.g.*, Kemp the quarterback turning blocker for Dole; Clinton running out the clock.) Nobody was complaining, though. The Republicans needed something to liven up the party, and Kemp was it. J.C. Watts, Republican congressman from Oklahoma and former University of Oklahoma quarterback, joked that Dole had selected the second best quarterback. Finally, the Republicans were in a lighthearted mood.

The Democrats were stunned by the choice. Strategist Ann Lewis and others labeled some of Kemp's views "extremist," but it wasn't an easy sell. Chris Dodd, in San Diego to provide a counterpoint to the Republican view of the world dominating the media during convention week, was placed on the defensive when asked about the allegations of extremism. They just weren't working, and the Democrats knew it. Next to Colin Powell, Jack Kemp had more prospects of reaching beyond the Republican Party to independents and Democrats than any of the other vice-presidential hopefuls—more than Dole himself. Unlike the Rockefeller Republicans, the pro-life Kemp would also not alienate the religious right, even if he wasn't their favorite candidate. Kemp might not have been the Democrats' worst nightmare, but he was close enough.

In a CNN/*USA Today* poll taken after the official announcement of Kemp as running mate, Dole had closed the gap to 12 points. In only a few days, approximately 10 points had been shaven off Clinton's lead and the famous "bounce" a candidate generally receives from a national convention was still to come.

Chapter 32

The Prelims

The eve of the Republican Convention had all the makings of a spoiler. On tap were the Reform Party Convention from Long Beach, California, and a preconvention speech in Escondido by Pat Buchanan. One month earlier, this lineup would have spelled disaster for Bob Dole. The Republicans, however, were on a roll and these preliminaries were not about to upstage them.

The Reform Party did give us a refreshing look at a different type of nominating process. Two men, Dick Lamm and Ross Perot, came before their convention to state their case. Afterward, Reform Party members around the country were to vote by fax, mail, E-mail, you name it. The winner would be announced the following week across the country in Valley Forge.

Dick Lamm made an effective presentation, criticizing both major parties for failing to provide honest solutions to the serious problems of a bulging national debt, campaign finance reform and immigration. He didn't have any criticism for his opponent, Ross Perot. Rather, his hopes were pinned on the theory that the torch must be passed, that the party must move beyond Perot if it were ever to become a real force in national politics, a winner rather than a spoiler. That message, though plainly correct, was not about to carry the day.

With one-third of the electorate independent and large numbers of Democrats and Republicans disaffected, it's hard to argue with the proposition that a well-organized third party could play a significant role. At the same time, there are substantial impediments to the formation of any meaningful new party in American politics, including the lack of an ideology separate and distinct from those of the major parties that could capture the imagination of the American people— actually, the lack of any ideology at all. Our disaffection with the major parties, the main source of whatever strength serious third party candidates have shown in the past (see John Anderson in 1980 as well as Ross Perot in 1992), has little to do with ideology. Rather, it stems from frustration with the apparent inability of government to solve obvious problems. Americans are upset with government because it is stale. We're not turning communist, socialist, anarchist (with some notable exceptions) or any other "ist." We just want our problems addressed. Don't bore us with the details or the analysis; just get it done. If and when we do have the time and desire to listen, we would appreciate some honesty in the presentation. Now that may be how many potential third party voters feel, but it's not much of an ideology.

The Reform Party, with its emphasis on a balanced budget, illustrates this point. You can't build a successful new political party around the balanced budget issue, at least not when both of the main parties have already conceded the importance of a balanced budget. With the Republican platform calling for a constitutional amendment requiring a balanced budget and the main Democratic criticism of Dole's economic plan being its potential adverse impact on the budget deficit, the Reform Party's central issue hardly served to distinguish it. Forming and funding a national political party is no easy task under the best of circumstances. If you haven't got anything exciting to sell, if your platform boils down to a plea for honest government, it would seem a far easier task to work within the existing party structures. Honesty may be the best policy, but it's not an ideology that rallies the troops.

Of course, if you're a billionaire, you can compensate for the lack of an ideology and get a new party off the ground. The obvious danger in such cases is the identification of the party with, and dependence upon, its founder, resulting in loss of credibility as an independent political party. That's why Lamm and others were saying it's time to pass the torch before Perot and the Reform Party both wore out their welcome.

Perot made very clear in his speech at the Reform Party Convention that he wasn't interested in passing any torches in 1996. Dropping his coyness of the past, he came right out and told them he wanted to be president. None of this business about him not liking politics and running only if the people insisted. He affirmatively wanted it. The rest was vintage Perot. Charts, numbers, clever lines, folksy style—if we hadn't seen it all before, it might have been refreshing. Under the circumstances, it looked like a television repeat. The performance was more than enough to take the nomination of the Reform Party, but one was left with the distinct impression that Perot's impact on the 1996 race would be minimal.

*   *   *

After the Reformers had finished, Buchanan took the podium in Escondido to deliver a preconvention speech at a "Thank you, Pat" party. They weren't letting him speak at the real convention, so he had a night for himself in front of his faithful supporters. Apart from celebrating a battle hard fought, there was news to be made: Buchanan would endorse the Republican ticket and stay in the party.

Notwithstanding Buchanan's endorsement, the Dole people were undoubtedly congratulating themselves on their decision to keep Buchanan off the list of speakers in San Diego. The image of the Buchanan Brigades taking over the Convention, as they had the party platform, was not what Republicans wanted to project to the nation. This was not the year for a cultural war, and Buchanan made clear in Escondido that the war had not ended. He merely called for a "truce," a suspension of the "battle" to achieve the immediate objective of dethroning Bill Clinton and

"Prince" Albert. Answering his own question of why he and his supporters should go to a convention where they call you names and don't let you speak, he credibly declared it's not just their party, it's our party, too. In case of doubt, read the platform, whole sections of which came right out of his speeches. According to Buchanan, one day the stone the builder rejected could become the cornerstone. For a party fearful of the political impact of allegations of extremism, such an endorsement of the party's ticket was better delivered from Escondido than the convention podium in San Diego.

The speech was not without light moments. Pointing out that had Lamar Alexander run second in the New Hampshire primary instead of third Dole would have withdrawn from the race, Buchanan said he had told Lamar the plaid shirts weren't enough. It was at once amusing and frightening, this thought that the course of history might have been altered had the plaid shirts been more effective.

Chapter 33

San Diego

The Republicans put on quite a show in San Diego. That huge Clinton lead, which had been cut in half following Dole's announcement of Kemp as running mate, was slashed again by the end of the Convention. A *Newsweek* poll actually placed it at two points, statistically a dead heat, the weekend after the Convention. Even the Democrats acknowledged the lead had shrunk to single digits. The seesaw was in motion again, this time more turbulent than the week of Dole's Senate resignation. The Democrats, who were hoping for a repeat performance of the 1992 Republican Convention in Houston (of Pat Buchanan's cultural war speech), were clearly shaken by the effectiveness of the show put on in San Diego, as they had been a few days earlier by the surprising selection of Kemp.

First on the Convention planners' agenda was tackling the serious Republican image problem. The Republican Party had been damaged by allegations of extremism and intolerance and its leadership was intent on projecting the image of an all-inclusive party, the big tent, the party of Lincoln. The gender gap that had plagued Dole throughout the campaign also had to be addressed. So the lineup of speakers featured Colin Powell, who referred to his differing views on abortion and affirmative action, and the young African-American star of the party, quarterback J.C. Watts, as well as a series of leading women, including keynote speaker Susan Molinari, Senator Kay Bailey Hutchison from Texas (who had almost been excluded from her state's delegation because of her position on abortion), Christy Todd Whitman and, most impressively, Elizabeth Dole. In a risky and unprecedented performance that ended up stealing the show, Elizabeth left the podium to roam among the delegates and tell the nation about her husband's qualities.

The Republicans also wanted to remind us of their rich presidential history. Before Colin Powell capped off opening night with his stirring speech, the former Presidents were trotted out: Gerald Ford with popular wife, Betty, George Bush with popular wife, Barbara, and, on screen, the Gipper. Nancy Reagan appeared in person and had the audience in tears.

None of these performances would have amounted to much without the grand finale. Democratic commentators had to concede the effectiveness of each of the individual speeches but kept repeating that none of those speakers was on the ticket. At the end of the day, it was still Clinton-Gore vs. Dole-Kemp (or, as the Democrats preferred, Dole-Gingrich). On Thursday night, both Jack Kemp and Bob Dole had to deliver, and deliver they did.

Kemp was himself—enthusiastic, genuine, positive, reaching out to voters from the burroughs of New York to the barrios of California, not leaving anybody out. The economic plan was just the beginning, he said; we were going to scrap the tax code and end IRS intrusiveness. Music to everyone's ears. It wasn't a great speech like Powell's, just good, solid Kemp, and that was good enough. He had set the stage perfectly for Dole. Referring to the modern presidential practice of introducing heroes in the balcony at the State of the Union address, he predicted there would be a hero at the podium in 1997. Was that another reference to Clinton's war record—negative campaigning—or was it simply highlighting a strength of Bob Dole? Close call.

The fear that Kemp might upstage the relatively inarticulate Dole was unfounded, as Dole delivered the speech of his career. He came across as a genuinely humble man with strong values, having worked hard for everything he had achieved in life. Following an interesting though dangerous strategy, he criticized the values of today, represented by the Clinton Administration, arguing that they had little to do with what we had accomplished in this country. What did? His values: God, family, honor, duty, country. It was dangerous because you never know how people are going to react to what sounds like a good old days routine. In this case, it was effective.

Dole also hammered home the message of tolerance, openness and all-inclusiveness that had been the primary theme of the week. In a dramatic passage, he seemed to recognize that the party had all too often been a cozy home for racists attracted to certain of its conservative positions, most recently its opposition to affirmative action. To the extent such people had been attracted, he showed them the door. There would be no room for *tolerance* on that issue.

The speech contained a lot of hard-hitting material aimed directly at the President, the First Lady and the White House staff. The attack was an integral part of the "values" theme. In effect, Dole's message was that he had values; the entire Clinton Administration didn't. The 1992 Clinton campaign theme of "It's the economy, stupid" was a reflection of Clinton's emphasis on materialism at the expense of values. The Administration consisted of a corps of the elite who didn't understand what it meant to sacrifice and who were spending our money on dubious schemes. In a not too subtle reference to the First Lady's book about child rearing, he said it didn't take a village to raise a child.

The Democrats were clearly shaken. Before the speech had even been concluded, George Stephanopoulos, presumably one of the young elitists to whom Dole had referred, called it the most negative, partisan and divisive speech since Goldwater. This time, however, the negative attacks had been mixed well with the affirmative talk of values and the humility exuded by Dole. Notwithstanding the rapid response of the Clinton camp, Dole was getting rave reviews; the speech was a "10."

So was the Convention as a whole, and that was the real news coming out of San Diego. The media, hungry for a conventional story and uneasy about its role in broadcasting a four-day "infomercial," simply missed the boat. They were looking for controversy, uncertainty, the stuff of old conventions, and weren't content merely to broadcast the show. Yet the story of San Diego was about how the Republicans got their act together, the distinct message they were sending out and how they were launching their fall campaign. It was a story as powerful and interesting as that of any convention of recent history, and the media wasn't prepared for it.

When it was all over, the big question was whether 1996 marked the end of the era of the national convention *as we know it*. The evolution of the primaries as the means of selecting major party candidates has removed most of the drama surrounding conventions because of the slim chance that any race would remain undecided going into the summer party. The function of the national convention has therefore changed from candidate selection to message formulation and dissemination. This is not necessarily a bad idea. Given the choice between 30-second commercials produced Hollywood-style and a few nights of live performances produced Broadway-style, the latter is by far preferable, more instructive and even more entertaining. We may not learn much of substance on particular issues, but the four-day extravaganza does convey a sense of the spirit, personality, grand themes and overall direction of a party, as reasonable a basis as any for a busy voter to make a decision. Until we figure out a better way to use the media, televised conventions (perhaps abridged versions thereof) do have a future, even if television itself remains disappointed in the role it will play in that future. All this assumes, of course, that political parties retain their nominating function, an assumption one could be forgiven for challenging based on the cumulative experience of recent elections.

Chapter 34
Chicago

Not to be outdone, the Democrats showed they could plan and program political events every bit as well as the Republicans, starting with preconvention week and going right through the Convention. Preconvention week was filled with staged events. Looking presidential, Clinton signed and took credit for the health care, minimum wage and welfare reform bills. The highlight of the week was the announcement that the Administration would treat tobacco as an addictive substance and regulate its advertisement and sale to children. It was a bold move that capitalized on Dole's tobacco gaffe and provided somewhat of a counterweight to official reports of increased drug use among teenagers during the Clinton Administration, an issue Dole planned to use as a strong second (to his economic plan) in the fall campaign.

The Sunday before the Convention opened Clinton was all over the airwaves. He was on his 21st Century Express (actually a slow train ride to Chicago), stopping along the way in small towns for speeches carried on television. The principal themes were Clinton's record on crime (a paralyzed policeman, a hero, introduced Clinton at one stop telling all how proud he was to be on the same stage as the most pro-law enforcement President of his lifetime) and a balanced budget (Dole's plan would blow a hole in the deficit). Not exactly traditional Democratic themes, but a sign of the conservative times. It seemed to be working, as Clinton's lead over Dole was back to double digits according to a CNN/*USA Today* poll.

The Convention itself followed suit—crime, the importance of a balanced budget, small but targeted and fully paid for tax cuts and family values. The stars of the show weren't politicians. Rather, the Democrats went for the strong emotional appeal with former Reagan Press Secretary Jim Brady, in his wheelchair, his wife speaking on gun control, and actor Christopher Reeve, in his wheelchair, speaking about the need to resist slashing necessary government programs on the way to balancing the budget. Regardless of the merits of the issues to which they spoke, you disagreed with either at your peril. When the politicians took the stage, there was more of the same. Al Gore again told the story of his sister's last breath as she died of tobacco-induced lung cancer; the President referred to his brother Roger's battle with drugs. None of this fostered intellectual debate of any of the issues of the day. All of it was good theater.

The two most important speeches were delivered by the Clintons themselves. Hillary, who had a tough act to follow in Elizabeth Dole's performance at the Republican Convention, focused on family values. Her treatment of this traditionally Republican issue was significant in two respects. First, adopting the same strategy often used with respect to "character," she redefined the issue in terms of policies that support families, such as health care, education and an assortment of government programs designed to improve family life. It was a dangerous strategy, a gamble that discussion of liberal programs smacking of the supposedly lost era of big government would be well received if cloaked in the mantle of family values. Second, Hillary's strong policy-oriented speech served notice she was back, reminding everyone of the 1992 Clinton slogan of buy one, get one free. If there was to be a second term for Bill, there would be one for Hillary, too.

Bill Clinton capped off the Convention in similar fashion. The video setting up his speech cleverly preempted the character issue. Clinton was seen praising Dole, acknowledging his strong record of service to his country. He would not attack Dole's character because he wasn't brought up that way. It sounded presidential, straight out of *An American President.* Of course, apart from his upbringing, there were other reasons for the President's refusal to engage in personal attacks on Dole, including the one about people who live in glass houses. This was one circumstance where there was little choice but to take the high road.

The speech picked up on the same themes. Dole, Kemp and Perot all love their country. This must be a campaign of ideas. What were Clinton's ideas? A little bit of everything, a convenient blending of old-fashioned liberalism and modern conservatism—extend the Brady Bill to prevent those involved in domestic violence from purchasing guns; ban cop-killer bullets; make sure those required to work by the welfare bill will have jobs; promise only fiscally responsible tax cuts. As might have been expected, Clinton also jumped all over Dole's bridge to traditional values. We didn't need a "bridge to the past," he claimed; we needed one to the future, presumably for his train to the 21st century. By the time he had finished, we didn't know the precise route the train would take to get to the bridge, right or left, but there was a sense that Clinton had accomplished his mission for this night, which was to restore his 20-point lead.

Ironically, the person credited by many with diagramming the plays that gave Clinton his commanding lead, strategist Dick Morris, almost ruined the night. The story had just broken that Morris had regularly visited with a prostitute, Sherry Rowlands, at the Jefferson Hotel in Washington, allowing her to read an advance copy of Hillary Clinton's speech and listen in on telephone conversations with the President. Morris immediately resigned and went home to an understanding wife, presumably occupying himself finishing what was to be another in a long line of "insider" books about politics—sure makes recruiting decisions tough when every advisor you hire is a prospective author, writing about *you.* Everyone was wondering whether the Morris story had "legs."

Not surprisingly, the new scandal had no immediate impact

on Clinton's standing. If the President had previously been able to withstand his own extracurricular activity, why shouldn't he be able to withstand that of an advisor? It was disappointing, however, that the opportunity wasn't seized to ask some basic questions about Morris that should have been addressed much earlier. I'm not referring to whether confidential information had been leaked by Morris or to whether the Morris affair reflects a White House culture of hypocrisy. Rather, the question we should have been asking is whether it is appropriate for a president to hire as a top strategist, someone in a position to shape policy, a person equally comfortable advising Bella Abzug and Jesse Helms.

Lawyers know what it means to advocate both sides of an issue at different times, depending upon the needs of a client, and to provide the best legal defense possible even when unconvinced of the merits of the client's position. Like it or not, and we all have times when we don't like it, society has long accepted the notion that the greater good requires lawyers to do nothing less in defending their clients' interests. Likewise, there is nothing wrong with a client seeking out the best lawyer money can buy to undertake that defense. The issue is whether the same is necessarily true of the relationship between politician and political consultant. I don't think so, notwithstanding the trend exemplified by Dick Morris.

How are we to know what a president's core beliefs are if they are shaped by someone whose business it is to submerge core beliefs in favor of political expediency? The natural result of reliance on such consultants is an even greater ideological void than already exists in American politics. In this new political era, candidates can maneuver left and right with relative ease, counting on slick campaign machines to explain away any inconsistencies. There is only one guiding principle: winning. If that means advocating a balanced budget, signing a welfare reform bill your own party considers virtually immoral or making uniforms for schoolchildren and family values issues in presidential campaigns (positions widely attributed to Morris), so be it. The problem, of course, is that we are supposed to be voting for candidates based on their own positions, not those of a political consultant focused on short-term electoral goals.

In addition, it would be nice to know enough about a candidate's guiding principles to be able to predict his or her positions on important issues that may arise in the future, after the election. If whatever a candidate says isn't reflective of core beliefs, why should we listen at all? A lot of people in New Jersey were asking themselves that very question after newly elected Senator Bob Torricelli announced his changed position on the balanced budget amendment. A balanced budget amendment may indeed be a terrible idea, but the way it went down to defeat won't do much to change our cynical view of politics and politicians.

The polls following the Convention didn't indicate that either the Dick Morris affair or the questions it should have raised were bothering too many people. On the contrary, Clinton's lead soared over 20 points again. As for the impact of Morris' departure on the campaign, the consensus was it would be minimal because the direction of the campaign had already been established, *i.e.*, Morris' influence would outlast his tenure. Congressman Clinger, however, had other ideas. He planned to call Morris and Sherry Rowlands to his committee hearings on Filegate to find out what the First Lady knew about the FBI files. Unfortunately for the Clintons, a Rowlands diary entry indicated Morris had told her Hillary Clinton was behind the obtention of the FBI files. Did the story have legs after all?

Chapter 35

Make My Day

I remember several conversations with friends in Europe in mid-August. As usual, they were watching the U.S. elections closely. The race was beginning to tighten as the Republicans headed into their Convention, and the main question was whether Dole had any chance of overtaking Clinton. After the normal "anything can happen" banter, I recall discussing how dangerous a time it was, anticipating the possibility of some sort of military action as we headed into the fall campaign. The likely target? Iraq, Iran or Libya. The groundwork had been laid for an attack on any of them—Iran had been blamed for the bombing of the building housing military personnel in Saudi Arabia, Libya for constructing a chemical weapons plant and Iraq, well, it was still the home of Saddam Hussein. All that seemed missing was the spark that would direct our attention to one of the three. Just as the Labor Day kickoff of the fall campaign was ending, the United States reacted to Iraqi troop movements in northern Iraq, home of the Kurds, launching cruise missiles against antiaircraft installations in the south. The attack was repeated the next day, purportedly to finish the job.

Hitting Iraq, where today's favorite archenemy rules, is almost always good politics, particularly if it can be done without suffering casualties. The Republicans could do nothing. Not wanting to appear unpatriotic during a military conflict, Dole was supportive. So was Powell. The only real criticism came from some members of Congress, principally Senator Trent Lott, Dole's successor as Senate majority leader, whose complaint that he had not been consulted in advance as required by the War Powers Act fell on deaf ears. There were also many who supported the President with the caveat that he should have done more. In this atmosphere, the attacks carried little political risk at home.

Nevertheless, I had some reservations about the attacks and the ensuing lack of analytical criticism. In the first instance, the supporting logic was tenuous at best. When I turned on the TV in my hotel room in Mexico City the morning of the first strike, Iraqi Deputy Prime Minister Tariq Aziz was on a live telephone hookup on CNN explaining that there had been fighting among the Kurdish factions in northern Iraq and that Iran had supported one of the factions, the PUK. According to Aziz, another faction, the KDP, requested the assistance of the Iraqi government. Saddam Hussein responded, rather than allow the Iranians to gain the advantage. The station then broke away to cover Defense Secretary Perry's press conference, which I thought would surely provide a very different version. Surprisingly, Perry began with exactly the same story—intra-Kurdish fighting in which Iran had supported the PUK and the KDP had requested Iraq's assistance. The principal difference in the versions was that Perry characterized the KDP's request for Iraq's assistance as a huge mistake. No satisfactory explanation was given for that characterization.

The remainder of Perry's presentation was equally difficult to fathom. Saddam Hussein's movement north required a response, but it didn't require a response in the north, where the fighting was taking place. Why? We had no national interest at stake in the north and didn't care who won the intra-Kurdish fighting. Our national interests, according to Perry, were in the south, where the oil was. However, when questioned whether there had been any threat in the south, Perry could only refer to previous threats, nothing in the past year. Without any basis for interfering in the north and without any threatening action in the south, Perry's only justification for the retaliation was that the failure to respond might embolden Saddam Hussein to take aggressive action in the future implicating our national interests. In this way, the Iraqi action posed a "clear and present danger" to Iraq's neighbors and the stability and security of the region.

While not too many people in the United States were questioning the Administration's explanations, people overseas weren't buying. The coalition delicately put together by George Bush was falling apart and the U.N. Security Council refused to endorse our position, an unusual occurrence in the post-Cold War era. The Administration's line was that there are times when the United States has to lead. I took that to mean international law must be respected when convenient for us; when not, the 700-pound gorilla can swing into action on its own.

This cavalier attitude toward the views of others, including our allies, in the international community is not cost free. Notwithstanding the fact that U.N.-bashing is now in fashion, there are times when we need the U.N. and where the strictest adherence to international law is essential to our national interest. It is difficult to provide "leadership" when we, under the guise of exercising it, consistently manifest a determination to do exactly what we please. If we had a monopoly on either wisdom or morality in international affairs, we could construct an argument in favor of such a posture. Since the preponderance of the evidence appears to be to the contrary, a more modest approach would seem to be in order.

Apart from the inherent dangers of international muscle flexing, the missile strikes on Iraq highlighted the absence of a coherent policy in this area. We don't like Saddam Hussein, but we also have problems with some of the people he doesn't like—Iran. We insist on maintaining the territorial integrity of Iraq, but we don't want the Iraqi government acting like a government in that territory or participating in any meaningful way in the international community. We call Saddam Hussein a ruthless dictator, but we impose sanctions that cause severe hardship on the people he is presumed to be oppressing, thereby solidifying his position and perpetuating his power. We would like to see Saddam Hussein go, but we aren't prepared to take any action reasonably calculated to yield that result. No wonder people outside the United States believe we actually prefer to see him stay rather than go. They are confused, and anyone at home analyzing our actions should be confused, too.

Confusion in our foreign policy is not limited to Iraq. We have obviously been suffering from an overall foreign policy void since the fall of the Iron Curtain. For decades the existence of the Soviet Union provided the focal point of our foreign policy. It was simple; we had to compete with, contain and ultimately defeat communism. The means varied, at times causing us to tear ourselves apart, as was the case during the Vietnam War. However, there was never any real dispute as to the end. With the extinction of the "evil empire," things aren't as clear anymore and it is harder to discern the guiding principles of American foreign policy. Not that we aren't in need of any; the world is still a dangerous place, with the prospect of military confrontations more frequent than during the Cold War. It's just that we haven't figured out, or at least haven't yet enunciated, precisely what those principles are to be. Given our standing as the world's only remaining superpower, that is a serious deficiency indeed.

The two presidential elections since the end of the Cold War have done little to clarify matters. Instead, they only highlighted the point that, despite the president's critical role as foreign policy architect and commander-in-chief, the presidential election process does not accentuate international affairs. Absent a credible rival or a foreign policy crisis, V-chips and uniforms for schoolchildren take precedence as presidential issues. Candidates move from primary to primary addressing more local issues, with no incentive to take on the challenge of constructing a new conceptual framework for the conduct of foreign affairs. In 1992, Clinton actually campaigned on the need to return the focus of the presidency back home and concentrate on the economy—"It's the economy, stupid." In 1996, after three years of unfocused foreign policy and with the country sorely needing a debate on that new framework, foreign policy remained a secondary (or tertiary) issue in the campaign. Far from debating it, the entire campaign went by with scarcely a mention of the world beyond our shores.

Consequently, our foreign policy, always slightly mercurial, has degenerated into a series of ad hoc actions such as the missile strikes. In this environment, talk straight out of Hollywood substitutes for statesmanship. We don't say Iraq is a threat; Saddam Hussein is the threat. He isn't often referred to as "president" or even "Saddam Hussein"; usually it's just "Saddam." He "pops" up, according to Colin Powell, and we "slap" him down. We "whacked" him, said then U.N. Ambassador Madeleine Albright, who a few months earlier during the mini-Cuban crisis had told us about "cojones." Saddam has to know he'll pay a heavy price, said all. It makes a lot of people feel good, but it's not classic diplomacy.

Another unfortunate consequence of this ad hoc approach to international affairs is the increasing temptation to view foreign policy as merely an extension of domestic politics. If there are no clearly enunciated principles to guide us, it is more likely that short-term political goals will fill the void. That's why I considered some military adventure a distinct possibility in mid-August, and that's why many suspected domestic politics weighed heavily in the political calculus of the attack. Holding a huge lead in the polls, Clinton didn't need to bolster his position. Nevertheless, nonaction on his part in the face of reports of Iraqi troop movements in northern Iraq ran the risk of erosion in his position if Dole was to capitalize on Saddam Hussein's unpopularity, and Dole had already begun his song about Clinton's weakness in foreign affairs. One can only hope politics was not the primary motivation of the attacks, but the lack of guiding principles for our foreign policy doesn't inspire confidence on that score.

Whatever the motive, the fact was Saddam Hussein had given the President a gift. Unlike the villain who didn't dare make Dirty Harry's day, he had made the move that made Bill Clinton's day. The attacks received wide approval at home and, together with Hurricane Fran, drove Bob Dole off the airwaves and out of the news for nearly an entire week. By week's end, Clinton's lead was still in the high teens, Saddam Hussein was in command in the north and we were wondering whether there was more to come.

* * *

The peculiar thing about international crises is that they can get out of control quickly, particularly when the actors are making it up on the fly. It's like playing with fire. Iraq was another example.

Just when everyone was adding up the score to determine the winner of the week's hostilities, Iraq fired antiaircraft missiles against American planes enforcing the no-fly zone (the modern expression used to describe the portion of a country's skies we decide it doesn't really need) in northern Iraq. They weren't actually threatening; to protect themselves, the Iraqis had turned off the radar that guided the missiles shortly after firing. Still, the incident escalated the crisis, leading to more tough talk out of Washington and a massive buildup of forces in the area.

This time there would be no free ride for the Administration. The Republicans came out of their shell, no longer backing the President. Jack Kemp, Jim Baker, Newt Gingrich, John McCain, Colin Powell and others spoke out in Congress, on the campaign trail and on television, sharply criticizing Clinton. They weren't consistent in what they had to say, some arguing for immediate tougher action, others urging caution in the absence of clearly enunciated goals. The lack of consistency didn't matter; the Republicans had sensed weakness on the part of the Administration and were pouncing.

The White House response was that the Republicans were playing politics in an election year, implying that such blatantly political activity was unseemly and unpatriotic in times of international crisis. It's in those times that the old "America, love it or leave it" mentality resurfaces. Indeed, had there not been widespread suspicion that election-year politics had motivated the attacks in the first place, the Administration's responsive criticism might have struck the right chord. Under the circumstances, it wasn't working and Clinton didn't seem to know quite how to get out of the crisis.

As the rhetoric escalated, a major attack seemed inevitable. The Administration had virtually advertised it, going out of its way to prepare the public for a "disproportionate" response. It was a novel theory of international law, this theory of disproportionality articulated by Secretary Perry. One can only hope the world was not taking it seriously. We didn't see the theory put into practice because Iraq took steps to defuse the crisis, signaling that it would not fire on American planes or rebuild the antiaircraft installations. Given the lack of international support for further action, and given the mounting criticism at home for an unfocused foreign policy, the Administration seized the opportunity to allow the crisis to ease. The world breathed a sigh of relief, wondering whether this was the last tremor it would experience before the November election.

Chapter 36

The Real Campaign

When the Iraqi crisis quieted down, it was time to refocus on the campaign on the home front. Initially, Clinton had obtained the expected boost from the military action. As the crisis eased and the criticism flowed, his lead had again dipped, another wild swing in a matter of days. Nonetheless, by mid-September the Republicans were getting nervous, uncomfortable with the thought that another big swing their way was necessary in the short time remaining before the election. The Democrats grew confident that not only would they hold on to the White House, they would take Congress back as well. Christian Coalition founder Pat Robertson didn't mince words in describing Dole's predicament—a "miracle" was needed.

Were things that bad for Dole? Yes and no.

Yes, because although Dole had managed to identify his two main issues, the tax plan and drugs, Clinton still seemed to be always one step ahead. The tax plan hadn't caught on with the public, which seemed to be responding to the notes of caution sounded by Clinton and to sense that the Dole plan was too good to be true. Polls showed people were starting to feel better, more optimistic, about the economy, that we were on the right track. When people *believe* the economy is headed in the right direction, a tax plan branded as risky won't thrive absent a selling job manifestly beyond the capacity of Bob Dole.

Clinton was also quick to respond on the drugs issue, which became the crime issue. While Dole hammered home the increase in teenage drug use, Clinton capitalized on the Democrats' new alliance with the law enforcement community. He received the endorsement of the nation's largest police union, the Fraternal Order of Police, a most unusual feat for a Democrat. Now the Republican hostility to gun control legislation, including the attempt to repeal the ban on assault weapons, was proving costly.

Despite these ominous signs, Pat Robertson was exaggerating when he spoke of the need for a miracle. There were six weeks left and, if history had proven anything, it was that a relatively short span of time can be an eternity in a modern political campaign. As Democratic Chairman Dodd warned, 45 days "is a millennium in politics." The volatility we had seen through mid-September had already made clear that Clinton's support was soft and there would be plenty more opportunities for Dole to make a more lasting breakthrough. In addition, the main events were yet to come: the presidential debates.

Like Super Bowls, presidential debates often turn out to be super disappointments. Still, the magnitude of the events broadcast on national television could not be ignored. One slip and an entire campaign could go down the drain. With so much at stake, both sides take the debates seriously— negotiators, handlers, sparring partners, the works. Naturally, the front-runner is never anxious to participate; there aren't too many Ted Williamses out there ready to step to the plate the last day of the season with a .400 average on the line. (Is that what they mean by character?) The candidate who is far behind anxiously awaits the opportunity to catch up with a good showing, even when, as in the case of Dole, a good showing is far from expected. British Prime Minister John Major reportedly put it this way in refusing to debate Labour's Neil Kinnock in 1992: "Every party politician that expects to lose tries that trick of debate, and every politician who expects to win says no." In 1997, with the Tories trailing badly, Major was more anxious to try that "trick." Tony Blair, whose Labour led by more than 20 points in the mercifully short British campaign, wasn't.

The principal issue surrounding the preparations for the debates concerned Ross Perot: should he or should he not be allowed to participate? Consistent with its approach to the Perot candidacy from the beginning, the Clinton camp wanted Perot in—or could it be the Clinton people were just acting as if they wanted Perot in, knowing he wouldn't pass the admission test? Consistent with its approach from the beginning, the Republican side didn't welcome Perot at all. Republicans argued that if Perot were to be included, so should other candidates, such as Ralph Nader, who presumably would not be welcomed by the Democrats. The decision was in the hands of the Commission on Presidential Debates, sponsor of the debates, whose guidelines called for the inclusion only of candidates with a "realistic" (as opposed to theoretical) chance of winning. On September 17, the decision came down against Perot.

What had become of the maverick who once struck fear in the hearts of both major political parties? He had hit rock bottom, hovering around 5 percent in the polls with no apparent prospect for improvement. Instead of getting a lift from the Reform Party Convention in August, he had slipped badly. Appearing on television shortly after the Convention, Dick Lamm had shockingly refused to endorse Perot in the presidential race. He didn't actually accuse him of foul play in winning the nomination, but he wasn't a happy camper. Subsequently, Perot seemed unable to find anyone to join him on the ticket. He finally settled on Pat Choate, an economist with little political experience who didn't quite provide Perot with a Kemp-like lift. It was clear the Reform campaign would go nowhere. Too bad—the taxpayers had just forked over close to $30 million in federal funds (outrageous as that amount sounds, it was less than half the amount received by each of the main parties), which Perot had earned the right to receive based on his 1992 performance.

Dole appeared to have won a mini-victory in excluding Perot from the debates. In my book, that victory and the strategy behind it were highly questionable. Given the state of the Dole campaign and his apparent inability to match up favorably with Clinton head-to-head, allowing Perot access to take his shots at the President didn't seem like such a bad idea. Moreover, the prevailing theory that Perot would divide the anti-incumbent vote was not borne out by history. In 1992, when Perot was allowed to take his shots at the incumbent, the main challenger was the beneficiary. Indeed, Perot was largely if not primarily responsible for bringing the incumbent down and allowing Clinton to win the election without a majority of the popular vote. For some reason, the Republicans didn't see it that way. After observing Perot in 1992 and in 1996 up to the presidential debates, the only theory they felt held water was a vote for Perot equalled a vote for Clinton regardless of season.

Excluding Perot came at a heavy price for Dole. Apart from that issue, the negotiations between the Clinton and Dole camps on the debates, led by Commerce Secretary Mickey Kantor for the President and former South Carolina Governor Carroll Campbell for Dole, went Clinton's way. There would be only two debates between the presidential candidates and one between Gore and Kemp, thereby limiting the number of swings the underdogs could take. The swings would come late in the game. The first presidential debate wouldn't be until October 6, less than one month before the election. The second would be in a town meeting format, playing to Clinton's strength. In short, the President seemed to have gotten his way on all important issues other than the participation of Perot.

A reasonable case could be made that Clinton had won the latter issue as well. He received credit for having supported Perot's participation, putting Dole on the defensive with whatever remaining support Perot had and providing Perot an inducement to save his harshest words for Dole. More significantly, Clinton avoided having to deal directly with the kind of uninhibited attack that was unleashed on him by Perot in the last few days of the campaign. Remember the civility normally prevailing in face-to-face confrontation? Well, it wasn't at all clear that a three-way debate with Clinton far ahead in the polls despite being awash in scandal would be civil. Anyone in the Clinton camp foreseeing Perot's election eve tirade on national television should have been quite pleased Perot would not be there in October to liven up the party.

It was a rough period for Dole physically as well. On the campaign trail in Californa he leaned over a fence on a stage, the fence gave way and he suffered a frightening fall of several feet that could have been disastrous had a photographer not caught him to break his fall. Amazingly, Dole bounced up smiling. He later showed off his sense of humor, gaining points for handling a difficult situation admirably. Nevertheless, an unfortunate photo in the *Washington Post* had Dole grimacing on the ground. It reminded one of those unflattering pictures of George Bush throwing up in Japan and Gerald Ford stumbling down steps coming off an airplane. Even television, which showed Dole's rapid recovery, repeated it so often that the fall became the story of the week.

It was hard not to feel sorry for Dole, not because he had been hurt, but because he seemed justifiably frustrated at being able to dominate the news only by falling off a stage. Certainly he was having difficulty explaining why he should be elected. Still, he had presented at least one sweeping proposal and touched upon a number of other issues worthy of consideration. And even if he hadn't managed to do so, there were real issues out there crying out for attention. Yet nobody seemed interested. One could sense that, absent some extraordinary developments in the last month of the season, we were headed for an unusually pronounced—even for us—display of apathy come Election Day. One could also sense that the frustration building inside Dole would be hard to contain as the campaign wound down.

Chapter 37

Things Get Ugly

As both parties began to spend their impressive war chests freely, the commercial wars heated up. Dole took the offensive on the drugs issue and Clinton responded in kind. In both cases, the product was embarrassing. Like the language of modern diplomacy, the commercials were drawing a caricature of the political process. Neither side seemed to pay much attention to the notion of truth in advertising, even when it was obvious the whole truth was not being told. Moreover, the cinematic techniques used at once provided comic relief and insulted the viewers' intelligence. Both sides had adopted the silly tactic of mixing black and white pictures of the opponent, often in slow motion, with regular clips of the candidate.

In one of those commercials the Dole campaign found a way to bring character into play while purportedly addressing a substantive issue. After tearing into Clinton's record on drugs, the commercial replayed—in black and white, naturally—a scene from a 1992 Clinton campaign appearance on MTV. A member of the youthful audience asked Clinton whether he would inhale if he had it to do over again, referring to Clinton's infamous contention in Campaign '92 that he had in his youth tried marijuana without inhaling—it was the one part of the character issue I truly had not expected to return in 1996. A smiling Clinton was then shown answering: "Sure I would, if I could. I tried once and didn't succeed." The Democrats were livid, but they didn't quite know how to respond. The statement on MTV hardly proved Clinton was responsible for the teenage drug problem. However, it not too subtly reminded people of the laundry list of questions about Clinton's character, an area the Democrats were not eager to have explored.

Smelling blood, the Dole campaign went after Clinton with another tough black and white ad that branded Clinton as a spend and tax liberal. According to the commercial, he had spent $76 million on midnight basketball and $2.5 million on Alpine slides in Puerto Rico and orchestrated the biggest tax increase in history. It was the tactic Clinton had seemingly spent his entire campaign preparing to defend. The Democrats had been hit hard in the past by the "L" word. When George Bush unleashed it on Michael Dukakis in 1988, Dukakis basically said so what; the voters told him to take a hike. Clinton wasn't going to repeat that mistake. Instead, he denied he was a "closet liberal." Nevertheless, Dole had shaken Clinton and the indications were that he would continue his attack through the first debate on October 6. In fact, Clinton's denial of closet liberalism was incorporated into yet another black and white commercial hammering home the message. Having taken enough of the Democrats' allegations of "extremism," the Republicans had rediscovered their killer instinct and retaken the offensive.

As amusing as was the debate over whether Bill Clinton is a liberal—it doesn't get much more amusing than Mario Cuomo, the quintessential liberal, appearing regularly on TV to argue the Clinton cause—the debate wasn't really significant on the merits. It did, however, underscore two points concerning the state of American politics, one substantive, the other not.

On a substantive level, both the attack and Clinton's denial made clear that, Cuomo and a few prominent Democrats in Congress aside, overt liberalism is dead in America. It may and probably will come back, perhaps even soon, perhaps by another name, but in 1996 few politicians proudly wore the label. That's why traditionally liberal Democrats running for the House and

Senate around the country were following Clinton's lead and loudly proclaiming their conservatism, particularly on the issues of crime and fiscal responsibility. Never have so many Democrats seemed so comfortable talking about balanced budgets and so tough talking about crime. It meant that there was less basis in 1996 than at any time in the recent past to distinguish between candidates on substantive grounds, and it made for lower campaigns than normal.

On a nonsubstantive level, the debate over Clinton's closet liberalism was another illustration of the silliness surrounding modern political campaigns and the dangers inherent in political commercials. Were we to believe that Bill Clinton is a liberal because of Alpine slides in Puerto Rico and midnight basketball? The biggest tax increase in history is somewhat more significant, but the Dole commercials didn't prove that case and didn't even touch the more complex issue of why the 1993 Clinton tax increase was the wrong move at the time. After all, if tax increases were never justified, we wouldn't have any taxes to complain about. Of course, the Dole commercials also made no attempt to explain precisely what it was about being a liberal that was so bad or—for those who may have forgotten—what it means to be a liberal.

The exaltation of form over substance was not confined to the presidential race. In Senate and House races around the country Democrats and Republicans alike acted as if "liberal" in the 1990s carried the same connotation as "communist" in the 1950s. The accusers used the word loosely. It was a convenient substitute for substantive debate, the best way to place the accused nervously on the defensive. For emphasis, an adjective was often added. Simply being "liberal" wasn't enough. Thus, Paul Wellstone, Democratic senator from Minnesota, was labeled "embarrassingly liberal," and Representative Bob Torricelli, in a tough battle with Republican Dick Zimmer to fill retiring Bill Bradley's Senate seat in New Jersey, was alleged to be "foolishly liberal." A Zimmer ad showed Torricelli stating, "I certainly do have a variety of positions which are liberal," as if he had been caught red-handed. Somehow, Wellstone and Torricelli both found a way to overcome their embarrassing and foolish liberalism on November 5.

There's no point in being overly critical of the candidates and their ugly ad wars. They use the commercials now and will continue to use them in the future until prohibition arrives. Why? Because they work. In the presidential race, the combination of the MTV inhaling episode and the "liberal" ads seemed to be doing just that, with some polls showing Clinton's lead dwindling again toward single digits. Then Benjamin Netanyahu decided to open a tunnel in East Jerusalem.

As matters deteriorated in East Jerusalem, it appeared that the peace process slowed by the May Israeli elections was about to either go into a deep freeze or turn into a hot war. Prospects for an immediate healing of wounds seemed dim. But Clinton had no choice; he had to act. With the outcome of the Iraqi adventure uncertain at best and the likelihood of American troops remaining in Bosnia beyond year's end becoming more obvious, it wasn't a great idea to stand by and watch Arabs and Israelis completely erase the image of Yitzhak Rabin, Shimon Peres and Yasir Arafat on the White House lawn. Clinton called for an emergency summit at the White House, which was attended by Netanyahu, Arafat and King Hussein of Jordan. The summit wasn't successful—at its conclusion the three leaders sat glumly behind the President with nothing to say to the press. There were, however, some warm handshakes, and the President once again had managed to appear presidential in a time of crisis.

The burst of activity on the international front had its usual effect on the polls, as Clinton's lead ballooned again. Like the other bounces each of the candidates had received during the course of the campaign, this one too was temporary, but Dole's momentum had again been broken and he had lost another week in his Sisyphian struggle. Benjamin Netanyahu, whom Clinton seemed to have worked so hard to defeat in his race against Shimon Peres in Israel, had perhaps unintentionally given the President a lift at a time when he was in danger of slipping. Dole, who had trouble putting together full sentences in speeches to *friendly* audiences, was now left to look to the debates to rescue his campaign.

Chapter 38

The Debates

The night of October 6 was important for Bob Dole. It was his chance to show millions of Americans and millions more around the world reached via satellite that he was indeed a serious candidate for the presidency. Nobody expected him to do very well, and those low expectations lightened his burden somewhat. Nevertheless, he trailed badly in the polls and needed to hit a home run in this first matchup, something that would energize his followers for the home stretch and begin to cut into Clinton's soft support. It wasn't meant to be.

Not that Dole's performance wasn't good in the first debate. He was civil, much more than expected, disappointing many Republicans who wanted him to go after Clinton more aggressively on the character issue; he was humorous, living up to his reputation in that regard; and he showed the public that if he were somehow to be elected president, disaster would not be the inevitable consequence. Not surprisingly, dispelling the myth that his election would be an unmitigated disaster was insufficient to generate any positive movement toward Dole. This wasn't the primaries, where the expectations game could magically transform a clear loser into a winner by virtue of a smaller than expected margin of defeat. This was the main event, the two candidates going head-to-head, the loser way behind on points and needing a knockout to win.

For his part, Clinton showed the viewers precisely why expectations for Dole were so low. Clinton was much better on his feet, more polished and more in command of his material. At debate's end, one was left to wonder why the Dole camp had placed so much hope in the debates. It never did make any sense, this notion that Dole, who by his own admission was at a distinct disadvantage in a debate format requiring responses in 30-, 60- and 90-second bursts, might be able to accomplish on this night what he had been unable to accomplish for months on the campaign trail.

The vice-presidential debate also did little to alter the dynamics of the race. The reviews were generally negative for both candidates, Kemp showing enthusiasm but seemingly unable to address any issue other than taxes, Gore living up to his reputation as a boring, robotic candidate. The matchup was billed as a preview of the race in the year 2000, a billing that was somewhat insulting to Bob Dole—since he had not announced his intention to be a one-term president, talk of a Kemp/Gore matchup in 2000 obviously presumed defeat for Dole in 1996. In any event, the debate didn't live up to its billing. It not only confirmed that vice-presidential candidates, and therefore vice-presidential debates, tend to have relatively little impact on the presidential election (*see, e.g.*, Bentsen/Quayle in 1988); it also revealed that both Kemp and Gore had a lot of rehearsing to do if they wanted to play the lead in 2000.

The second presidential debate was Dole's last chance to hit that home run. Once again, there was no rational basis for the Dole camp's hopes. The format of the second debate, a town meeting where the candidates could roam around the stage answering questions from the audience, was tailor-made for Clinton, who could have replaced Donahue if he hadn't been otherwise employed. Yet six of us crowded into a hotel room in Mexico City for the last debate party. Like millions of others attracted by the previews, we wanted to see if Dole would finally get nasty, whether he would be able to get under Clinton's skin and whether Clinton would make the critical mistake that would turn things around. None of that happened. Although Dole repeatedly raised the character issue—not unlike Kemp's reliance on tax cuts as the solution to virtually all problems—he still seemed to hold back. Well-trained for the challenge, Clinton wisely ignored much of the disjointed attack and emerged largely unscathed. We all knew we had witnessed a master at work. Like Muhammad Ali in the Rumble in the Jungle, Clinton had used the rope-a-dope, allowing Dole to take his swings, not wasting his energy and retaliating with well-placed blows that more than offset the sting of Dole's attack.

As the last debate concluded, I felt somewhat guilty, guilty of having watched for the wrong reasons. I knew or should have known there was little of substance to be learned from the debates. Was the economy—not the perception of the economy, the actual economy—in good or bad shape? Were those 10.5 million new jobs a sign of a healthy economy or of more people holding more jobs just to get by? What was the real explanation for the drop in the crime rate and the rise in teenage drug use? Would a 15 percent tax cut blow a hole in the deficit? Is our economic growth rate satisfactory or disappointing and, in any case, what can a president do to affect it on a short-term basis? Most importantly, how are we to make a judgment on any of the above based on the nonsense we heard from both candidates in those 30-, 60- and 90-second bursts? I've practiced law for more than 20 years and am still learning. That tells me most people who formed strong opinions on the issues presented in the debates on the basis of what either Clinton or Dole had to say should have stopped and reconsidered.

If the debates don't provide us with the knowledge necessary to make an informed decision on substantive issues, what use are they? I think this question has a four-pronged answer.

First, like the national conventions, though not as effective, the debates offer a glimpse of the overall philosophy of the candidates. For example, Dole spoke of trusting the people and getting the government out of their hair, Clinton of giving the people the tools they need to improve their lives. It was a subtle but important difference, the former message more clearly reflecting the conservative view that government is not helpful, the latter a '90s formulation—without using the "L" word—of the liberal philosophy that government has an important role to play in improving our lot. In the national conventions, we saw these messages honed over a period of four nights. In the debates, you had to listen more carefully, avoid falling asleep when the discussion drifted toward substance and catch the same message from one burst or another. That had value if you hadn't been paying any attention to Clinton's performance during his first term or to what Dole had been saying for more than a year on the campaign trail. For those not fortunate enough to live in a state of political unconsciousness, however, the debates served only to reinforce the message already delivered by the time October rolled around—marginal value indeed.

Second, and perhaps more valuable, the debates tell us much about the candidates' personal strengths and weaknesses in certain areas. We like to think that the president is articulate and witty, able to think quickly and maneuver in unscripted situations. At some point during a four-year term in the White House, those skills are likely to come in handy. Like the combines run by the NFL before its famous annual draft, the debates allow us to measure technical skills. Unfortunately, that's not enough, any more than a football draftee's time in the 40-yard dash can guarantee success come game time. In football, teams don't rely solely on such athletic tests. They conduct extensive interviews, do psychological testing, research the background of the player, study game films and send scouts to watch live performances. All this to make sure they find a gem in the seventh round. When it comes to selecting the president of the United States, most of us don't seem to feel that same sense of urgency.

Beyond message and evaluation of debating skills, there are two areas that explain the true significance of debates and the emphasis we place on them. Both highlight the ills afflicting the presidential election process.

From the candidates' standpoint, the debates present the opportunity to rally the troops while at the same time winning new friends quickly. How can this be done? Catchy phrases, one-liners, the stuff of TV comercials. Just as *Dirty Harry* and *The Terminator* have made their way into international diplomacy, cleverness predominates over substance at home. What do you remember most from the performances of the great communicator, Ronald Reagan—are you better off now than you were four years ago? It's a powerful line often used and abused since then, in 1996 by the incumbent. It doesn't matter whether you are better off in spite of, rather than because of, the incumbent's actions. Nor does it matter whether things have been bad notwithstanding the incumbent's best efforts, and might have been worse without them. In fact, it doesn't even matter whether it is true that you are better or worse off now than you were four years ago, as long as you can be led to believe it through a barrage of statistical information you have no way of analyzing or digesting. Reagan proved that one line born out of the same genius that produces the best of TV commercials can do more for a candidate than volumes and years of serious work. In the face of that reality, how much seriousness do you think the candidates will allow themselves?

From our standpoint as viewers, we can't deny the single most obvious benefit we get from the debates: entertainment. We enjoy seeing the candidates engage in a battle of wits. We're also curious as to how low the candidates will go. Would Dole really get nasty as advertised in the second debate and, if so, how nasty? Polls show the voters are turned off by nastiness. I'm not convinced. It seems to me more likely that many who proclaim their antipathy toward negativism and personal attacks in campaigns can't wait to see some of the old-fashioned mudslinging in the debates.

Finally, there is the ever-present danger of the slip, the blunder, the gaffe, the possibility that one or both of the candidates will utter something nonsensical or embarrassing that will result in one of those memorable moments only live television can provide. It happened to Gerald Ford in 1976, when he inexplicably declared in a debate with Jimmy Carter that there was no Soviet domination of Eastern Europe. Ford and vice-presidential running mate Bob Dole came back from an enormous early deficit in that campaign, only to lose by a hair. That one slip may have cost them the election. With so much at stake, the entertainment value of the debates is high. We watch, we listen, and we wait for the break that could make one candidacy and destroy another. When it doesn't happen, we call the event boring, as was the case in 1996. A few more debates like Clinton/Dole, Gore/Kemp and the intra-Republican debates in the 1996 primaries and television just might shut down the show for good.

Chapter 39
The Home Stretch

Campaign '96 ended with one of the worst periods of campaigning we had ever had the privilege of witnessing. Dole had been thwarted at every turn, completely unable to get his message across. For most of the campaign, he had no message. When he developed one, the economic plan, it didn't catch fire. His gaffes, such as the tobacco fiasco, had attracted more attention than his positions on important issues. Ditto his fall off stage. Every time he seemed to get his act together and gather some momentum, one event or another, often on the international front, intervened to disrupt his timing. The debates had only brought more failure—not in the sense of a poor showing, but rather in his inability to hit the home run. All this seemed too much for Dole, who was now faced with the harsh reality that his dream was being denied by a man perceived to lack character and guiding principles. An obviously frustrated Dole was now going after the President more aggressively, no longer holding back. Finally, belatedly, he was doing what the Republican hard core had wanted him to do all along.

At the same time, bad news was hitting the Clinton camp in alarming doses. Most of it concerned Democratic fund-raising practices, both domestic and international. At home, news broke that a drug felon had made a substantial contribution to the Democratic Party and been rewarded with a visit to the White

House. Shortly thereafter, he had been arrested and convicted on drug charges. More embarrassingly, the Administration was linked to questionable international fund-raising activities. The Party had received huge contributions from Indonesian, Korean and Taiwanese interests that caused many to conclude either flagrant violations of the law had taken place or the loopholes in the law were large enough to drive a locomotive through. And Vice-president Al Gore raised eyebrows with a lucrative visit to a Buddhist temple.

More seriously, a man named John Huang, formerly employed by an Indonesian banking group, had allegedly left that group with a handsome severance to take up a senior position at the Department of Commerce, where he had allegedly attended meetings regarding Indonesia. From there he took up a position with the Democratic Party, enjoying enormous success in raising money for the Democratic National Committee from Asian interests. Critics strongly implied that not only was much of the fund-raising illegal, it also had sinister consequences, including a marked softening of the Administration's trade policy toward Indonesia. Serious stuff indeed, notwithstanding Bob Dole's joke that foreign aid had finally come to America. It didn't help that Huang had made dozens of visits, some rather lengthy and after hours, to the White House during the course of the campaign. Another gate had been opened at the White House. They called this one "Indogate"—the scandal was named before the Chinese connection was uncovered. Like Filegate and Travelgate, Indogate had to be kept shut until after the election.

The allegations concerning Taiwan were just as serious. Reports circulated that Taiwanese businessmen had been pressured into making contributions to the Democratic Party. Coming in a year in which the country had faced a crisis over Taiwan—the war games played by China during the period leading up to the Taiwanese elections—the notion that such political contributions may have been solicited was particularly offensive.

When it rains, it pours. Jerome Zeifman, former chief counsel to the House Judiciary Committee during Watergate, declared there was probable cause that Clinton was a felon. In an appearance on "Crossfire," he chided his friend Bob Beckel for supporting Clinton, saying Beckel would be holding his nose while voting. And *The American Lawyer*, the country's most entertaining publication for lawyers, ran an article by Stuart Taylor, Jr., which argued that the evidence supporting Paula Jones' allegations against Clinton was stronger than the evidence supporting Anita Hill's allegations against Clarence Thomas. The accumulation of charges painted an ugly picture of an ethically challenged Administration stumbling to the finish line.

The Democrats didn't have much to say about all this. Most of the bad news was ignored. When that wasn't possible, there were three tactics that had served them well throughout the campaign to fall back on.

First, the Democrats showed again that the best defense is a good offense. Nobody really wanted to defend the fund-raising practices, regardless of the legalities. So they didn't. The Democrats' primary rebuttal became "They do it, too." It was a tactic that captured the spirit of modern American politics, in which too frequently right and wrong are measured not by any legal or ethical standard. The theory of political relativity and electoral fairness justifies, even requires, all sorts of unsavory conduct as long as somebody else is, or might be, breaking the rules as well.

As the full extent of the obsession of the Clinton White House with reelection became apparent in the months after the election, some Democrats elaborated on this theory, justifying their party's conduct by referring to the grand issues of policy at stake in the 1996 election. If there were excesses, they were necessary to stop the Republicans from carrying out their misguided policies. The defense assumed a certain moral tone as it moved beyond the argument that Democrats were no worse than Republicans to the triumph of good over evil. To lend crediblity to this version of the end justifies the means, it was necessary to bring out the evil in the Republicans, a difficult task considering the Democratic strategy throughout the campaign of co-opting the Republican agenda. The fact that the Democrats managed to pull it off was testimony to their mastery of campaign tactics, and in particular their ability to use the media to brand the Republicans as dangerous extremists. If a few rules had to be bent to defeat them, at least it was for a worthy cause.

The second tactic was reliance on a fundamental principle of our criminal law: the defendant is innocent until proven guilty. It is a principle so deeply rooted in American culture that it is often invoked in contexts having nothing to do with the criminal justice system. Here it served to appeal to the American voter's sense of fairness. If O.J. was entitled to the presumption of innocence, isn't that the least to be accorded the president? The answer is clearly yes if the question is asked in the context of a criminal case. When asked in the context of a presidential election, the issue is a bit more complex. If there really was "probable cause" to believe Clinton was a felon, that might not be enough to put him in jail, but the White House is a different story. That's not to say every time someone makes an allegation we should dismiss the president; it's simply to point out that the innocent until proven guilty routine has its limitations.

Like the first tactic, the second was refined after the election in the face of the dizzying revelations of abuses. Vice-president Al Gore, responding to charges that he had made fund-raising calls to major contributors from the White House, repeatedly asserted that his counsel—lawyers always get the blame—had advised him there was no controlling case or legal authority establishing the illegality of his conduct. Not only were criminal standards imported into the realm of politics, they were conveniently modified to suit the occasion. Unless someone else had been tried and convicted of the same offense, there was no offense. Just make sure you're not the first and things will work out. How many times do you think we'll be seeing Gore's carefully delivered defense replayed in those black and white pictures in the future?

Third, as long as it was working, was the strategy from *An American President*: take the high road. The President didn't answer the charges that proliferated during the home stretch. His mission, as the Clinton camp advertised it, was to stay on the substantive issues that were important to the American people, not to get down in the gutter with his adversaries. Under different circumstances, it might have been a noble strategy. Given the number and nature of the charges, it sounded a lot more like Jack Kemp's "running out the clock."

Frustrated as were the reporters following Clinton in the home stretch, you can't really blame the Clinton camp for playing it safe. It was deep in the fourth quarter and Clinton still led by a wide margin. Is there anyone (or any Giant fan) in America who hasn't seen or heard of The Fumble? Rather than falling on the ball with a lead and time running out, then Giant quarterback Joe Pisarcik attempted a handoff to Larry Csonka. Fumble, touchdown, Eagles win! Answering reporters' questions about Indogate would have unwisely risked fumbling away the election when the battle had been won. The questions surrounding the fundraising activities were serious, but there was no way anybody could piece it all together in time to make a difference in Election '96, at least not unless Clinton helped by dignifying the questions with a response. He didn't need a great coach or political consultant to avoid that mistake.

None of the tactics employed by the Democrats seemed to be fooling anyone. Most people I talked to felt that where there's smoke there's fire—how much they didn't know. There was also a sense that the strategy of taking the high road was borne more out of necessity than nobility. Polls indicated a majority of Americans were not impressed with the President's honesty or trustworthiness. Yet the concerns about his character and ethics didn't seem to be cutting into his substantial lead. That fact clearly exasperated Dole, who was furious as the campaign wound down. Where is the outrage in America, he cried repeatedly. When will America wake up?

In one of the strangest and most desperate moves of the campaign, Dole's campaign manager, Scott Reed, held a widely publicized private meeting with Ross Perot to urge him to withdraw from the race. Perhaps the idea was something akin to Boris Yeltsin courting Alexander Lebed to seal his victory over Zyuganov in the 1996 Russian presidential election. Perot's main theme of balancing the budget was largely Republican, and now his second issue, campaign finance reform, had been revived by Indogate. Why would Perot want to hand Clinton the White House a second time when he was obviously much closer in ideology to the Republicans? Presumably, that was the logic behind the approach.

It was a flawed logic. Perot wasn't about to disappoint his

few remaining supporters with another withdrawal; nor was it likely he would have so soon forgotten who had excluded him from the presidential debates. For the first time, however, Perot did focus his attention on Bill Clinton rather than the Republicans. In the last few days of the campaign, he unleashed a scathing attack on Clinton, just what the Republicans had expected from Bob Dole. Perot shockingly speculated that if elected, Clinton, like Richard Nixon, might be forced to leave office early. Echoing Dole's cry, he asked why there is no sense of shame. The American people should not allow a smooth-talking President without a strong ethical or moral base to have control over sending their sons and daughters to do battle. Nor could the country afford to spend the next two years in Watergate II.

On election eve, Perot bought time on network television, devoting much of the full hour of prime time to a continuation of his harangue against Clinton. Would you allow a person with pending criminal charges to babysit your children? The outrage Dole was looking for, and much more, was being colorfully expressed by the man whose participation in the campaign the Republicans had dreaded from the beginning. If nothing else, it called into question the wisdom of the Republican strategy of opposing Perot, including Dole's resistance to Perot's participation in the debates. How much worse could Dole have done if Perot had been there?

While Perot seemed to be giving Dole a hand, the Republicans weren't. Once again, they were bailing out. Candidates across the country, apparently taking their cue from the national leadership, were campaigning on the premise that Dole would lose. The line was vote for us so Clinton won't have a blank check. It was the theory of ballot box checks and balances: a Democratic president needs a Republican Congress and vice versa. If you listened carefully, it sounded a lot like we know the only reason you're voting for Clinton is Dole's a lousy candidate, but don't make that mistake with Congress.

Dole himself fought valiantly until the end. He wound up his campaign with a 96-hour dash that exhausted his younger entourage, going "round the clock, round the clock, round the clock." He seemed in good spirits, as if he had somehow been liberated by the virtual certainty of his imminent defeat. The spark missing for his entire campaign was there. It was too little, too late. By then, nothing was going to stop Bill Clinton.

*   *   *

Less than one-half of the eligible voters turned out to vote on November 5. Of those who did, less than one-half voted for Bill Clinton, who nevertheless won reelection by a landslide in the electoral college. The late-breaking scandals obviously hurt Clinton, denying him the majority of the popular vote he had sought and pushing Dole over 40 percent, a barrier he had not been able to pierce for most of the campaign. Ross Perot climbed a few points at the end to 8 percent, thanks to the fund-raising scandals, but he still finished far below his 1992 level. The Republicans, meanwhile, managed to maintain control of both houses of Congress, slipping slightly in the House and gaining two seats in the Senate.

What did it all mean? One of the privileges of victory is the opportunity to proffer an interpretation of the message sent. Predictably, Clinton warned Republicans to listen to the voters' plea to curb partisanship and work together in the interests of the country. It was an extension of the high road theme he had been developing all campaign. Early post-election comments coming out of the Republican camp reflected a concern that perhaps Clinton was right. A kinder, gentler Republican leadership was talking more of legislation and less of investigation.

It was all so unnatural—Bill Clinton, the consummate politician, calling upon Republicans to put politics aside; the Republicans, led by Gingrich and Lott, letting bygones be bygones. The betting was it wouldn't take long for both sides to start acting naturally. The last campaign of the millenium had just left us holding our noses and left people around the world covering their eyes and ears. Now the ride to that bridge to the 21st century promised to be just as uplifting. But there was no point in complaining. We had been duly entertained by the campaign and it looked like a new show was about to start.

Chapter 40

Lessons

There are plenty of lessons to be learned from Election '96, some big, some small. Let's not bother with the small ones, such as don't snub a major civil rights organization to go to an All-Star Game, lay off popular TV personalities, make sure at least a majority of your close friends don't get indicted and get your staff to check the railings on stages in advance. Assuming we're interested in lessons going beyond the procedural issue of how to win an election, we can start with the news flash that the system is indeed broken and needs fixing. Fixing doesn't necessarily entail sweeping legislative or constitutional changes. After all, who's there to carry out that overhaul, and why should we assume that the fix provided by products of a broken system would work? No, I'm afraid it's going to require some hard thinking and self-analysis to come up with the proper medicine for what ails the presidential election process. A good start would be recognition of the problem. If we're going to let the system continue to evolve into a caricature of democracy, that's our right and privilege, as long as it is exercised consciously.

Here's my take on the situation after observing Election '96. See if you agree.

Not Much Democracy. The experience of Election '96 challenges the wisdom of Churchill's famous characterization of democracy—it may not be great, but it beats anything else (loose translation). I don't mean to advocate an undemocratic form of government. It's just that too often what are plainly unhealthy practices are excused in the name of democracy, in much the same way that bad policy is occasionally justified by the "My country, right or wrong" philosophy. In fact, one has to wonder how much democracy is left in our presidential election process. The way I've always understood it, a pure democratic system is one in which the majority rules, directly or indirectly, subject only to the basic safeguards necessary to protect the minority. That's not what we saw in 1996, and, although the system has clearly been in a state of continuous degeneration, we haven't seen it in some time.

If you have any doubt about the prevalence of minority rule (I don't mean minority in the sense of religious, ethnic or other groups, but only in terms of sheer numbers of voters), reflect a bit on the numerology of November 5 and work your way back through the campaign. With less than 50 percent of eligible voters turning out (pathetic in comparison to the much more robust turnouts in mature European democracies) and less than 50 percent of actual voters voting for Bill Clinton, less than one-quarter of the electorate selected the President who will—unless Ross Perot's Watergate II prediction comes true—lead us into the 21st century. That turnout wouldn't be enough to constitute a quorum at most shareholders' meetings.

Maybe the numbers wouldn't be as disappointing if the menu of candidates had been developed through some sort of democratic process. If you were paying any attention in 1996, you know that wasn't the case. Bill Clinton wasn't even challenged in his own party. Yet I can't seem to find anybody who voted for him without reservation (the holding your nose point). The Republicans put on more of a "democratic" show to select their nominee, complete with primaries, caucuses and a slate of nine candidates. What could be more democratic? Well, one of the lessons of Election '96 is that we shouldn't take the proliferation of players and games as empirical evidence of a healthy democracy. More likely, the opposite is true.

The dynamics of the process, including the rules of the expectations game and the role of momentum, can reduce if not eliminate the impact of late-season primaries, thereby depriving a majority of voters of any meaningful participation in the selection of the main party candidates. Even in the early, small-state primaries and caucuses that play a disproportionately large role in shaping the nomination process, a relatively small number of voters can carry the day. A small minority of Republicans finished off Phil Gramm in Iowa and by the time California, purportedly the biggest prize of all, rolled around, it was already over for the seven other Republican pretenders.

As for the candidates themselves, there were slim pickings in 1996, and not just in the Democratic Party. The main point the nine candidates on the Republican side drove home to us was that the only persons who dare run for president these days are those with virtually no chance of winning—that's if you put aside Bob Dole, who appeared to be calling in the chit we owed him after his distinguished career in public service. Presumably, somewhere out there were plenty of other fine Democrats and Republicans who might have had an easier time capturing our imagination and commanding our respect, but none showed up for the party.

There were a number of third party candidacies in 1996, as there always are. Apart from Ross Perot and Ralph Nader, Larry King introduced us to candidates of the Natural Law Party, the Libertarian Party and the U.S. Taxpayers Party. However, only Perot managed to attract more than 1 percent of the popular vote. Assuming, *arguendo*, that he counted as a serious alternative to the main party candidates, his nomination was hardly more democratic than the others. Reformers didn't exactly turn out in droves for their first party nomination, another minority decision. This is a brand new political party we're talking about; it hasn't had time to lose the fire in the belly. If only a small fraction of Reformers bother to select their own nominee in their first election (it's not as if they actually had to go to a polling booth; E-mail or fax would have done it), you can probably color their future Democratic or Republican.

Thus, wherever you look, the numbers are telling the same story. The system is not designed to give effect to the wishes of the majority, and the majority, whether of members of our political parties or of the electorate as a whole, is allowing the system to dictate to it. If majority rule lies at the heart of any democracy, the majority in this country must be thinking our brand of democracy stinks.

Out of Control. Perhaps not entirely unrelated to our democracy deficiency is the fact that so few of us have the time or the inclination to acquire the information necessary to make an intelligent choice. People who don't know how to swim or ski tend not to spend much time in the deep or on the slopes. Golf is the rage among my peers, but I never learned how to play and don't talk much about seven-irons. The same is true in politics, a field dominated by professional politicians and their handlers, advisors and consultants. The main difference is that in politics, unlike other sports, the winner is determined by fan voting. What the professionals have done to win the fan vote has sent the system spinning out of control.

If you're looking for reasons why we're in this mess, you can start with our apolitical culture. While it is always dangerous to generalize, there's little doubt the average American voter is, from a political standpoint, as unsophisticated as they come when it comes to *nonlocal* politics—national and international. For an unusually large number of Americans, politics is a combination of civic duty rarely carried out and entertainment to be turned off when unexciting. By and large, we feel we have better things to do than talk politics. Although that may not always be true, the fact is that in 1996 we felt relatively secure in the knowledge that the sky wasn't likely to fall regardless of who won. Our way of life and place in the world would remain intact.

In many other countries, politics is a way of life, often an obsession. People eat, drink and breathe politics, at virtually every social gathering, at the dinner table, at work, everyplace. Ironically, what they're talking about frequently is the latest bit of irrational behavior to come out of the world's lone remaining superpower. We may not be interested in what our government does, but the rest of the world *has* to be.

This cultural trait of ours isn't necessarily unhealthy. A reasonable case can be made that the incessant political talk one hears in some corners of the world is the product of frustration, a dearth of other forms of entertainment, paranoia and other ills indicative of a separation from reality. We should be grateful we don't have that problem. Nevertheless, our cavalier approach is starting to prove costly. It's one thing to *choose* not to get too excited about politics, to *choose* to preoccupy ourselves with other pursuits, knowing that we're still in control when it counts. It's quite another to lose control of the system to minorities, both political and apolitical, taking advantage while we're out on the course or doing whatever else we do for recreation outside politics.

Political minorities are nothing new. It's a fact of life in any democracy (not to mention other forms of government) that small but organized and motivated groups can wield disproportionate political power. That power is magnified in a country in which less than half the eligible voters vote. Since organized and motivated groups by definition are more likely to vote than others, our overall apathy transforms miniscule percentages into powerful voting blocks that cannot be ignored. That is particularly true in states with high electoral college votes, as strong voting blocks there can swing all of those votes to one candidate or another under the winner-take-all rule prevailing in the obsolete electoral college.

More troubling than conventional democratic problems is the power wielded in our brand of democracy by the apolitical forces. The combination of money, obscene amounts of it, the *business* of political management, and the power of the mass media is distorting the system in ways unanticipated a relatively short time ago. We can no longer choose not to be bothered by politics, at least not with any comfort that nothing funny's going on while we're otherwise engaged.

In 1996, a year in which records were either broken or threatened in a number of unflattering categories, we saw exactly how dangerous those apolitical forces can be. Like Ross Perot before him, Steve Forbes was able to spend his way to political prominence, using more than $30 million of his own money to explain to us his message of hope, growth and opportunity. Was his message so unique that we needed to have him deliver it? Was he the best qualified person in the country to discuss taxes and the economy? Not likely, any more than Ross Perot is the country's top expert on international trade. The one indispensable asset Forbes and Perot both had was money, and the one thing both have proven is we're not likely to see too many fresh faces from the private sector in the race for the presidency unless their bank accounts are up to the task.

That's just the price of admission. Once you're in, even a personal balance sheet as healthy as Forbes' or Perot's won't get you there (assuming you're not completely irresponsible with your own money). As we saw when the real campaign began in 1996, the main parties were raising and spending hundreds of millions of other people's money (OPM) on Election '96. Spending's a lot freer when it's OPM—that's why some corporate executives find it easy to spend millions of corporate funds on projects in which they wouldn't invest a dime of their own money.

Most of the attention in the waning moments of the campaign was focused on the developing scandal concerning how the money was raised and where it came from—"Indogate." One can hardly complain about that focus given the scale of the questionable activity. It would take an unusual dose of good fortune, even for the Clinton White House, to escape from the scandal completely unscathed. The standard response that there is no proof the contributions influenced decisions is insufficient. That's why we have presumptions. They fill the gap in proof when experience teaches us a proposition otherwise difficult to prove is nonetheless true. Considering the public's apparent disgust with money in politics and the anger and frustration of the Republicans, who weren't shy about raising and spending OPM themselves, one had the feeling we would be hearing a lot more about John Huang and company in 1997, not to mention some very expensive cups of coffee and socializing at the White House. And that was before news broke about a Chinese connection that raised the spectre of improper foreign governmental influence in policy-making, introducing a whole new dimension to the scandal.

Important as it is to investigate the fund-raising activities, I was a touch disappointed with that focus. One of the main lessons to be learned from Campaign '96 is that we should be more concerned with what the money was doing than how it was being raised. Channelled into multimillion dollar advertising campaigns, it was turning our gray matter to mush. Too many people bought the idea that the Republican extremists were trying to destroy the environment, Medicare and Medicaid and didn't care about education, largely on the basis of those black and white commercials that depicted good and evil for those who didn't have the time or the information to figure it out for themselves. The Republicans were no better than the Democrats, just less effective. The fact that their attempt to recycle the "L" word didn't succeed wasn't because they had taken the high road and engaged in an intellectual discussion of the deficiencies of modern liberalism; it was because they had been totally outclassed on the campaign trail by the Democratic team. Both sides took advantage of our apathy; neither seemed concerned that we might be misled by the incomplete pictures produced with those impressive war chests.

In focusing on how money is put to use, I'm assuming Congress will devote enough attention to the fund-raising side of the money equation, especially the loopholes allowing hundreds of millions of "soft" dollars to be raised legally from corporations and other organized groups notwithstanding the relatively strict limitations on campaign contributions by individuals. (Will Justice Breyer ever again say, as he did in the *Colorado Republican Federal Campaign Committee* case, that "Unregulated 'soft money' contributions may not be used to influence a federal campaign, except when used in the limited, party-building activities specifically designated in the statute.") I'm also assuming that those on both sides who crossed the line in 1996 and committed illegal acts under the existing rules will either be caught and punished or sufficiently deterred not to repeat the offense—admittedly a shaky assumption. With actor turned Senator Fred Thompson playing the leading role in the Senate investigation of the "money trail" and Representative Dan Burton (of Helms-Burton fame) doing the same in the House, there was plenty of firepower to address the obvious fund-raising abuses.

The problem is that when Congress has finished its work—after hearings in the tradition of the Watergate, Irangate, Clarence Thomas and Whitewater spectacles of the past—we're still likely to be left with a system that allows candidates and political parties to raise and spend obscene amounts of money, legally, on political campaigns. Campaign '96 had barely ended when both parties reminded us how comfortable they were with the status quo, continuing their highly visible fund-raising activity as if in defiance of public opinion. And as the Supreme Court has made clear, only a constitutional amendment can prevent you from spending your own wealth freely. That's why it's at least as important to focus on how the money is spent as on how it is raised.

Which brings us back to those television commercials. They used to get people to smoke. Now they get them to believe one candidate or another, or one party or another, has answers to some fairly complex questions about which, judging by the material they're feeding us, neither the candidates nor the parties have a clue. Where does that leave us? Given the power of television in the hands of professionals who know how to use the medium to maximum effect, it looks like we no longer have the luxury of not paying attention to politics. We're going to have to work at it, find new ways to inform ourselves and take back our democracy.

Winning Is Everything. Like the others, this is not a new ill, just one that became painfully obvious in 1996. It's to be expected in a country that, on the one hand, abhors ideology and, on the other, has a political environment inhospitable to well-meaning men and women who want to serve their country. The absence of ideology can be a plus if the gap is filled by honest and competent civil servants bringing their expertise to bear on the problems of the day. If, however, most of our experts wouldn't even consider paying the price to enter the political arena or public service, we end up with the worst of both worlds.

How did the winning is everything philosophy manifest itself in 1996? In matters of form as well as substance. On both counts, the Democrats outdid the Republicans, earning themselves another four-year lease on the White House. From the standpoint of form, one couldn't help but admire the manner in which the

Democratic rapid response machine handled adversity in the campaign. The Democrats beat the Republicans to the punch every time. Before Dole announced his economic plan, the Democrats had managed to brand it their way, a brand that stuck throughout the fall. Before Dole finished his Convention speech, the highlight of his campaign, the Democrats were prepared with the response. When the Republicans put on a hit show in San Diego, the Democrats came right back with one of their own in Chicago. There was also an answer for Kenneth Starr, the guilty verdicts in Arkansas and the D'Amato Committee report. The Dick Morris affair was sidestepped with ease. Not even Filegate or Indogate could derail the campaign. The team didn't permanently dispose of the problems besetting the White House; it simply did what was necessary to get Bill Clinton across the goal line on November 5.

Deserving of the game ball as the entire Clinton campaign team may be, I kept asking myself how it could be possible for any team to become so proficient in one part of the game without sacrificing something, and if something was being sacrificed, what? A football team practicing nothing but power sweeps can't be expected to do well in the passing game. Is the same true of an Administration that devotes so much effort to reelection, *i.e.*, could it possibly be paying any serious attention to governing, other than whatever may neatly fit into the reelection plan? We're not talking about a couple of weeks or even months. The focus of politics in the United States for an entire year is the presidential election, and many feel Election '96 was actually won in 1995, when Bill Clinton returned from his state of irrelevancy and sowed the seeds for the strategy of posing as the centrist defending the public against extremism from the right. One lesson to be learned from a comparison of the performances of the Clinton and Dole teams is that obsession with reelection has its reward. The odds are, however, we're paying a heavy price in the process.

In early 1997, as the revelations of the extent of the White House obsession with fund-raising came at an accelerated pace, the questions became more serious. Apart from those coffees, it was reported that there were nearly a thousand sleepovers at the

White House during the Clinton tenure. The Lincoln Bedroom was seemingly the favorite guest room of the rich and famous, at least those of them who contributed huge sums to the Democratic National Committee. According to papers provided by ex-Deputy Chief of Staff Harold Ickes to the House Committee investigating the scandal, the idea of using the sleepovers may have come from the President himself. The revelations raised new concerns that a bright line had been crossed by the Democrats in their fund-raising frenzy, assuring that Congress and prosecutors would be busy for some time to come.

What I found most troubling was the confirmation the revelations brought that reelection must have been the Administration's top priority since 1994, if not earlier. Coupled with the organized, massive effort to counter every move made by the Republicans and to stay one step ahead every step of the way, the relentless fund-raising couldn't have left much time or energy for governance or policy. With all those "friends" roaming the White House at all hours of the day and night, it's a wonder the first family didn't take more vacations to get away from the crowd.

On the substance, there is reason to suspect that the winning is everything philosophy permeated both camps in 1996, although here again the Clinton team appears to have outdistanced its rival.

I don't profess to know whether Bill Clinton is indeed a closet liberal. Part of the criticism of him is precisely that—we don't really know. What we do know is that he certainly seemed to take a lot of liberal advice in the first half of his first term. No one was accusing him of co-opting the conservatives' agenda when he issued his order regarding gays in the military, when he cut the deficit by raising taxes, when he pushed Hillary Clinton's mammouth health plan or when he vetoed earlier attempts at welfare reform. Nor were the liberals then complaining that their leader had betrayed them. After the shock of the midterm elections, we began to see a very different Bill Clinton. Was this the product of some spiritual transformation, a sudden recognition that the principles he had stood for were wrong, or was it a case of a man indoctrinated in the winning is everything philosophy sticking by his principles and doing whatever it took to win? You decide.

If Clinton's transformation was in fact attributable to a burning desire to be reelected, everyone lost in 1996. The right might be pleased that, regardless of motive, a large part of its agenda—including a large part of the discredited Contract with America—was placed front and center, but it would have been a lot more pleased, and secure, if the man at the helm hadn't made a living trashing the Contract. As for the left, unhappy as it may be with Clinton's conservative strategy, it can find solace in the hope that Clinton was indeed only faking right, as Haley Barbour said. However, its confidence on that score had to be severely shaken when Clinton finally signed the welfare reform bill, notwithstanding the theory that sometimes it's necessary to stand up and do the wrong thing.

All of us, right, left and center, lost an opportunity to have an open and honest debate on the direction of the country, particularly on how far right we want to go, how dead should liberalism be in America and whether we should completely abandon the notion that governent can be and do good. Does the failure of past government programs necessarily mean all programs are bad? Maybe the Clinton health plan was a bad idea, but surely something is wrong when tens of millions of Americans have no health insurance, when the homeless are freezing on the streets of New York in the dead of winter and when our child poverty rate is abysmal in comparison to our supposed level of development.

I wonder whether it's possible anymore to have such a debate, one in which liberals can't invoke Newt Gingrich or the "extremists" in Congress and conservatives are not permitted to throw around the "L" word, alone or in conjunction with any of the adverbs used in 1996, where liberals are not permitted to wage class warfare and conservatives must go beyond the argument that big government doesn't work. We were deprived of that debate in 1996, and I have a feeling it had something to do with the winning is everything philosophy.

It would be nice to be able to say Bob Dole stood for something different, and maybe to some extent he did. At least you never had the impression he was comfortable playing the game. Nevertheless, it's hard to overlook some of the bizarre moves of his campaign, including his shifting on the abortion plank in the party platform. By far his most shocking moves were the Gamble and the Choice.

Not every change in beliefs, even fundamental ones, can be attributed to political expediency. As discussed earlier, the strength required to change one's mind based on sound argument is one of the definitions of character. Unfortunately, one doesn't get the feeling that Bob Dole ever bought into his own economic package. If he didn't, his leap to the supply side was one of the most desperate campaign moves in recent memory and perhaps the single most glaring illustration of what's wrong with the system. Regardless of your position on the merits of Dole's economic package, which included the selection of supply-sider Jack Kemp as running mate, it is hard to reconcile the Gamble with the principles defended by Dole during his career and harder still to explain it without reference to the winning is everything philosophy and all its negative connotations. If a man with such a distinguished record as Bob Dole can get caught up in the game, we shouldn't be surprised when candidates with lesser self-assurance and character succumb.

What About the Rest of the World? A hopefully erroneous conclusion one might be tempted to draw from the proceedings in 1996 is that, frankly, we just don't care what goes on in the rest of the world, or what it thinks. Consequently, the professionals in this sport have little incentive to articulate a coherent foreign policy, one that provides a measure of predictability missing in a policy of ad hoc reaction to crises.

As in the case of the direction we should be taking at home, we sorely needed a debate on international affairs in 1996. It was natural for some confusion to exist in the immediate post-Cold War period as we sorted out what our role would be in world affairs, but several years have gone by without clear progress on defining the new world order. Our role as leader of the free world was in the process of transformation, but into what? Characterizing our status as that of the lone remaining superpower doesn't begin to answer the question of how a lone superpower is supposed to act. We needed to think about whether we should have more or fewer troops abroad and how and when to use them, what should be the level of our defense spending and what types of defense spending we should stress, whether to expand NATO, whether to pursue a policy of constructive engagement toward China, whether our Russia policy is too dependent on one man, what will be the future role of our intelligence agencies and a host of other political, economic and military issues crucial both to us and to people around the world. In general, we needed to define the overarching theme and objectives of our foreign policy in the post-Cold War era, something that could substitute for beating back the red menace.

There was no room for that debate in 1996; neither side could afford to take a crack at it. Since we didn't put any pressure on the candidates to explain themselves, they were able to devote their attention to some issues of a relatively trivial nature and others unlikely to occupy the president's attention once elected.

Absent guiding principles, our foreign policy in 1996 had all the earmarks of that 700-pound gorilla on the loose. Even worse, the perception grew at home and abroad that, for us, international affairs were relevant only in the context of domestic politics. Thus, Congress passed and the President immediately signed the controversial Helms-Burton Act, an arrogant extension of U.S. jurisdiction that puzzled the international community. Friends and foes alike condemned the legislation, taking it for granted that it was the product of election-year politics. The bombings of Iraq were also frowned upon abroad, including by the impressive anti-Iraq coalition that had been organized by George Bush, as there was wide agreement with the implications of the Iraqi expression "electoral bombing." In the United Nations, we defied the 14 other members of the Security Council and insisted on ousting Boutros Boutros Ghali from his post as secretary general, despite our status as the U.N.'s largest debtor. Imagine how your local club would react if you didn't pay your dues on the grounds you were displeased with the job performance of the club president—whom do you think would be more likely to be thrown out?

Thankfully, when we faced one serious crisis with China over

Taiwan and another potential one involving Russia during Boris Yeltsin's illness, we weren't mouthing off as usual. But there was still nothing clear about the direction in which we were heading, a deficiency which could prove costly when we encounter problems that don't solve themselves.

Our friends abroad have just about had it with all this nonsense. The combination of the end of the Cold War, with its own brand of checks and balances, and the ever-increasing length of our presidential campaigns leaves little room for serious diplomacy, particularly in a president's first term. Except for Ronald Reagan and Dwight Eisenhower, we haven't seen much second term foreign policy since World War II and, given the legal problems besetting the Clinton Administration, one has to wonder whether foreign policy will take a back seat again. If Ross Perot's predictions of a rocky road for the President prove accurate, we may be in for more ad hoc action, with the possibility of foreign ventures serving to distract national attention rather than to promote the national interest.

Is all this an argument for term limits? We already have them in the presidency and it doesn't seem to be sufficient. Maybe a limit of one, longer term, at least as long as that of a U.S. senator, would be an improvement. It's an idea that deserves serious consideration if there's no better way. If there is, a single, longer term may be far too long to rectify a mistake and far too short in case the system manages to produce a real winner. I prefer to think we can find that better way.

What then? By way of introduction to the plan outlined below, I first readily acknowledge I have no idea whether it would work. Nor do I have any expectation anything like it has any serious chance of ever being adopted. I'm not yet sold on it myself. Doesn't matter. Given the state of our politics, anything is worth discussing, if only as an academic exercise.

I start with the assumption that my first suggestion, banning paid political advertisements on television, is not really controversial. Apart from those in the business of advertising and media consulting, the networks profiting from television advertising, big money, big business and those First Amendment absolutists from the right as well as the left, who would want to defend them? If they stay, don't get your hopes up for substantial progress. If they go, don't worry too much about the flow of funds to political candidates and parties. As long as existing laws are enforced, we should be able to withstand the effect of money in a commercial-free environment. And even without strict law enforcement, "decommercialization" is like fighting drugs by cutting demand; it removes the incentive presidents and other politicians have to engage in obsessive fund-raising behavior, thereby devaluing the contributions so imaginatively sought by both parties today. Simply put, if you can't put the money to good use, why make the Herculean effort necessary to raise it?

Having conveniently assumed away the principal vice of the times, I set my sights on the candidate selection process. Looking back over the year, it was easy to see that something had to be done about the games conducted by the major political parties on the road to their respective nominations. Whatever good originally had come from the primaries and caucuses had been eradicated by the time 1996 rolled around. A logical conclusion to be drawn from the experience of Campaign '96 would be that we should scrap them entirely before they do any further damage in 2000. No more retail politics in small states wielding disproportionate voting power; no more dictation of the political agenda by small groups of political activists; no more sports coverage of political contests; no more ignoring issues of national and international concern in favor of local issues outside the scope of a president's jurisdiction; and no more requiring that presidential candidates begin their marathon campaigns two years before the election.

If no more primaries and caucuses, how are the parties to nominate their candidates? The defense of the current system is usually based on the theory that it's better than having party bosses selecting candidates in smoke-filled rooms. Can't you just picture those dark, smoky rooms, in black and white? Well, I'm not convinced we'd be any worse off returning to the party conventions their long-lost nominating function. Given what the primaries and caucuses have been serving up for us, it doesn't seem likely that the candidates would be any less impressive, and we would at least be spared the embarrassment and disgrace emanating from the current prolonged process. If for some inexplicable reason a ridiculous choice is made, the voters seem to have no hesitancy in answering by crossing party lines. That's not to argue in favor of smoke-filled rooms—today they would probably be smoke-free rooms. Rather, it's to point out, as a first step, that we did fine without the primaries and caucuses before and can do fine again without them now.

A good second step would be to challenge the assumption that political parties are indeed the best vehicles for filling out the ballot. Once again, the experience of Election '96 indicates our political parties may be uniquely unsuited to the selection of presidential candidates commanding wide support among the electorate, whether the selection is made through primaries, even a single national primary, or by party leaders at a convention. Moreover, the conservative face put on by the Democrats in 1996 also indicates that, as Ralph Nader said, the main political parties are not offering us a meaningful choice. The Reform Party is to be commended for its efforts to break the monopoly of the Democrats and Republicans, but its efforts fell woefully short of the goal of energizing the large mass of unaffiliated voters unimpressed with the conventional choices. No, there are better ways to select candidates than asking political parties to do it for us.

Since the parties have consistently shown they aren't up to the task, why not let the candidates do it themselves? Let anyone who wants it announce his or her candidacy, regardless of party affiliation—the more the merrier—and then let's find some practical way to narrow down the field that doesn't involve money, train rides, funny hats, chicken dinners or dress rehearsals. If we managed to find a way to determine which candidates were eligible to participate in the 1996 presidential debates, we should be able to do the same for ballot eligibility. Actually, we should be able to do a lot better, with more institutional and refined procedures and safeguards to avoid even the relatively modest amount of controversy generated by Ross Perot's exclusion from the presidential debates.

Suppose an independent agency of stature were entrusted with the task of selecting candidates from the list of declared interested parties. The only basis for selection would be whether the candidate had demonstrated a certain minimum level of support, say 10 percent. Anyone meeting that threshhold gets on the ballot, allowing for a maximum of 10 candidates. Theoretically, all 10 could belong to the same political party—we shouldn't be deprived of the opportunity to choose from among our preferred candidates merely by virtue of their common party affiliation.

Admittedly, figuring out precisely how the 10 percent requirement is satisfied presents some challenges. However, if we're not up to that task, what are we going to do with the really tough ones? The more independent and respected the deciding agency is, the less mechanical the rules have to be. Failing all else, we could always rely on a combination of demonstrated support through verified signed petitions and more modern forms of communication, taking a cue from the Reform Party, coupled with a (horrors) single national primary. I would prefer to take more care in selecting the selectors, and then trust them to engage in regular, transparent, administrative rule-making in implementation of the basic 10 percent standard. As a last resort, anyone who feels unfairly left out should still be able to get on the ballot by affirmatively demonstrating support through the petitions and other means referred to above, or by getting a good lawyer.

When does all this happen? Labor Day Weekend. With all the polling conducted on a regular basis throughout election year, it's not likely that there will be many surprises; we should know well in advance what the slate of candidates will be come Labor Day. But the official designation should not be made until two months before the election, when the campaign would officially begin. Potential candidates would be free to announce their candidacy at any time up to two weeks prior to Labor Day and could spend their time up to that date concentrating on presidential issues rather than walking across states and dressing up in cowboy hats and boots.

With the possibility of several serious candidates on the ballot in November, we would need some way to narrow the field further. Other countries have little difficulty doing this. Runoffs are the norm in systems allowing several candidates to run regardless of party affiliation. Until we make the necessary changes to allow runoffs, finally dismantling the electoral college in the process, we can always fall back on the method currently envisioned for selecting the president when nobody receives an electoral college majority, a vote of the House of Representatives by state delegation.

What might have happened in 1996 if we had used anything like the foregoing? Here's my guess. In addition to the bundle of candidates we saw, Bill Bradley, Colin Powell and Jack Kemp, among others, would have declared their interest in getting on the ballot. Labor Day Weekend, Clinton (29 percent), Powell (29 percent), Dole (22 percent), and perhaps one other selected from among Bradley (a lock had the second Whitewater trial ended in guilty verdicts), Kemp, Perot and Buchanan, would have made the cut—only three or four candidates in all, hardly an overcrowded or unmanageable situation.

I'm not sure who would have won such an election. To assume that the outcome would have been different would be to grossly underestimate the political talents of Bill Clinton. However, the fact that Bill Clinton, campaigner extraordinaire, may have done well under any system doesn't justify applying the no harm no foul rule to the sorry excuse for an electoral process that gave him a second term. If nothing else, we should all have no trouble agreeing after 1996 that the way we elect our president is hazardous to our democracy—it wouldn't be a bad idea for some group to spend a few hundred million driving that point home through a Madison Avenue ad campaign.

No, the changes to be made are not for the purpose of denying any particular candidate the office, and the merits of the system should not be judged by the winner of any single election. Let's devise some rules that make sense, rules that don't permit or induce the candidates to embarrass us or themselves. After that, let the best candidate win. Only then will the winner command the respect he or she deserves for getting there, and, if 1996 is an accurate reflection of what our process has become, only then can we enjoy a greater sense of assuredness that all is well while we're out on the course.

I know all this is simplistic, but who's going to stand up and proudly defend what we saw in 1996? If it ain't broke don't fix it just doesn't cut it anymore. After 1996, the burden of proof has shifted. It's no longer necessary to prove that the system is broken. Adjustments are necessary; it's only a question of which ones. A starting point would be to search for the holes in the plan outlined above and compare it, with all its flaws, to the current system. Assuming you won't be entirely satisfied with either, force yourself to come up with your own plan—what you would do if you had the power to change the process in any way you wanted.

*   *   *

It wasn't all bad news in 1996. We were entertained, perhaps not as much as by the Olympics or the Super Bowl, but it was a longer-running show. Recall Lamar Alexander in plaid shirts, Morry Taylor and B-1 Bob Dornan in the pre-New Hampshire primary debate, Pat Buchanan in cowboy dress in Arizona, Jesse Helms and Madeleine Albright during the mini-Cuban crisis, the Whitewater trials, the scandals, Jack Kemp throwing spirals, the marvelously choreographed shows in San Diego and Chicago, the fall debates and Ross Perot—the only thing missing was a close race at the end. Then again, a lot of Super Bowls are blowouts, too.

It was fun following Election '96. I learned some things, confirmed others and generally had a good time. However, entertaining as the proceedings were, they weren't pretty. In some respects, they were enough to shake one's faith in democracy, although the problem isn't so much what democracy has done to us, it's what we have done to democracy.

I have a feeling the excesses we saw in 1996 will cause a lot of people to ask some serious questions about the presidential election process. Don't expect major progress in developing cures for the ills that afflict the process in the near future. Election fatigue usually prevents us from thinking about elections until it's time to start the next campaign, not such a bad idea when one considers the potential damage that might be inflicted by hastily developed solutions. What we should hope for, if not expect, is that the recovery process will have begun by the time Election 2000 rolls around. If not, we'll be embarrassed once again, as people everywhere watching the show will be rolling their eyes, shaking their heads and muttering: *You Must Be Joking!*

Appendix

Awards

Awards are handed out after every season. Allow me to present the following nominations for Election '96, in no particular order:

MOST VALUABLE PLAYER
Dick Morris, if everything they say about him is true.

COMEBACK PLAYER OF THE YEAR
Bill Clinton, for his comeback from a state of irrelevancy in 1995.

STRATEGY OF THE YEAR
The Democrats, for running against Newt Gingrich and the Republican "extremists" in Congress.

PLAY OF THE YEAR
Fake right, run left.

MISPLAY OF THE YEAR
Dole's reverse field on supply side economics.

DUMBEST MOVE OF THE YEAR
Dole's making an issue out of the addictiveness of tobacco. Close second: following it up with his snub of the NAACP.

WORST EXCUSE OF THE YEAR
Dole's explaining he had a scheduling conflict, which turned out to be baseball's All-Star Game, that prevented him from accepting the NAACP's invitation.

WORST DEFENSE OF THE YEAR
Even though it came in early 1997, it's worth stretching a bit to count Al Gore's imaginative defense, on the advice of counsel, that no controlling case or legal authority existed making his conduct illegal.

DUMBEST ARGUMENT OF THE YEAR
Whether we need a bridge to the past or one to the future. Close second: whether it takes a village to raise a child.

LINE OF THE YEAR
U.N. Ambassador Madeleine Albright, for her explanation that the Cuban action in downing the planes in March showed cowardice, not *cojones*.

IMAGINATIVE DOCTRINE OF THE YEAR
Secretary of Defense Perry, for his theory of disproportionality expounded during the Iraqi crisis.

WORST LEGISLATION OF THE YEAR
The Helms-Burton Act. It's hard to make up stuff like that.

WORST EXPLANATION OF VOTE OF THE YEAR
On the Democrats' support of welfare reform: sometimes it's necessary to stand up and do the wrong thing.

LARGEST MEANINGLESS VICTORY OF THE YEAR
Dole's victory in the California primary, when the race for the Republican nomination was already history.

PERFORMANCE OF THE YEAR
Elizabeth Dole, for her performance on the floor of the Republican National Convention.

POSTURE OF THE YEAR
Clinton voters holding their noses while voting.

BREAK OF THE YEAR
Not guilty verdicts in the second Arkansas trial. Without them, who knows?

MISCALCULATION OF THE YEAR
Dick Lamm, for actually thinking Ross Perot wouldn't run.

WORST DRESS OF THE YEAR
Lamar Alexander—as Buchanan said, the plaid wasn't enough. Close second: Buchanan's cowboy outfit in Arizona—it wasn't enough, either.